AF477893

Palgrave Studies in Minority Languages and Communities

Titles include:

Anne Judge
LINGUISTIC POLICIES AND THE SURVIVAL OF REGIONAL LANGUAGES IN FRANCE
AND BRITAIN

Máiréad Nic Craith
LANGUAGE, POWER AND IDENTITY POLITICS

Máiréad Nic Craith
EUROPE AND THE POLITICS OF LANGUAGE

Anne Pauwels, Joanne Winter and Joseph Lo Bianco (*editors*)
MAINTAINING MINORITY LANGUAGES IN TRANSNATIONAL CONTEXTS
Australian and European Perspectives

Glyn Williams
SUSTAINING LANGUAGE DIVERSITY IN EUROPE
Evidence from the Euromosaic project

Forthcoming titles:

Maya Khemlani David, Vanithamani Saravanan and Peter Sercombe
LANGUAGE, IDENTITIES AND EDUCATION IN ASIA

Gabrielle Hogan-Brun (*editor*)
MINORITY COMMUNITIES IN A CHANGING WORLD

Nancy Hornberger (*editor*)
CAN SCHOOLS SAVE INDIGENOUS LANGUAGES?
Policy and Practice on Four Continents

Yasuko Kanno
LANGUAGE AND EDUCATION IN JAPAN

Dovid Katz
TEN LIVES OF YIDDISH

Vanessa Pupavac (*editor*)
LANGUAGE RIGHTS IN CONFLICT
Serbo-Croatian Language Politics

Graham Hodson Turner
A SOCIOLINGUISTIC HISTORY OF BRITISH SIGN LANGUAGE

Palgrave Studies in Minority Languages and Communities
Series Standing Order ISBN 1–4039–3732–X
(*outside North America only*)

You can receive future titles in this series as they are published by placing a standing
order. Please contact your bookseller or, in case of difficulty, write to us at the address
below with your name and address, the title of the series and the ISBN quoted above.

Customer Services Department, Macmillan Distribution Ltd, Houndmills, Basingstoke,
Hampshire RG21 6XS, England

Also by Máiréad Nic Craith

AN tOILEÁNACH LÉANNTA

COMMUNICATING CULTURES (*editor with Ullrich Kockel*)

CULTURAL HERITAGES AS REFLEXIVE TRADITIONS (*editor with Ullrich Kockel*)

CULTURE AND IDENTITY POLITICS IN NORTHERN IRELAND

EUROPE AND THE POLITICS OF LANGUAGE: Citizens, Migrants, Outsiders

MALARTÚ TEANGA: An Ghaeilge i gCorcaigh sa Naoú hAois Déag

PLURAL IDENTITIES, SINGULAR NARRATIVES: The Case of Northern Ireland (*editor*)

WATCHING ONE'S TONGUE: Aspects of Romance and Celtic Languages (*editor*)

WATCHING ONE'S TONGUE: Issues in Language Planning (*editor*)

Language, Power and Identity Politics

Edited by

Máiréad Nic Craith
Academy for Irish Cultural Heritages
University of Ulster

First published 2007 by
PALGRAVE MACMILLAN
Houndmills, Basingstoke, Hampshire RG21 6XS and
175 Fifth Avenue, New York, N.Y. 10010
Companies and representatives throughout the world

PALGRAVE MACMILLAN is the global academic imprint of the Palgrave
Macmillan division of St. Martin's Press, LLC and of Palgrave Macmillan Ltd.
Macmillan® is a registered trademark in the United States, United Kingdom
and other countries. Palgrave is a registered trademark in the European
Union and other countries.

ISBN-13: 978–1–4039–8818–8 hardback
ISBN-10: 1–4039–8818–8 hardback

This book is printed on paper suitable for recycling and made from fully
managed and sustained forest sources. Logging, pulping and manufacturing
processes are expected to conform to the environmental regulations of the
country of origin.

A catalogue record for this book is available from the British Library.

A catalog record for this book is available from the Library of Congress.

10   9   8   7   6   5   4   3   2   1
16   15   14   13   12   11   10   09   08   07

Printed and bound in Great Britain by
Antony Rowe Ltd, Chippenham and Eastbourne

Contents

List of Tables

Series Editor's Preface

Worldwide migration and unprecedented economic, political and social integration in Europe present serious challenges to the nature and position of language minorities. Some communities enjoy protective legislation and active support from states through policies that promote and sustain cultural and linguistic diversity; others succumb to global homogenisation and assimilation. At the same time, discourses on diversity and emancipation have produced greater demands for the management of difference.

This book series has been designed to bring together different strands of work on minority languages in regions with immigrant or traditional minorities or with shifting borders. We give prominence to case studies of particular language groups or varieties, focusing on their vitality, status and prospects within and beyond their communities. Considering this insider picture from a broader perspective, the series explores the effectiveness, desirability and viability of worldwide initiatives at various levels of policy and planning to promote cultural and linguistic pluralism. Thus it touches on cross-theme issues of citizenship, social inclusion and exclusion, empowerment and mutual tolerance.

Work in the above areas is drawn together in this series to provide books that are interdisciplinary and international in scope, considering a wide range of minority contexts. Furthermore, by combining single and comparative case studies that provide in-depth analyses of particular aspects of the socio-political and cultural contexts in which languages are used, we intend to take significant steps towards the fusing of theoretical and practical discourses on linguistic and cultural heterogeneity.

Gabrielle Hogan-Brun
University of Bristol

Acknowledgements

Palgrave Macmillan has been entirely supportive of this project from the beginning. Jill Lake, the Commissioning Editor and Melanie Blair were particularly helpful in refining the focus of the book while the process of peer review identified many key questions for contributors. Gabrielle Hogan-Brun, the series editor, has consistently encouraged interdisciplinary research in the field of language planning. A special thanks to Koldo Larrea and Philip McDermott of the Academy for Irish Cultural Heritages at the University of Ulster for their help in preparing the text for publication. Cultural Encounters is one of the research themes of the Academy for Irish Cultural Heritages, and the support of the Community Relations Council, Northern Ireland, in developing various aspects of this research should be acknowledged.

Two chapters in this book draw on previously published material. Diarmait Mac Giolla Chríost is grateful to Routledge for permission to use material from his book *Language, Identity and Conflict*, which was published in 2003. Parts of John Dunlop's chapter in this book draws on material in his *A Precarious Belonging – Presbyterians and the Conflict in Ireland*, published by Blackstaff Press in Belfast in 1995. That material has been used with the permission of the publisher.

Notes on the Contributors

Mary Delargy is a Research Associate for Ethnic Minorities at the Academy for Irish Cultural Heritages, University of Ulster, Northern Ireland. A graduate of Queen's University, Belfast, with an MA in Irish Studies, she previously held a research post at the Institute of Ulster Scots Studies, University of Ulster. Before that, she worked as Irish language librarian in the Linen Hall Library in Belfast for 14 years. She is currently undertaking a doctorate exploring British and Irish identities among Indian and Chinese communities in Northern Ireland. In 2005–2006 she was commissioned by the Community Relations Council, Northern Ireland, for research on multiculturalism in schools in the North West region. She has a keen interest in concepts of shared cultural heritages and has worked extensively in Northern Ireland as a cross-community Irish language teacher.

John Dunlop is a Minister of the Presbyterian Church in Ireland. He worked with the United Church in Jamaica from 1968 to 1978 and then as the minister of Rosemary Presbyterian Church in Belfast from 1978 to 2004. He was Moderator of the General Assembly of the Presbyterian Church in Ireland in 1992–1993. A graduate of Queen's University Belfast and the University of Edinburgh, Dr John Dunlop was an Eisenhower Fellow in 1989. In 1996–1997 he was a member of the Independent Review of Parades and Marches in Northern Ireland. From December 2001 to May 2002 he chaired the North Belfast Community Action Project. He was awarded the CBE in 2004 and honorary doctorates from the Presbyterian Theological Faculty of Ireland, Trinity College Dublin, Queen's University Belfast and the University of Ulster. He has also authored *A Precarious Belonging: Presbyterians and the Conflict in Ireland* (1995).

Rebecca Fong is a Senior Lecturer in English as a Foreign Language at the University of the West of England, Bristol, UK, and teaches modules on intercultural communication, area studies, cultural anthropology and linguistics (phonology). She holds an MA in Modern Languages from Oxford as well as an M Ed from Bristol. Rebecca is a working partner on the European Modular Programme for Intercultural Learning, which is based in Munich and involves a number of universities in Germany, Greece, the UK, Bulgaria and Turkey. Rebecca has spent many years living and working in Asia and Europe. She is also a photographer and her research interests lie in the field of intercultural communication, visual anthropology and Asian students. She has published *Working Knowledge: English for Business* (1997). She was also involved in *Who on Earth are We?*, 12 BBC World Service Radio Programmes on Intercultural Communication broadcast in 2000.

Diarmait Mac Giolla Chríost is a Lecturer in the School of Welsh at Cardiff University, UK. A native of Ireland, he is an authority on linguistic minorities and language planning. He has a range of research interests, which include the situation of the Irish language and the nature of the relationship between language and conflict from a comparative, European perspective and also language in city contexts. He is the author of numerous books including *Language and the City* (2007), *The Irish Language in Ireland from Goídel to Globalisation* (2005) and *Language, Identity and Conflict* (2003). Dr Mac Giolla Chríost has published numerous scholarly papers in learned journals on Irish studies, the social sciences, human geography, material culture studies and the sociology of language. He is a Fellow of both The Royal Geographical Society and The Royal Historical Society.

Gabriele Marranci holds a doctorate from the Queen's University, Belfast, and is currently a Lecturer in the Anthropology of Religion at the University of Aberdeen, Scotland. His main area of interest is the cultural and identity aspects of the Muslim communities in the West. He has conducted fieldwork in different European countries. Author of many articles on different aspects of Muslim life in the West, he is the founding editor of the international journal *Contemporary Islam: Dynamics of Muslim Life,* and the author of *Jihad Beyond Islam* (2006), *Anthropology of Islam* (forthcoming) and *Understanding Muslim Identity, Rethinking Fundamentalism* (forthcoming).

Philip McDermott is currently a Doctoral Student at the University of Ulster's Academy for Irish Cultural Heritages, Northern Ireland. His research is sponsored by the Department for Employment and Learning Northern Ireland and explores the potential for holistic language planning in Northern Ireland for indigenous, minority ethnic and migrant worker languages in the region. He has presented papers on his research at international conferences in Łódź, Liverpool and Leeds. Prior to this he worked as project officer on the *When Words Collide: John Hume Colloquium*. He has a keen interest in the issue of language and its potential for peacebuilding. He holds an MA in Peace and Conflict Studies and a BA in Media Studies.

Máiréad Nic Craith is Director of the Academy for Irish Cultural Heritages at the University of Ulster, Northern Ireland. She has previously held an Irish government-sponsored lectureship at the University of Liverpool and tutored at University College Cork. In 2000, she held a visiting fellowship at the Department of Politics in University College Dublin. She is author and editor of several books, including *Europe and the Politics of Language* (2006), *Culture and Identity Politics in Northern Ireland* (2004) and *Plural Identities, Singular Narratives* (2003). Prof. Nic Craith's research interests include culture and identity politics, European integration and regional cultures, and European Ethnology. She was joint winner of the 2004 Ruth Michaelis-Jena Ratcliff research prize for folklife. In 2006, she was awarded a Senior Distinguished Research Fellowship at the University of Ulster.

Robert Phillipson is a graduate of Cambridge and Leeds Universities, United Kingdom, and has a doctorate from the Faculty of Education of the University of Amsterdam. He worked for the British Council in Spain, Algeria, Yugoslavia and London before settling in Denmark. He currently holds a Chair at the Faculty of Languages, Culture and Communication of Copenhagen Business School. Prof. Phillipson previously worked as Head of the Department of Languages and Culture at the University of Roskilde. He has also held attachments to universities in Australia, Hungary and India, and in 2005 was a Visiting Fellow at the Centre for Research in the Arts, Social Sciences and Humanities (CRASSH), of the University of Cambridge. Author and editor of many distinguished books, his recent publications include *English-only Europe?* (2003), *Rights to Language: Equity, Power and Education* (2000) and *Language: a Right and a Resource* (1999) co-edited with Kontra, Skutnabb-Kangas and Várady.

Javaid Rehman currently holds a Chair in Law at Brunel University, West London, UK. He was formerly a Professor of Law at the University of Ulster (2002–2005), and Lecturer and Senior Lecturer in Law at Leeds University (1996–2002). He has acted as a Visiting Professor at a number of institutions including Emory University (United States),

Tezukayama and Kagawa Universities, Peshawar University and University of Maine. Author and editor of many books, his recent publications include *Religion and Human Rights Law: A Critical Examination of Islamic Law and Practices* (2006), co-edited with Susan Breau, *Islamic State Practices, International Law and the Threat from Terrorism: A Critique of the 'Clash of Civilizations' in the New World Order* (2005), and *International Human Rights Law* (2003). He is also the editor of the *Journal of Islamic State Practices in International Law* (JISPIL).

Jane Saville is a Senior Lecturer in English as a Foreign Language and European Studies at the University of the West of England, Bristol, UK. As part of her MSc in Development Studies, she started to explore the political and socio-economic aspects of language teaching and policy and contributed a chapter entitled 'Language and Equity: A Development Perspective' to *Culture and Economy. Contemporary Perspectives* (edited Kockel, 2002). Her other current research and teaching interests are aspects of identity such as transnational identities, liminality and regionalism from the perspective of social and cultural anthropology. Jane is an exponent of an increasing move towards a multi-disciplinary approach in research and teaching.

Markus Warasin holds a PhD in Political Theory and History of Ideas from the Leopold Franzens Universität Innsbruck (Austria), an MA in International Relations from the Université Libre de Bruxelles (Belgium), and two Italian lauree from the Università degli Studi di Verona and from the Free University of Bozen/Bolzano. He began his career as a trainee in the Economic and Social Committee of the European Communities. Having worked as a Lecturer and Journalist in Italy, Austria and Hungary, from 1999 to 2001, he worked as a parliamentary assistant to an Italian Member of the European Parliament and to an Austrian Member of the Convention that drafted the Charter of Fundamental Rights for the European Union. From 2001 to 2004 he was Secretary General of the European Bureau for Lesser Used Languages. He is currently working in the European Public Service as a Civil Servant in the Citizens' Rights and Constitutional Affairs Directorate of the European Parliament, Brussels, Belgium. He has published on various aspects of European integration and on Austrian Foreign Policy.

1
Languages and Power: Accommodation and Resistance

Máiréad Nic Craith

Interconnections between language and power in the context of identity politics provide the focus for this book. One of the primary issues for contributors is the process of globalisation and its consequences for languages at all levels, major, regional and migrant. The emerging deterritorialisation of all languages is a new and important consideration in the process of language planning. This applies not just to major world languages such as Chinese or Spanish, but is relevant at all levels. Minorities are no longer restrained by a national geographical context and are not dependent solely on national state bureaucracies for recognition. Speakers of all languages operate in a modern transnational framework which has been considerably enhanced by the development of new media and technology. People and their languages are 'on the move'. As individuals and communities migrate from one location to another, new linguistic minorities are formed and fresh issues arise. There are novel cultural contexts which are not easily translated and the field of intercultural communication has important resonances for language planners.

Globalisation has sparked numerous debates on religious issues and Samuel Huntington's seminal essay in 1993 suggested that civilisational identity would become increasingly significant in the twenty-first century. The world would be shaped by a number of major civilisations such as Western and Islamic. Moreover, the most significant conflicts of the future would occur 'along the cultural fault lines separating these civilizations from one another' (1993: 25). The predicted 'Clash of Civilisations' has linguistic as well as religious implications and in an age of increasing anxiety, certain languages have become associated with particular religious perspectives and terrorist atrocities. While such implications are of current import for speakers of languages such as

Arabic, the association of violence with languages is hardly original, and minority languages such as Irish and Basque have suffered from such connotations in the past (Conversi 1997, Kockel 1999, Nic Craith 2006).

Globalisation and global languages

Concepts of language and power are inherently related and strongly connected with the notion of 'cultural capital' – an idea that was first proposed by Pierre Bourdieu in the early 1970s. Bourdieu extended the concept of capital beyond its traditional economic categories and broadened it to include social as well as linguistic capital. For Bourdieu, the concept of 'cultural capital' is not an economic term. It involves a broad range of linguistic abilities as well as orientations which are present in the family and nation-state. In the case of the state it may exist in an institutionalised form (such as educational qualifications) or in the form of cultural artefacts such as books (Bourdieu 1991, 1997).

Language is also a form of cultural capital, and linguistic capital can be defined as 'fluency in, and comfort with, a high-status, worldwide language which is used by groups who possess economic, social, cultural and political power and status in local and global society' (Morrison 2000: 471). This implies that individuals and groups speaking global and majority languages have considerable advantages over their counterparts whose mother tongues are ranked low on the social scale – a matter which is hardly a point for debate in an economic context. Many benefits accrue to those speaking a major language. These include prestige, honour and educational credentials, that is speaking the 'right' language becomes a form of capital or investment which can consolidate or enhance one's credibility in the non-material sector. 'Moreover, privilege and prestige can be transmitted intergenerationally through forms of cultural capital' (Swarz 1996: 76).

In the twenty-first century we tend to think of languages in international rather than national terms and there are many sources of information on languages spoken at a global level. Although many assume that English is the most widely spoken language in the world, it has not yet attained that position. The most widely spoken languages in the world according to the Global Language Monitor Service are outlined in Table 1.1. Not surprisingly, the six official languages of the United Nations are all included on this list.

There are incredible difficulties with statistics such as these. How does one define the concept of a speaker of a language? Does one count native and non-native speakers alike? How does one assess fluency?

Table 1.1 Most Widely Spoken Languages in the World

Language	Approx. Number of Speakers
Chinese (Mandarin)	1,075,000,000
English	514,000,000
Hindustani	1,496,000,000
Spanish	425,000,000
Russian	275,000,000
Arabic	256,000,000
Bengali	215,000,000
Portuguese	194,000,000
Malay-Indonesian	176,000,000
French	129,000,000

Source: Global Language Monitor (http://www.infoplease.com/ipa/A0775272.html)

Nevertheless such statistics are useful as a guide to the escalation in numbers of speakers of certain languages and to the spread of particular tongues at a global scale.

Moreover, there is the issue of international languages which are interlingual versus those that are intralingual. This distinction put forward by Ammon (1991) proposes that languages can only be deemed to be international in a rigorous sense if different nation-states with diverse languages use the same international language in addition to their own. Here one could cite the example of English which is widely used in international communications by many nation-states in addition to or instead of their national language. In contrast, Ammon reserves the concept of international-intralingual languages for forms of communication such as German which are spoken in different nation-states such as Germany, Austria, Switzerland and Liechtenstein. These states are unified by the same language which is spoken as a first rather than as an additional language (Ammon 1991; see also Ussai 2003). Such distinctions may be useful in predicting the future status of many 'international' languages – especially when used as an indicator along with statistics such as those cited in Table 1.1.

Linguistic capital is closely tied to the process of globalisation and especially with the spread of online technology. Speakers of many languages are united across the globe through the Internet in an imagined virtual community. The Global Language Monitor outlines the top ten languages currently used on the Internet as shown in Table 1.2. It is interesting to note that certain languages such as Hindustani and Malay-Indonesian which currently feature on the list of the top ten

Table 1.2   Top Ten Languages Used on the Web

Language	Internet Users (by language)	Percentage of all Internet Users
English	312,924,679	30.0
Chinese	144,301,513	13.8
Japanese	86,300,000	8.3
Spanish	78,166,075	7.5
German	58,214,778	5.6
French	45,807,499	4.4
Korean	33,900,000	3.2
Portuguese	32,372,000	3.1

Source: Global Language Monitor (http://www.internetworldstats.com/stats7.htm)

languages spoken worldwide are not present on the Internet list – a feature which is probably explained by a lack of widespread access to technology in India and Malay-Indonesia. What is more interesting is the presence of languages such as German, Korean and Japanese on the Internet language list although these do not feature on Table 1.1. It would be interesting to speculate whether or not the strong Internet presence of these languages will alter the spoken language ranking in time to come.

Of course, it is incredibly difficult to arrive at statistics on a global scale. A survey by Global Reach of Internet users in 2004 exhibits different statistics for users of languages over the Internet (see Table 1.3). Interestingly, however, the ranking order of languages is the same. Classifications on the Global Reach website are 'by languages instead of countries, since people speaking the same language form their own online community no matter what country they happen to live in' (http://www.glreach.com/globstats/index.php3). These are the top ten languages currently in use over the Internet according to the Global Reach statistics.

The emergence of online technology inevitably has an impact on language policy and strategy. A shift of focus has occurred and Diarmuit Mac Giolla Chríost's contribution points to the concentration of new information and communication technologies in cities, and other urban centres more generally. He advocates a move from primarily territorially based language policies to strategies that recognise the significance of space rather than place in our contemporary globalised world, although notions of community and sovereignty still remain important. In the context of technological advances, language-planning approaches that

Table 1.3 Global Internet Statistics (by languages)

Language	Internet Access (millions)	Percentage of World On-line Population
English	287.5	35.8
Chinese	102.6	14.1
Japanese	69.7	9.6
Spanish	65.6	9.0
German	52.9	7.3
Korean	29.9	4.1
French	28.0	3.8
Portuguese	25.7	3.5
Italian	24.3	3.3
Russian	18.5	2.5

Source: Global Reach (http://www.glreach.com/globstats/index.php3)

are entirely territorially based are unlikely to generate long-term success. Mac Giolla Chríost argues that policy makers who ignore the changing infrastructure of power relations will ultimately fail in their efforts to cultivate or maintain specific languages, while global languages such as English which are no longer identified with a particular territory will continue to gather momentum.

The late twentieth century has witnessed a rapid spread of English in particular. A publication by the British Council in 1997 confirmed that very few languages in the world could now rival English (Graddol 1997). The 'normalisation' of British and American English in a global context is at the expense not just of other languages but of other varieties of English. The major dialects of British and American English are virtually the only varieties to be seen in print or heard in broadcasting, and the status of these two varieties is overwhelming. However, the picture is hardly entirely simplistic.

Central to Foucault's theorisation of power was the notion that power is not monolithic. Resistance, contestation and struggle are accompaniments of power (Foucault 1978: 93) and 'power relations depend on a multiplicity of points of resistance, which serve at once as adversary, target, support, foothold' (Sheridan 1980: 185). This applies to language as much as to other social phenomena. The apparent continuing domination of English is queried in Jane Saville's contribution. In the first instance Saville notes the increasing recognition of English as spoken by non-native speakers. The range and variety of English spoken worldwide is unparalleled (http://www.ic.arizona.edu/~lsp/main.html).

Varieties of American English are spoken in Canada and the United States. British English has diversified in many locations in the British Isles, Africa, South and South East Asia, and Australasia. Even within England, the diversity of English is immense (Crystal 2004).

But the growth of English has not necessarily continued at the predicted pace. The American television channel CNN failed to reach a mass market when operating solely through English. In consequence it has produced editions of news programmes in different languages because English has not spread as far as the corporation had originally anticipated. A visit to the CNN US website (http://us.cnn.com/) offers news in Arabic, Japanese, Korean and Turkish. Saville's chapter explores the relationship between language and culture in an international context with special reference to English. In particular she examines the extent to which linguistic and cultural rights have permeated into educational systems in three continents, South Africa, The Philippines and Peru and how this permeation ultimately affects the life chances of individuals living in these locations.

The role of language in education – especially in colonial and post-colonial contexts has prompted much debate at international levels. In many colonies English became the language of education and ultimately stemmed the intergenerational transmission of indigenous languages. In France, Belgium, Spanish and Portuguese colonies, only European languages were recognised and permitted for official and educational purposes (Spolsky 2004: 83). However, this policy was not universally applied. In some instances, British cultural policy promoted primary education in the local languages but with a transition to English at higher levels – a strategy which gave English a higher status in social and educational contexts.

Moreover, such a strategy had political as well as educational and linguistic consequences. Until the Second World War, only 2 per cent (or less) of the 15–19 age group went to high school. This was the norm even in countries with a reputation for democracy such as Denmark and the Netherlands. The net effect was that only the literate (i.e. the elites) had access to state power and could engage effectively with political structures (Hobsbawm 1996).

The dominance of English is a key concern in the writings of Robert Phillipson. In previous publications, he has pointed to the phenomenon of linguistic imperialism as a key factor in the spread of English (Phillipson 1988, 1992). He defines linguistic imperialism as a strategy of linguistic planning which occurred in many colonial contexts when the colonial elite promoted its own language through power structures. This argument has been countered by Bernard Spolsky (2004), who suggests instead that historical immigration to the colonies has served as the primary catalyst for the spread of English. In core English-speaking countries such as Australia, New Zealand and much of Canada, English-speaking emigrants quickly outgrew the native population. Once the number of colonists was larger than the indigenous Maori in New Zealand, for example, there was a change in school policy in favour of English. Internal migrations also helped the emergence of English.

In this book, Phillipson focuses on the pro-English pressures of the European linguistic market, which have received clear impetus from the United States. Phillipson argues that as a global language, English has impacted negatively on major languages within the European Union such as French, German and Swedish, and suggests that there are several forms of linguistic apartheid in EU institutions. Since minority language users are not entitled to speak their languages in EU affairs, Phillipson argues that these languages are in a perilous state. He focuses on what he terms 'the Janus-faced dimension' (or double-edged sword) of English which can be seen to enhance opportunities in economic and employment sectors but only for those who are fluent in the language. Such opportunities are counterbalanced by the threat of English for the autonomy of many national languages, and in particular, French. The process of 'Englishisation' in continental Europe has served as the impetus for a number of countries to take measures to counteract the growing influences of English and protect their own national tongues. Whether such strategies can be successful in the long term remains to be seen.

The quest for recognition

Globalisation has traditionally been interpreted as a process which offers endless opportunities to speakers of global languages at the expense of those who speak regional and minority languages. However, there is increasing evidence that this is not necessarily the case, and Roland Robertson (1994) is credited with coining the term 'glocalisation' to indicate the increasing significance of the local in the global context and the counter-trends that can occur in the globalisation process. Although glocalisation is frequently used in a business context, it also has relevance for language planners, and speakers of many minority languages have come to regard the international context as an opportunity rather than a threat.

Using Bourdieu's concept of the field, one could argue that the EU linguistic domain is essentially a field within which there is rank and hierarchy. Moreover, the European Union could operate as a 'force field where the distribution of capital [i.e. linguistic status] reflects a hierarchical set of power relations between competing individuals, groups and organisations' (Swarz 1996: 79). The European Union has served as a forum in which speakers of minority languages can operate in collaboration at a transnational level with one another rather than in isolation. Just as proponents of official, working languages of the European Union seek to co-operate in an endeavour to prevent the total domination of English, speakers of languages classed as 'minority' or 'regional' have worked together for a number of years on matters concerning their lack of official, working status. The transnational context has offered many such speakers an opportunity to bypass unco-operative central powers in their respective nation-states and work together on common issues. Early collaboration led to the establishment of the European Bureau for Lesser Used Languages (EBLUL) in 1994, which has proved a not insignificant champion for the cause of minority languages (http://www.eblul.org/).

Markus Warasin's contribution to this book considers the achievements of speakers of lesser-used languages in the process of designing a new Constitution for Europe. When the Convention began its work on 28 February 2002 under the presidency of ex-French Prime Minister Valéry Giscard d'Estaing, minority protection or the promotion of lesser-used languages was not on the agenda and was hardly considered relevant. However, the efforts of speakers of minority languages to profile issues of concern prompted several debates and conferences on questions related to minorities in general and to regional or minority languages in particular within the context of the future European Union. Several organisations working in the field of minority protection promoted an open dialogue about these questions and generated responses from academics, think tanks as well as individual members of the European Convention. Although ultimately the Convention was not endorsed by all member states, and the final document could hardly be regarded as a 'Minority Charter', the process offered opportunities and clear perspectives for a potentially significant step forward in the standard setting of European minority protection and lesser-used language promotion.

Promotion of minority languages is also a key feature of the chapter by Philip McDermott, which focuses on the significance of broadcasting and the media in the Celtic regions in Ireland, the United Kingdom and France, where English and French have consistently dominated. For such languages, access to power structures in the public sphere is a key issue. Without such access, the significance of these languages for public recognition of one's identity remains problematic since an important influence on the promotion of identity-cohesion is missing. Broadcasting is extremely significant in maintaining the vitality of one's own linguistic community. Moreover, the media has the capacity to introduce the language to non-speakers and therefore serves an important role in augmenting numbers. 'In short, it is no longer necessary to make a language official if it is to be moved out of the house and off the street into a wider world' (Hobsbawm 1996).

Some theorists such as Joshua Fishman (1991: 473) argue that there is an overemphasis on the power of the media in contemporary society which detracts from the effectiveness of other means of restoring a minority language, such as the role of education and the family, but McDermott emphasises the impact of the broadcast media on the consolidation of a language within family and education systems. At the beginning of the twenty-first century, the media have become a focal point in many homes. If the language of the home is neither visible nor audible in the broadcast sector, this is highly likely to have an adverse impact on the status of the language at societal level, and the lack of recognition in the public space has been an important factor in the decline of many languages.

Many minority communities have recognised the importance of the media in the promotion of small or lesser-used languages (Kirk and Ó Baoill 2003). For example, the growth of a feeling of community among the indigenous Sámis in the Arctic Circle has been made possible through technological innovations. In particular, the use of radio has overcome physical distances and borders in a new way. Radio has provided an international tool for the communication of Sámi culture and protects it against the overwhelming force of other Scandinavian and international cultures (Nic Craith 2004, Niezen 2004).

In his analysis of the James Bay Crees, Niezen (2004) explores their increasing use of computer technology for traditional language preservation in a non-European context. The James Bay Crees have developed a cultural programme that includes the promotion of indigenous language on the Internet. In response to the challenges posed by the dominance of English and French in Quebec, the Cree Regional Authority has developed a Cree Cultural Institute which is devoted to language preservation (http://www.creeculture.ca/e/institute/index.html). One of its more significant initiatives has been the cultivation of computing resources which facilitate the Cree syllabic alphabet (http://www.creeculture.ca/images/content/syllabics.gif).

The European Union has traditionally supported minority languages in their quest for recognition through the offices of the EBLUL. However, such support has only extended to indigenous and autochthonous languages in the continent, and the growing numbers of non-European languages spoken in Europe are virtually ignored by many official bodies. Speakers of migrant languages in Europe have virtually failed to gain access to power structures. In the EU linguistic field, specific forms of struggle (i.e. between majority and minority languages) are regarded as legitimate whereas others are excluded. There is tacit fundamental agreement that only those indigenous to Europe are permitted to engage with its hierarchy of power structures and there is a fundamental distinction between the established actors and the newcomers who are denied entry. Bourdieu (1971: 178) suggested that in all cultural fields there is inherent opposition for the monopoly of cultural legitimacy along with the right to withhold and confer it.

The principle of indigeneity has remained central to the mindset of many bureaucrats in Brussels, and languages which are regarded as 'in Europe', but not 'of Europe' have been virtually excluded from many international documents and charters. This occurs despite the fact that the whole notion of what constitutes a 'European language' remains problematic. In the *Encyclopaedia of the Languages of Europe*, Glanville Price makes a strong case for Arabic as a European language. He supports his argument with a number of reasons. Historically, Arabs occupied extensive territories in Southern Europe, sometimes for lengthy periods of time and especially during the Middle Ages. Price also notes the existence of a long-standing Arabic-speaking people in Cyprus. He highlights the large numbers of Arabic-speaking peoples in contemporary Western Europe and especially France (Price 2000: 11). One could also point out that Maltese, which is historically a dialect of Arabic, has acquired the status of official, working language in the European Union (Nic Craith 2006).

Price also extends the umbrella term 'languages of Europe' to the community languages spoken in Western Europe, especially in Britain, France and the Netherlands. He uses the concept 'community language' to denote the vernaculars of 'reasonably settled communities of (in most cases recent) incomers from areas such as Asia, Africa or the Caribbean'. Price suggests that if these tongues 'are not, in the usual sense of the term, "European languages", it seems difficult not to recognise them as having achieved the status of "languages of Europe"'.

Chapters by Mary Delargy, Rebecca Fong and Gabriele Marranci in this book feature such community languages in the United Kingdom. Unlike Great Britain, which has had a Race Relations Act since 1976, Northern Ireland has had legislation relating to race only since the Race Relations (NI) Order of 1997 (http://www.opsi.gov.uk/Sr/sr2003/20030341.htm). This Order has led to a significant change in the relationship between the host community and the incoming communities in Northern Ireland in the last 10 years, and Delargy's chapter aims to outline some of the changes which have occurred in the Chinese community since it was first established in Northern Ireland in the early 1960s.

One of the key issues raised here is the influence of English in several sectors. Not only does the global language impact on the use of migrant languages in the public space, it also generates anxiety about which language is spoken in the home. In the case of Chinese migrants in Northern Ireland, children acquire fluent English through their everyday contact with the language in schools and in the public environment but many of the older generation have limited skills in the language leading to inter-generational problems of communication and understanding (Holder 2003). Moreover, some of these elders have been advised by the well-meaning officials not to speak Chinese or Cantonese with their children and to use English instead (Man-Wah Watson 2000: 98).

This is a process which is hardly confined to Northern Ireland, and examples of such advice are available on an international scale. In his autobiography *Hunger of Memory*, Richard Rodriguez, the son of Mexican immigrant parents in Sacremento, recalls similar advice being given to his parents. On one occasion, 'with great tact' nuns from the local convent visited his parents at home and enquired whether it would be possible for Richard's mother and father to encourage their children to practice English (instead of Spanish) at home. The response was predictable. 'Of course my parents complied. What would they not do for their children's well-being? And how could they have questioned the Church's authority which those women represented' (Rodriguez 1982: 20). The change was immediate. 'In an instance they agreed to give up the language (the sounds) that had revealed and accentuated our family's closeness.' In such cases, there are social consequences which go beyond a simple language change. Frequently, there are different levels of fluency between one generation and the next. Children typically learn the language 'fluently, accent-free and with confidence'. In contrast, the language of the parents is all-too-often broken and a potential source of embarrassment for the children (Bammer 1994: 101).

Of course the counsel given is well-intentioned and aims at enhancing the linguistic capital of the children involved. In Delargy's case study, however, such concerns are incredibly ill-advised when one considers the global scale on which Chinese is spoken. Current statistics indicate that Chinese is the most widely spoken language in the world and It ranks as one of the most widely used languages on the Internet. However, such advice does point to the greater esteem in which English is held (especially in primarily English-speaking countries!). English has become one of the major business *lingua franca* internationally, and there is a general perception that 'English is indispensable to personal material success and to the performance of a technologically advanced economy' (Grin 1999: 175).

Perhaps there was a perception on the part of the advisor in Northern Ireland that Chinese was a language spoken at 'the other side of the world' which would be of no practical value to children living in Northern Ireland, but such matters are changing rapidly. Rebecca Fong's chapter addresses the increasing presence of speakers of Chinese within Britain and argues for a new conceptualisation of intercultural communication in Academia. There is no doubt that there have been extraordinary changes in our communications between and across cultures in the past 50 years. One of the consequences of globalisation has been the increase in international students in UK Higher Education. Fong's chapter highlights the role that culture plays in the curriculum and the manner in which this affects teaching and learning expectations. She proposes that the process of 'cultural awareness' needs more explicit treatment in the curriculum to heighten issues of identity and to facilitate the cross-cultural experience. In addition, it is argued that the practice of bridging the gap between theory and practice is a reflexive issue for each individual in his or her own right and more recognition needs to be given to two processes: methodology, or more specifically an 'anthropological approach' to underpin a search for meaning, and pedagogy that trains teachers to be more aware of the issues concerning migration and intercultural communication.

Religion and communication

Migration is essentially a process of 'up-rooting' and 're-grounding' in a new cultural context and different forces influence the adaptation to the host society. Language can prove an important barrier to communication in such contexts. Religious belief can also constitute a significant hindrance in the process of communication and accommodation in a new society. The final chapters in this book feature case studies where issues of language, religion and power are intertwined to such an extent that efforts at genuine communication are difficult to resolve.

Marranci's essay focuses on Muslim migrants in Scotland and Northern Ireland and their different approaches to cultural negotiation with the host society. Arabic is a language of considerable cultural standing among the Muslim community worldwide. As the liturgical language of Islam, Classical Arabic, the language of the Koran is regarded as sacrosanct and is used in mosques throughout the world (Suleiman 2003). Although the majority of the world's Muslims do not actually speak Arabic, many are familiar with phrases in Islamic prayer and would respectfully participate in services conducted in that language.

In his contribution, Marannci considers the relationship that his Muslim respondents in Northern Ireland and Scotland have with language and worship. In particular he focuses on the official role of Arabic within the community (*ummah*) and the differences in approach to this language by Muslims in Northern Ireland as opposed to Scotland. In the case of Northern Ireland, the local Muslim community has made the unusual decision to conduct their Friday sermons (*khutbas*) in English rather than Arabic. This has been explained as a gesture towards peace in a largely English-speaking political context that has been sectarian and violent. As such it could be regarded as a genuine attempt at intercultural communication by a group that may feel under threat from its immediate environment. (Alternatively, a cynic might suggest that this is more likely an excuse to avoid the use of a language which the majority cannot understand.) This approach contrasts sharply with that of the Muslim communities in Scotland, many of whom have sought to retain the symbolic importance of Arabic as the only acceptable language of the *ummah* in a society which is hardly devoid of sectarian conflict either.

Marranci's contribution sets the language question in the context of a fundamental shift in the understanding of Islam among the different generations and its significance as part of a wider national and international ideology. It addresses the question of how language plays an integral role in both dividing and uniting peoples of different faiths and ethnic backgrounds. The chapter by John Dunlop looks specifically at barriers to communication between Catholics and Protestants in the course of the Northern Ireland conflict. Although both groups speak English as their mother tongue, there is still a genuine lack of communication between them.

While this could possibly be explained simply in terms of a clash between Hiberno- and British-English, Dunlop tends to look for a more complex rationalisation. He explores approaches to what is basically the same language from different religious groups. The Presbyterian Church in Ireland has great respect for the authority of the written word of the Bible. This religious group has traditionally placed great importance on education and continuous study of the scriptures and theological writings (Hamilton 1992, Holmes 2000). Dunlop suggests that Presbyterian language does not have too many layers to it and is not very flexible. (For this reason, they are probably not very good negotiators.) Political statements of negotiators influenced by Presbyterianism tend to contain a straight analysis of the situation along with a blunt statement of their 'bottom line'. There is no movement either contemplated or even possible unless you can convince Presbyterians that the primary analysis is incorrect.

In contrast, he suggests that Catholics adopt a more flexible approach to the English language. Historically, the language was spoken by the coloniser rather than the native, and many Irish still have an ambivalent relationship with English and speak it using syntax that is inherited from Irish Gaelic (Todd 1999). Although the English spoken in Ireland is largely similar to that spoken in the United Kingdom, there are subtle differences between Hiberno-English and British-English – and this includes variations in nuances even when the same words are spoken.

James Joyce, one of Ireland's most notable writers in English and a Nobel Laureate, noted the differential experience of the same language in one of his more famous novels written in the early twentieth century. In Joyce's *Portrait of the Artist as a Young Man*, the principal character, Stephen Dedalus, senses the shadow of imperialism while having a conversation in English with an English (Catholic) priest. Dedalus feels that the English language in which they are conversing ultimately belongs to the priest and his English tradition and is still the language of the coloniser. Dedalus remarks on the difference between 'the words home, Christ, ale, master' on the priest's lips in contrast with his own efforts. Dedalus 'cannot speak or write these words without unrest of spirit'. The priest's language which in one sense is 'so familiar' will always remain 'an acquired speech' for Dedalus because he has not made or accepted its words. His voice holds them at bay. Dedalus remarks that his 'soul frets in the shadow' of the coloniser's English (Joyce 1916: 172).

Although these comments were written early in the twentieth century, they reflect the differences still current in nuances between English as spoken by the British and that spoken by the Irish. Dunlop's contribution focuses on diverse interpretations of the same English by individuals from different denominations. Research has already been conducted on whether there is any variation in the English spoken by different denominations in Northern Ireland. According to Milroy 1981, any differences are regional rather than denominational. Others (e.g. Kirk 1997, Todd 1984) have countered this research. Presumably, Irish (Gaelic) has had a more significant influence on the English spoken by Catholics, although the ancestors of some Protestants were speakers of Irish and Scots-Gaelic (Blaney 1996, Ó Snodaigh 1995).

According to an account written by a medical doctor in the mid-1970s, most Catholics and Protestants recognise one another's religious denomination by their accent difference (Fraser 1974: 115–6). This view seems to be supported by individuals, such as Polly Devlin (1983: 383), who grew up in Northern Ireland and describes her early experience of being recognised as Catholic (Papist) in the following manner. She and a childhood (Catholic) friend were playing when they were pursued by a Protestant girl calling them 'papishes' (i.e. Papists): The Protestant girl urged them to say the Lord's Prayer which Polly began with 'Our Father Who art in Heaven'. When the Protestant girl heard ' "Who art in Heaven" instead of "which art" which is how they [Protestants] said it, she said, "You dirty wee papishes, you wee bitches, get on home." ' They ran on home crying asking their father the meaning of the word 'papishes' (cf. Nic Craith 2002: 131).

Although this incident refers to formal prayers rather than colloquial conversation it illustrates the manner in which Protestants and Catholics are aware of clues in one another's speech which confirm the denomination of the speaker. For her part, Devlin (1983: 384) suggests that the vocabulary of Catholics is antique and is more full of meaning than the 'pale nimble English' spoken by Protestants. She explains the constant use of violent imagery and exaggeration in Hiberno-English in terms of the 'damage done to Ireland' in its colonial past.

This view would concur with Dunlop's thesis that although Protestants and Catholics speak the same language, it can have inherently different meanings and it does not necessarily mean that they are communicating. From a Catholic perspective, it would appear that political statements are open to interpretation and re-interpretation. They tend to 'read between the lines' and may comprehend the same words in an entirely different manner from their fellow Presbyterians – a phenomenon which does not aid the resolution of conflict.

This premise is not entirely new and was noted by John Dunlop, Godfrey Brown and others at the Opsahl Commission in Northern Ireland some years previously. Both contributors argued that Protestant ideas of honesty had little time for ambiguous statements and approached politics in a literal fashion. One commentator suggested that Protestants were 'puzzled by what they feel is the ambiguous attitude of Catholics and their failure to define ordinary concepts in a clean, straightforward way'. Moreover, Protestants found it difficult sometimes to 'understand the sophistry, the playing with words which [they] sometimes get from Catholics' (Opsahl et al. 1993: 37).

This issue of the extent to which our language embraces our worldview is not a new one in applied linguistics. As early as 1929, Sapir proposed that our perception of the world is inevitably shaped by our mother tongue. Human beings, he suggested, viewed life through the filter of whatever particular language had become the medium of expression for the society in which they lived. He was convinced that languages predispose individuals to a specific interpretation of their environment (Sapir 1929: 69).

In the 1930s this position was endorsed by Whorf (his student), who extended it to argue that society cuts nature up. We 'organize it into concepts, and ascribe significances as we do, largely because we are parties to an agreement to organize it in this way – an agreement that holds throughout our speech community and is codified in the patterns of our language' (Whorf 1940: 213–4). While, generally speaking, this hypothesis is no longer accepted in its strict form, it is not entirely inconceivable to suggest that our mother tongue in particular has some impact on the way we view the world. But what is interesting about Dunlop's contribution is his suggestion that speaking the same 'mother tongue' does not necessarily guarantee a similar worldview.

Words have always had a sensitive role to play in the debate of cultures, traditions and civilisations, and the final chapter explores the perception of Islam in the wake of 9/11 atrocity and the subsequent war on terrorism. In 1993, Samuel P. Huntington published an essay on the theme of a clash of civilisations in which he anticipated a new variation in conflict in the twenty-first century. For Huntington, territorial politics were no longer relevant. The new faultlines were civilisations which were essentially cultural entities which he defined as 'the highest cultural grouping of people and the broadest level of cultural identity people have short of that which distinguishes humans from other species' (Huntington 1993: 24). Language, history, culture and tradition were common objective elements which held civilisations together, but the most important factor was religion (Huntington 1993: 25).

For Huntington a clash of civilisations was inevitable as differences between civilisations became ever more real in a world that was becoming smaller. As the process of globalisation gathers momentum, people become even more aware of the other in their presence. 'North African immigration to France generates hostility among Frenchmen and at the same time increased receptivity to immigration by "good" European Catholic Poles' (Huntington 1993: 25). He felt that faultlines between civilisations were going to replace the political and ideological boundaries of the Cold War and he predicted the re-emergence of the 'cultural division of Europe between Western Christianity, on the one hand, and Orthodox Christianity and Islam, on the other' (Huntington 1993: 29–30).

However, Javaid Rehman argues that this clash of civilisations predicted by Huntington should not be accepted without question. Instead he queries key words and concepts such as 'civilisation' and 'human rights' and argues that our interpretation of such words is highly dependent on the cultural context. The atrocities of 11 September 2001 generated considerable concern about the rise of terrorism and many problems have arisen as a result of the differential usage of words and values such as 'terrorism' in an international context. Rehman's contribution considers the extent to which the application (or misapplication) in the usage of such words has had a major role in exacerbating divisions between contemporary Muslim societies and the Western world.

Overall, contributions to this book address the issue of language, power and identity from a variety of perspectives – from global to transnational to local. The book explores powerful languages such as English, minority and regional languages such as Irish, and immigrant languages such as Chinese and Arabic. The issue of power, however, is highly contextual. Several contributions focus on languages such as Arabic and Chinese which are powerful in their homeland but lack any access to power structures abroad. The recognition of one's own language has important ramifications for a sense of identity in all cultural contexts, and all chapters query the implications of language in the quest for the ongoing negotiation of identity.

References

Ammon, U. (1991) *Die internationale Stellung der deutschen Sprache*. Berlin and New York: de Gruyter.

Bammer, A. (1994) 'Mother Tongues and Other Strangers: Writing "Family" across Cultural Divides', in A. Bammer ed., *Displacements: Cultural Identities in Question*. Bloomington and Indiana: Indiana University Press, pp. 90–109.

Blaney, R. (1996) *Presbyterians and the Irish Language*. Belfast: Ulster Historical Foundation and ULTACH Trust.

Bourdieu, P. (1971) 'Intellectual Field and Creative Project', in M. Young ed., *Knowledge and Control: New Directions for the Sociology of Education*. London: Collier-Macmillan, pp. 161–88.

Bourdieu, P. (1991). *Language and Symbolic Power*. Cambridge: Polity Press.

Bourdieu, P. (1997) 'The Forms of Capital' (http://www.viet-studies.org/Bourdieu_capital.htm).

Conversi, D. (1997) *The Basques, the Catalans and Spain: Alternative Routes to Nationalist Mobilisation*. London: Hurst.

Crystal, D. (2004) *The Stories of English*. London: Penguin.

Devlin, P. (1983) 'A Bogsider's Education', in Patricia Craig ed., *The Rattle of the North: An Anthology of Ulster Prose* (1992). Belfast: Blackstaff Press, pp. 379–93.

Fishman, J. (1991) *Reversing Language Shift*. Clevedon: Multilingual Matters.

Foucault, M. (1978) *Discipline and Punish: The Birth of the Prison*, translated by A. Sheridan. New York: Vintage Books.

Fraser, M. (1974) *Children in Conflict*. Harmondsworth: Penguin.

Graddol, D. (1997) *The Future of English: A Guide to Forecasting the Popularity of English in the 21st Century*. London: The British Council.

Grin, F. (1999) 'Market Forces, Language Spread and Linguistic Diversity', in M. Kontra, R. Phillipson, T. Skutnabb-Kangas and T. Várady eds, *Language: A Right and a Resource: Approaching Linguistic Human Rights*. Budapest: Central European Press, pp. 169–86.

Hamilton, T. (1992) *History of Presbyterianism in Ireland*. Belfast: Ambassador.

Hobsbawm, E. (1996) 'Language, Culture and National Identity (Multiculturalism based on Language)', *Social Research* (Winter) (http://www.findarticles.com/p/articles/mi_m2267/is_n4_v63/ai_19100677).

Holder, D. (2003) *In Other Words? Mapping Minority Ethnic Languages in Northern Ireland*. Belfast: Multi-Cultural Resource Centre.

Holmes, F. (2000) *The Presbyterian Church in Ireland*. Dublin: Columba Press.

Huntington, S. (1993) 'The Clash of Civilizations', *Foreign Affairs*, 72(3), (http://www.alamut.com/subj/economics/misc/clash.html).

Joyce, J. (1916) *Portrait of the Artist as a Young Man*. New York: Huebsch.

Kirk, J. (1997) 'Ethnolinguistic Differences in Northern Ireland', in A. Thomas ed., *Issues and Methods in Dialectology*. Bangor: Department of Linguistics, University of Wales, pp. 55–68.

Kirk, J and Ó Baoill, D. eds (2003) *Towards our Goals in Broadcasting, the Press, the Performing Arts and the Economy: Minority Languages in Northern Ireland, the Republic of Ireland, and Scotland*. Belfast: Cló Ollscoil na Banríona.

Kockel, U. (1999) *Borderline Cases: The Ethnic Frontiers of European Integration*. Liverpool: University Press.

Man-Wah Watson, A. (2000) 'Language, Discrimination and the Good Friday Agreement: The Case of Cantonese', in J. Kirk and D. Ó Baoill eds, *Language and Politics: Northern Ireland, the Republic of Ireland and Scotland*. Belfast: Cló Ollscoil na Banríona, pp. 97–9.

Milroy, J. (1981) *Accents of English*. Belfast: Blackstaff Press.

Morrison, K. (2000) 'Ideology, Linguistic Capital and the Medium of Instruction in Hong Kong', *Journal of Multilingual and Multicultural Development*, 21(6), 471–86.

Nic Craith, M. (2004) *Transfrontier Co-operation And Cross-Border Languages in Europe*, unpublished report for the European Bureau for Lesser Used Languages.

Nic Craith, M. (2006) *Europe and the Politics of Language: Citizens, Migrants, Outsiders*. Basingstoke, NY: Palgrave Macmillan.

Niezen, R. (2004) *A World Beyond Difference: Cultural Identity in an Age of Globalization*. Oxford: Blackwell.

Opsahl, T., Pollak, A., O'Malley, P., Gallaghar, E., Elliott, M., Faulkner, L., Lister, R. and Gallagher, E. eds (1993) *A Citizen's Enquiry: The Opsahl Report on Northern Ireland*. Dublin: Lilliput Press.

Ó Snodaigh, P. (1995) *Hidden Ulster: Protestants and the Irish Language*. Belfast: Lagan Press.

Phillipson, R. (1988) 'Linguicism: Structures and Ideologies in Linguistic Imperialism', in J. Cummins and T. Skutnabb-Kangas eds, *Minority Education: From Shame to Struggle*. Avon: Multilingual Matters, pp. 339–58.

Phillipson, R. (1992) *Linguistic Imperialism*. Oxford: Oxford University Press.

Price, G. ed. (2000) *Encyclopaedia of the Languages of Europe*. Oxford: Blackwell.

Robertson, R. (1994) 'Globalisation or Glocalisation?', *Journal of International Communication*, 1(1), 33–52.

Rodriguez, R. (1982) *Hunger of Memory: The Education of Richard Rodriguez*. New York: Bantham Books.

Sapir, E. (1929) 'The Status of Linguistics as a Science', in M. Toolan ed. (2002) *Critical Discourse Analysis: Critical Concepts in Linguistics*, Vol. 1. London: Routledge, Taylor & Francis, pp. 207–14.

Sheridan, A. (1980) *Michel Foucault: The Will to Truth*. London and New York: Tavistock Publications.

Suleiman, Y. (2003) *The Arabic Language and National Identity: A Study in Ideology*. Edinburgh: Edinburgh University Press.

Swarz, D. (1996) 'Bridging the Study of Culture and Religion: Pierre Bourdieu's Political Economy of Symbolic Power', *Sociology of Religion*, 57(1), 71–85.

Spolsky, B. (2004) *Language Policy*. Cambridge: Cambridge University Press.

Todd, L. (1984) 'By their Tongue Divided: Towards an Analysis of Speech Communities in Northern Ireland', *English World-Wide*, 5, 59–80.

Todd, L. (1999) *Green English: Irish Influence on the English Language*. Dublin: The O'Brien Press.

Ussai, M. (2003) 'Asserting Ethnic Identity and Power through Language', *Journal of Ethnic and Migration Studies* (http://www.highbeam.com/doc/1G1-111933628.html).

Whorf, B. (1940) 'Science and Linguistics', *Technology Review*, 42(6), 229–31, 47–8.

Websites

CNN (US) – http://us.cnn.com/

Cree Cultural Institute – http://www.creeculture.ca/e/institute/index.html

Cree syllabic alphabet – http://www.creeculture.ca/images/content/syllabics.gif
European Bureau for Lesser Used Languages – http://www.eblul.org/
Global Internet Statistics (by Language) – http:// www.glreach.com/globstats/
    index.php3
Global Language Monitor – http://www.languagemonitor.com/
Race Relations Order (Amendment) Regulations (Northern Ireland) 2003 – http://
    www.opsi.gov.uk/Sr/sr2003/20030341.htm
Varieties of English – http://www.ic.arizona.edu/~lsp/main.html

2
Globalisation and Transformation: Language Planning in New Contexts

Diarmait Mac Giolla Chríost

In this chapter, I examine the impact of globalisation on the relationships between language, identity and conflict, and begin with an exploration of the concept of globalisation itself. This is understood as a combination of key characteristic features involving the development of a transnational, global infrastructure and stretched social relations. The process inevitably entails the intensification of flows and interactions and an increasing interpenetration of global and local social activities. While globalisation can be seen as a threat to local identities and cultures, it can also be a force for reinvigoration.

New information and communication technologies are understood to be an important factor in understanding the dynamics of globalisation. Their impact may only properly be evaluated in the social context of their use and appears to relate to how people behave, organise and interact as shifts occur in the nature of interpersonal relations, participation and cohesion. Underlying this is a view that the effects of new technologies are not necessarily determined but are rather socially constructed. At the same time the users of the new technologies are themselves configured, or constrained, by the technology itself. This may contribute to the emergence of new forms of sociality as concepts of information, power, organisation and knowledge are reshaped.

A further consideration for this chapter is the apparent concentration of new information and communication technologies in cities, and other urban centres more generally. In this context, questions about language, identity and conflict do not relate primarily to territory, but instead to access to technology, but notions of community and sovereignty, however, remain common denominators. This insight raises a critical issue for language policy and planning practitioners concerned with minority languages. In this context of flows, networks and global cities, language-planning approaches that are entirely territorially based have limited engagement with the power. Empowerment, of course, is central to the sociological continuity of all languages.

Globalisation, nation-state, community

Developing an understanding of the place of language in relation to the postmodern condition, characterised by a society in a state of flux, instability and fracture, is a central issue for this chapter. According to May (2001: 156) the relationship between language and the modern nation-state may be variously defined as comprising a 'single linguistic community', or 'unified linguistic market', or, finally, as a 'homogenous civic culture'. May relates the emergence of this phenomenon during the modern period to the historical conjuncture, or fracture, between the premodern and the modern (Smith 1986) whereby premodern ethnic communities, or *ethnies*, become modern nations. The current erosion of the hegemony of the nation-state under the challenge of contemporary globalisation suggests that it is pertinent to ask whether the present historical conjuncture signals a break with the modern relationship between language and the organisation of society.

'Globalisation' is a term often associated with the myriad and rapid changes that much of the world is currently experiencing. The meaning of the term relates to a number of issues including more extensive global interconnectedness, a reconfiguration of interactions between local and global processes and increasing organisation and exercise of power at a local level. While globalisation can be seen as a threat to local identities and cultures, it can also be seen as a positive force in their remaking and reinvigoration. In addition, globalisation may be described as a multidimensional process that incorporates all social relations – cultural, economic and political – and, as such, the effects of globalisation can be seen in all aspects of society.

In the context of a globalising world, it has become common currency to think that the contemporary nation-state is too small to cope with the big issues, and too big to cope with the small ones (Davies 1997: 1120). That is not to say that the nation-state is no longer a key player in the world of geopolitics but rather that its authority as a sovereign, autonomous and independent political unit is subject to challenge. It now shares the stage with other players both at local and at global levels.

Evidence that globalisation is impacting upon the nation-state is considerable and diverse. For example, one might point to the flows of migration across nation-state boundaries and the continuity of diaspora communities, sustained in part by new information and communication technologies (e.g. Karim 1998) but also by increasingly affordable and rapid forms of international transport. Similarly, transnational flows of trade and investment or of environmental pollution could equally be presented as evidence of the erosion of the capacity of the nation-state to determine or shape events in a globalising world. Also, the global reach of new technologies along with their historically unprecedented rate of uptake by comparison with previous communications technologies and their accessibility to agents other than the nation-state could be cited (e.g. Appadurai 1995).

One could add that increasing accessibility to and identification with global icons – both of people and products – undermines the notions of national identity and culture that are central to the nation-state. The emergence of new forms of governance such as the Scottish Parliament or the Autonomous Community of Catalonia impacts on the role of the nation-state. The growth of supranational institutions of governance such as the World Trade Organisation, the North Atlantic Treaty Organisation and the United Nations as well as the increasing salience of Non-Governmental-Organisations [NGOs] such as Greenpeace, the Red Cross and Oxfam as agents in the global political landscape also appear to serve notice on the hegemony of the nation-state. In short, globalisation marks a shift in the geography of local and global socio-political relations. As a process that is multi-dimensional, the associated geographies are, rather unsurprisingly, both complex and overlapping.

One of the impacts of globalisation has been to cause nation-state sovereignty to be redefined. In a world of multi-layered governance, nation-state sovereignty is no longer absolute but negotiable as public power and authority is increasingly shared. The autonomy of the nation-state has been similarly reconfigured, it is no longer exclusive but rather is embedded in multilateral co-operation among diverse polities which include the nation-state. In this sense, the nation-state is a more and not a less important player as it is required to be more active in a globalising world in which a multiplicity of polities, authorities and movements lay claim to the allegiances and identities of its citizens.

The information technology revolution of recent years has been characterised by the massive growth of new electronic technologies. These new technologies promise to transform society fundamentally. Some initial reactions to the likely impact of these developments on linguistic diversity have been negative (e.g. Dixon 1997, Fischer 1999, Laver and Roukens 1996). Insights into the real impact of these technologies, however, are only now beginning to emerge. In some cases the impact runs counter to that which had been anticipated (e.g. Crystal 2001). Such impacts appear to be directly related to the social context of the use of new technologies. Underlying this is a tension between the social construction of the effects of the new technologies and the configuration of the users of technology by the technology itself. This contributes to the emergence of new forms of sociality as concepts of information, discourse and knowledge are reshaped (Woolgar 2000, 2001). In this virtual society (see e.g. http://www.virtualsociety.org.uk) power is dislocated from its modern points of anchorage and, in this context, questions of conflict do not relate to territory but rather to access to technology.

New technologies have the effect of fragmenting existing social organisations (Guéhenno 1995, Rondfeldt 1992, Solomon 1997) as they enable the development of electronically linked communities defined by especial single interests including those of language and ethnicity. Such virtual communities are not fixed to specific geographical locations, nor are they restricted by political boundaries. In this way they are removed from the structures of power and authority associated with traditional, territorially bounded and sovereign nation-states.

The term 'virtual community' might suggest that the community in question lacks a sense of real, or physical, presence. The virtual community may be dispersed in both space and time but yet it functions as a community via the new technologies of the electronic media in much the same way as Benedict Anderson (1983) conceives of the nation functioning as a community through the technology of print. The relationship between on-line and off-line domains is fundamental. It is of considerable significance that the new technologies tend to supplement rather than to substitute for existing practices and forms of organisation (Woolgar 2001). In this sense virtual communities are not created *ex nihilo*.

Everard (2000) pushes the case for the reality of virtual communities further in another direction. Drawing from the work of Turkle (1996), he argues that through membership of on-line communities, the individual, understood as the product of a process of social formation within a given symbolic order (e.g. language), is able to articulate a range of *personae* or identity structures (Everard 2000: 125) which more expansive than that normally available to the individual. The result of this is to enable the individual to achieve a fuller sense of self. In cyberspace, therefore, the multi-dimensionality and the fluidity of identity, so crucial to developing inclusive notions of relationships between language and identity, are reinforced.

Everard also asserts (2000: 126–7) that online communities can be more meaningful to individuals than other more immediate, in the geographical sense of the word, communities to which the individual could potentially claim membership. Accepting that this is the case, it may be of particular significance for language communities whose geographical integrity is greatly threatened. For example, in the case of the Welsh language in Wales a number of commentators suggest that the traditional Welsh-speaking heartlands of rural west and north Wales are currently so vulnerable as to be on the verge of an irreversible fragmentation. In this scenario Welsh-speaking communities would be so dispersed as to be re-constituted as nodes within a more fluid and plural socio-linguistic context and in turn become communities without propinquity (James and Williams 1997: 295).

Something of the urgency of the issue may be underlined upon noting the re-appearance of the language issue as a matter of substantial controversy in the broadcast and print media in both Wales and the rest of the United Kingdom since the language war was declared by some Welsh nationalist politicians to be at an end several years ago (Aitchison and Carter 1994, 2000). In such a situation the notion of virtual community may offer particular advantages in seeking to sustain a reality of community.

This point is also clear with regard to diaspora, or transnational, communities. Karim (1998) shows how new communication technologies, digital broadcasting technologies in particular, are being increasingly deployed by such communities in their efforts to sustain a coherent sense of cultural identity across international borders and continents. While underlining the preliminary nature of academic observations in this field, Karim also notes that the impact of the new technologies upon members of transnational communities is uneven. It would appear to vary according to a number of factors including socio-economic class, age and gender.

The case of the substantial Kurdish community in Europe may be used to illustrate the point. In 1998, following the Gulf War during which the Kurdish population of Iraq were attacked by the Iraqi armed forces with gas and chemical weapons, the issue of the state of the Kurds in the Middle East was at its most prominent in the European media. The *Independent* newspaper (9 March 1998) in the United Kingdom carried a story entitled 'The Kurds fight back on guerrilla TV'. The article recounts how a unique Kurdish language television service, styled Med-TV, is made available free from state censorship via satellite technology. It continues, claiming that the service is having a galvanising effect on the Kurdish diaspora suggesting that 'Kurds separated by borders, languages and political differences have unanimously embraced the intrepid station.' This was particularly the case in south-eastern Turkey, where 'satellite dish sales have soared. People sell their livestock to scrape together the money...Throughout the diaspora, cultural centres turn into mini-cinemas at news time. As one viewer in Paris explains, 'Med-TV has helped many people realise what it means to be Kurdish' (Serafin 1998: 5).

Wahlbeck (1998) not only concurs on the general assertion that modern technology has greatly facilitated the creation and maintenance of the social networks necessary to the functioning of the Kurdish transnational community as a whole but also notes that the expense of new technologies is also prohibitive for many individuals. Graham (1997: 3) previously noted similar inequalities in other more prosperous societies, including the United States. Besides the rather material barrier of cost, other more conceptual challenges relating directly to the idea of attachment to territory may be noted. While adapting to the revolution in new technologies may well enable embattled groups to create more effective national and global strategies of self-representation and cultural survival through the construction of virtual communities (Appadurai 1995: 218), the accompanying distancing from territory dislocates group identity from a sense of place in traditional geographical terms. Some view this process of de-localisation as emancipatory: 'in our Global Age, communities have become liberated from dependence upon direct inter-personal relations and, like cultures, from the need to operate primarily within the limits set by particular physical locations. Locality is no longer the only or even the primary vehicle for sustaining community' (Kennedy and Roudometof 2001: 21).

Whatever its merits, this process sets afresh the challenge of constructing meaningful senses of place. Geography, however, is not dead for, as Woolgar (2000, 2001) notes, the meaningful use and experience of new technologies, notwithstanding the attractiveness of the abstract notion of virtual community, is at its best when built upon existing social relations. Therefore, the notion of virtual space is best viewed as an extension of locale and not as an alternative. In the context of the proliferation of diverse virtual communities and the increasing virtuality of all communities, Guéhenno (1997) anticipates the greater need for institutions to facilitate interaction and cohesion between such communities across *e*-borders. Existing institutions may well need to respond through becoming increasingly virtual, and entirely new forms of virtual institutions may need to be devised. Present trends suggest that virtual states and city polities may be the key drivers in such trans-formations.

Transformation, information technology and resistance

For some commentators the revolution in information technology is as significant for contemporary society as was the invention of the printing press for early modern European society (Guéhenno 1997, Laver and Roukens 1996). If this is the case it has profound implications for conceptualisations of the nation as an imagined community and also for the idea of the nation-state and its institutions. Castells (2000a, b) has asserted that most social institutions, including government, have not yet been transformed by the advent of new technologies, in particular the Internet. What has happened so far, he claims, is that governments have been forced to react to the information technology revolution because of the new economy, characterised by the centrality of the Internet and networking to economic activity in general.

It is this new economy with its very different social and institutional requirements which is driving changes to the institutions of society. Part of the challenge facing the nation-states engaged in this new economy is increasing and irreversible multi-ethnicity. The resultant changes will reflect the national and local cultural contexts but the institutions of the nation-state will have to be so radically overhauled that a new form of state which he terms 'the network state' will inevitably emerge (Castells 2000a, b). This network state will comprise, briefly, nation-states in conjunction with international institutions, local and regional government, and NGOs functioning together in a complex interaction.

The exact nature of this conjunction is not clear but the immediate implications of the information technology revolution appear however, in the first instance, to turn upon notions of the sovereignty of nation-states and, secondly, the matter of the relationship between state and citizen. Castells (1997: 42–50) has previously identified the Autonomous Community of Catalonia in Spain as an exemplar response to the challenges of the global economy:

> This differentiation between cultural identity and the power of the state, between the undisputed sovereignty of apparatuses and the networking of power-sharing institutions, is a historical innovation…It seems to relate better than traditional notions of sovereignty to a society based on flexibility and adaptability, to a global economy, to networking of media, to the variation and interpretation

of cultures. By not searching for a new state but fighting to preserve their nation, Catalans may have come full circle to their origins as people of borderless trade, cultural / linguistic identity, and flexible government institutions, all features that seem to characterize the Information Age. (Castells 1997: 50)

Others have pointed to an unresolved geographical tension relating to Catalonia. Morata (1997), for example, notes that the Autonomous Community of Catalonia and the city of Barcelona are engaged in strategies that are in competition with one another. The regional government of Catalonia is committed to the idea of Europe of the Regions. To this end it has constructed what is described as a western Mediterranean Euro-region, a cross-border entity that includes Languedoc-Roussillon and Midi-Pyrénées. In contrast, Barcelona has created a network of cities, described as the C6 network, including Montpellier, Palma de Mallorca, Toulouse, Valencia and Zaragoza.

Morata (1997: 297) notes these two projects as representing two very different ways in which the space that is Europe might be shaped. For Taylor (1999) the tension is characterised as that between a territorially based strategy and a network-based strategy and that, given the nature of the forces of globalisation, the latter was most likely to prevail:

[I]t is at this continental level that the emergence of competition between alternative spatial configurations is occurring as network versus territorial strategies. This competition is expressed as a choice between a Europe of Regions and a Europe of Cities … In general, with the Maastricht Treaty setting up the Committee of Regions the territorialist strategy has a head start over the Euro-cities approach but, in contradiction to this, contemporary forces of globalisation would seem to privilege a space of flows in a world city network. (Taylor 1999: 9)

In general terms, the implications of the weaker attachments between territory and power for territorially defined polities are profound; most particularly they amount to an erosion of the modern hegemony of the nation-state (e.g. Guéhenno 1995). In itself this has certain consequences for language in socio-political context for, as we have already seen, the nation-state is a polity which is disposed towards the adoption of a single official and national language for all business of the state, including relationships between citizen and state and, in many cases, relationships among citizens as private individuals. Returning once more to Everard (2000), it is the transformations pertaining to questions of cultural identity which he claims are most significant: 'It is this shift of power into the cultural sphere that perhaps most marks the shift into a globalised political milieu' (Everard 2000: 53).

For the postmodern state the most fundamental challenge of all resides in charting the flows of the identity economy and in this language remains, and is likely to remain, a critical point of navigation. 'Language influences the way we come to conceive of ourselves – our identity – and, as we have seen, identity is at the seat of power, politics and the global economy. So an information technology that changes the terms by which we see the world is also a technology that shapes the way we structure the world' (Everard 2000: 158).

In this respect, the global dominance of the English language constitutes a formidable challenge to all other languages. May (2001: 198) records that English-speakers presently number at least 700 million worldwide. This is accounted for in part by historic structural reasons, such as the British Empire, but also by the place of English in globalisation. Crystal (1997: 360) summarises the contemporary foundations of English language hegemony as follows:

English is used as an official or semi-official language is over 60 countries, and has a prominent place in a further 20. It is either dominant or well-established in all six continents. It is the main language of books, newspapers, airports and air-traffic control, international business and academic conferences, science, technology, medicine, diplomacy, sports, international competitions, pop music, and advertising. Over two-thirds of the world's scientists write in English. Three quarters of the world's mail is written in English. Of all the information in the world's electronic retrieval systems, 80% is stored in English. People communicate on the Internet largely in English. English radio programmes are received by over 150 million in 120 countries. Over 50 million children study English as an additional language at primary level; over 80 million study it at a secondary level (these figures exclude China). In any one year, the British Council helps over a quarter of a million foreign students to learn English in various parts of the world. Half as many again learn English in the USA.

Picking up on Crystal's observation on English as the predominant language of electronic information systems at that point in time, Fischer (1999: 214) locates the English language at the heart of the transformations associated with globalisation; English is at the fore-front of international linguistic change, riding the new techno-language wave. He claims that the English language is on the verge of becoming a natural world language, an assertion which follows from his observation that '[t]he world's economic and political future is now being secured on a technological basis that is English-speaking and English-defined' (1999: 218).

Everard concurs to the extent that '[t]he Internet, for all its rhetoric of globalisation, is primarily conducted in English' (2000: 36). He continues to note the broader socio-economic and cultural ramifications of this in that the acquisition of English necessary to gaining such access to the Internet requires education that may or may not be available at public expense. Also, engagement with the Internet as an English language domain carries with it, on the part of many users whose first language is English, a presumption of knowledge of the cultural framework associated with the English language by all other users they encounter.

Everard also notes a significant technical problem namely that scripts other than Roman and Cyrillic, such as Japanese, Hangul or Hindi, are difficult to deploy on electronic information systems. As a result, in South Africa, for example, while there are 12 official languages of state, only English is available on the Internet (Everard 2000: 37). Thus the dominant position of English as the language of the Internet raises questions of sovereignty, or empowerment and disempowerment, for both the networked individual and wired communities where English may be the second or third language of users (Everard 2000: 54–5). Therefore, the acquisition of the English language, and its use, can be both empowering and disempowering. In some situations of conflict the relationship between language and the new technologies media can impact at more mundane levels, literally on-the-street.

> Among the processes of change being brought about by globalisation and the advent of digital communications is the change in the face of the political. When demonstrators in Russia and Albania hold up placards and banners written in English, it is clear that electronic media and the adoption of English as the lingua franca of the elec-tronic media has rewritten the nature of political life at a global level. (Everard 2000: 52–3)

Woolgar (2000, 2001) draws a cautionary note in the face of the hyper-bole, which appears to typify much debate on the impact of new inform-ation technologies on the society. He points out that many of the more fashionable visions of the information revolution are based upon intuitions derived from top–down views of the relationship between technology and society, too little attention has been paid to real, mundane applications of ICT in local social contexts.

Crystal has attempted to remedy this situation with particular reference to relationships between language and the Internet (2001). Counter to the conclusions reached by some by the mid-1990s that the most telling impact of the information revolution would be to further underline the role of the English language as the natural global tongue, the Internet and the World Wide Web are becoming increasingly multilingual. Crystal reports (2001: 218) that some commentators are now suggesting that the World Wide Web will very shortly be predominantly non-English. Crystal concludes (2001: 218–9) that the virtual presence of languages on the World Wide Web is increasingly a reflection of their presence in the real world.

> A Global Reach survey estimated that people with Internet access in non-English-speaking countries increased from 7 million to 136 million between 1995 and 2000. In 1998, the total number of newly created non-English Web sites passed that for newly created English Web sites, with Spanish, Japanese, German, and French the chief players. Alta Vista had six European sites in early 2000, and were predicting that by 2002 less than 50% of the Web would be in English. (Crystal 2001: 218)

Crystal suggests that this medium is not the exclusive domain of imperial-style languages. He also asserts that the World Wide Web is the ideal medium for minority languages (Crystal 2001: 221) due to the relatively low levels of cost and the moderate technical difficulties encountered by comparison with other media. Thus, he is able to find a virtual presence for the European minority languages and estimates that around a quarter of all of the world's languages has a presence on the World Wide Web (Crystal 2001: 219–20). Ongoing developments in the field of machine translation, the extension of the character set which may be supported by operating systems coupled with an increasing concern with localisation, 'the adaptation of a product to suit a target language and culture', indicates to Crystal (2001: 223) that the future of the World Wide Web and the Internet is multilingual.

Thomas (2000), however, sounds a note of caution. He points out that while languages other than English are increasingly marking out a presence on the Internet and that the Internet will become increasingly multilingual, the costs for deepening the virtual presence of a minority language are likely to be prohibitive, at least in the short term. Therefore, investment in multilingual infrastructures will probably be limited to an inner circle of languages for which it is commercially viable (Thomas 2000: 2). The ongoing struggle between Iceland and Microsoft regarding the localisation of products is, perhaps, going to be more typical of relationships between smaller language communities and Information Communication Technologies (ICTs) than that relating to the Basque language whereby the government of the Basque Autonomous Community commissioned Microsoft, at very substantial cost, to localise Word and Windows into Basque.

Some areas of difficulty were also revealed. The main issues related to accessibility – particularly the location of public access points to the Virtual Decision Making Environment (VDME) and the comprehension of the material made available via the VDME – and also to accountability, for example the task of ensuring the fullest possible representation of the community within the decision-making process. Morley and Robins (1995) note the issue of exclusion or marginalisation. In this case it is with specific regard to the televisual media. According to them, ICTs have special role in mediating what they describe as the global–local nexus, the dynamic tension noted previously between the global and the local, and in contributing to 'a new geographical disposition and new senses of community' (Morley and Robins 1995: 5). This causes us to reconfigure the idea of the border and 'increasingly we must think in terms of communications and transport networks and of the symbolic boundaries of language and culture – the spaces of transmission defined by satellite footprints and culture – as providing the crucial, and permeable, boundaries of our age' (Morley and Robins 1995: 1).

In the context of the televisual media, this tension between the global and the local, configured as an *e*-border, is manifest as a conflict between network and community, for example 'these global systems in information networks, satellite "footprints" – also lay an abstract space over concrete territorial configurations. Consequently, older communities and older, localised, senses of community are undone. The question then is how network and community can be reconciled' (Morley and Robins 1995: 75). Reconciliation may be sought in balancing 'market integration and market diversity' (Morley and Robins 1995: 17), that is a balance between the global possibilities of the technology and the local cultural specificities.

A response in many European regions, typified by local televisual institutions such as ETB [The Basque Autonomous Community] and Sianel Pedwar Cymru (S4C) [Wales], has been to seek to re-territorialise using the regional vernacular as the critical point of reference. As Maxwell (1996) notes, however, the aspirations of ETB have not been entirely realised in this respect and a part of the reason for this is the diverse nature of the Basque language community that the broadcaster seeks to address as a single unified market. To this extent one might agree with Morley and Robins in that the global–local nexus is not merely dynamic but also ambiguous, while failing to concur with the implicit suggestion of hierarchies of identity:

> Local cultures are overshadowed by an emerging world culture – and still, of course, by resilient national and nationalist cultures. It may well be that in some cases, the new global context is recreating a sense of place and sense of community in very positive ways, giving rise to an energetic cosmopolitanism in certain localities. In others, however, local fragmentation may inspire a nostalgic, introverted and parochial sense of local attachment and identity. If globalisation recontextualises and reinterprets localism, it does so in ways that are equivocal and ambiguous. (Morley and Robins 1995: 118)

The notion of *e*-borders might even be extended to within the home. Graham (1997), for example, expresses concern with regard to the matter of Monopolised Gateways. Gateways will be essential to digital TV in form of Electronic Programme Guides [EPGs]. Only through one of these will the user gain access to a full range of digital channels. Eventually the TV will offer reception for all sorts of services including shopping, advice, education, entertainment and so on and, similarly, access to these will only be gained through an EPG.

For Graham the question is which one and who will control it for the issue at stake is not merely a matter of ease of viewing but of exposure to content and the control the individual will be able to exercise over it. Government regulation on this matter is the answer in order to make EPGs subject to public interest considerations and also in order to ensure that content is local and interactive, that is reflective of local priorities and to involve local input (Graham 1997: 6–7). The defining and maintenance of electronic borders then is a critical issue for local culture on the one hand and the government on the other. For minority language communities the negotiation of culture and boundary which this entails is certain to be problematic.

Cities, distribution, language

A final observation on the impact of new technologies relates to the unevenness of distribution. A number of commentators confirm that the take-up rate of ICTs is much higher in urban centres than elsewhere (e.g. Loader 1998, Tsagarousianou et al. 1997). This may encourage agreement with Taylor's view on the relative strengths of the networked, as opposed to the territorial, response to globalisation. For Taylor the networked, de-territorialised urban centres hold many attractions and opportunities in the postmodern realm of identity. He speaks of '*Fin de siècle* opportunity' and 'cosmopolitan cities' and argues that with cities to the fore, cosmopolitan identities can again begin to rival national identities. The world of global cities is also the world of global diasporas leading to multiple layers of identity with state, national, regional, diasporic and city identities all available (Taylor 1999: 10).

Cities could function in the global world as vital multi-ethnic and multilingual polities. If this were to happen, it would represent a significant transformation in the relationship between urban centres and linguistic diversity. Historically the city of the modern nation-state has been a graveyard for languages other than the language of the state (e.g. Withers 1991). There are some indications that such a transformation might already be underway. In the case of the Welsh language, Aitchison and Carter (1987) have outlined a quiet revolution in the capital city, Cardiff. In this transactional city the Welsh language has undergone something of a renaissance, driven in part by the increasing institutionalisation of the language in the education system and also by a burgeoning Welsh-medium televisual industry. Such is the extent of the transformation that the ability to speak Welsh would appear to offer considerable socio-economic advantages. The concentrations of Welsh-speakers in the upper levels of the socio-economic register suggest that Hechter's model on the cultural division of labour in Britain's Celtic fringe requires modification. The fact that a similar phenomenon has been identified in relation to the Irish language in Northern Ireland (Mac Giolla Chríost and Aitchison 1998) serves to reinforce the point.

While the urbanised autochthonous language communities in these cases appear to be breaking free from a disadvantageous cultural division of labour, there is evidence from research on other urban centres of a new cultural division of labour (Castells 1989: 172–228, Sassen 1991: 299–317). In this case it is recent immigrants who are the victims. In a European context the new immigrations are as much a consequence of Empires coming home (to paraphrase Taylor) and of the collapse of the

USSR as they are a consequence of the various challenges and opportunities presented by the new global economy. These new migrations open up new questions of citizenship and rights:

> [T]raditional conceptions of the citizen and citizenship are vigorously in question at every geographic level of the world system – for we are all of us rapidly coming to be, at one and the same time, participants in local, national, plurinational, and global communities – but nowhere as immediately or urgently as in the large global city-regions of the new world system. (Scott 2000: 8)

In this context, the appeal by Williams and Van der Merwe (1996) for more sustained and interdisciplinary research on urban multilingualism becomes urgent. Moreover, relationships between language planning and citizenship are also of central concern:

> [T]he plight of minority cultures and of ethnolinguistic religious groups have become central in the social fabric of metropolitan life. This has a number of implications for urban planning, particularly in the fields of education, social services and employment. Central to such service provision is the question of language choice and official usage in the public domain … This, in turn, leads to the wider question of the balance of rights between the individual and the group, and between constituent groups and the sovereign state. (Williams and Van der Merwe 1996: 49)

They draw on a substantial body of literature in which it is demonstrated that language in an urban context is best understood in terms of social networks rather than territory. For example, 'community without propinquity seems a more accurate characterisation of contemporary social interaction for many urban residents. Thus attention has switched somewhat from an analysis of cities as containers to an analysis of cities consisting of transaction flows and competing social networks' (Williams and Van der Merwe 1996: 53). Given this complexity, urban sociolinguistics requires Geographical Information Systems [GIS] applications to discern language behaviour in the urban realm. The sensitive analytic tools available via GIS should enable more effective language planning on the basis of much more sophisticated insights into the working of language in urban context. As we have seen earlier, the same GIS apparatus could also be used to engage community level participation in language planning processes and decision making.

In general terms, language has a significant social presence in the city but is substantially under-researched and therefore poorly understood, and a further number of themes which might guide research in this context may be identified. Notwithstanding the years that have passed since Jackson's (1989: 155–70) insight about the necessity of recognising the active role of language in constructing the social world, there remains considerable scope for exploring the cross-fertilisation of sociolinguistics/language planning and urban planning. The urbanisation of the global population, involving dramatic and complex flows of people within and between countries and creates socially diverse and divided cities. In the North, for example, 'cities are increasingly becoming a site of aggregation and representation of different interests' (Le Gales 2005: 243), key loci in a complex web of governance within which an order related to scale is less and less evident (Newman and Thornley 2005).

Language remains a potent marker of difference, with linguistic difference often elided with, or subsumed within, ethnic-racial differences (e.g. *The Future of Multi-Ethnic Britain* 2000). The management of diversity has long been a task of urban governance (Cochrane 1999). However, over recent decades the context within which it has been undertaken has created new challenges and tensions. With contemporary globalisation, cultural difference, of which linguistic diversity is a central feature, is re-shaping the social fabric of cities of all sizes and in all parts of the world. This is reflected in new, or re-newed, forms of cultural identity, of cultural division in urban labour markets, of political mobilisation, of conflict and cohesion (Eade and Mele 2002). Deepening the understanding of these changes for urban planning and language planning must be a priority for a research agenda in this area.

Within urban planning, the discussions of how the state and planners more generally should understand and respond to cultural mix in cities have rarely made references to language and its significance (e.g. Sandercock 2003). The implication is that language is a neutral and inert medium for the transmission of culture. This attitude is reminiscent of discredited notions of how to understand the spatiality of social processes, and is just as misguided. Language is an ever-changing artefact that is both shaped by and helps shape social life, sometimes contributing to, sometimes undercutting, constructions of identity and Otherness. Taking full account of language, for example, can enrich discussions of cultural hybridity (e.g. Hall 1992, 1996). It is important to understand why, and in what ways, being able to speak a particular language may (or may not) play a part in the construction of social identities as bases for popular mobilisation or, indeed, governance. In brief, how is linguistic diversity implicated in urban management of the 'mongrel city' (Sandercock 2003)? Reviews of urban policies which omit any reference to language or linguistic diversity (e.g. Le Gales 2005: 245) are illustrative of the inability of existing analyses to address this question.

On the other hand, the discipline of language planning and policy remains dominated by a concern with language issues in 'national contexts' (Kaplan and Baldauf 1997: 324–40). The nation-state is the focal point of the craft of language planning. That is despite the fact that in sociolinguistics more generally the city is recognised as being 'innovative, unstable linguistically' (Wardhaugh 1992: 136) and thereby central to understanding linguistic variation and change (e.g. Bulot 2003, Calvet 2002). Typically, studies in language planning have concentrated on individual languages or the relationship of a single minority language to a dominant one (e.g. Fishman 1994, Kaplan and Baldauf 1997, Levine 1990, Skutnabb-Kangas 2000). They have tended to ignore the broader cultural politics within which language use is embedded (e.g. Extra and Yagmur 2004, Farr 2003). They have often prioritised small settlements, often in rural areas despite, in some cases, the empirical geography of the language (Aitchison and Carter 2000, Nettle and Romaine 2000).

This, in some ways, reflects historical concerns with the modernist project of nation-state building and its associated emphasis on the desirability and efficacy of a single language for state and citizen (May 2001, Ricento 2000, Williams 1994, Wright 2004). In this historical context the city has tended to severely reduce the extent of linguistic diversity (Withers 1984). In some societies language policies have been very oppressive, giving the cities a distinctive geography of language (Christopher 2004, Williams and Van der Merwe 1996).

Moving beyond this modernist paradigm is a central challenge to language planning. A key question is the extent to which linguistic diversity might be sustainable in urban contexts – sustainable in the sense that it contributes to the 'holding together' of the city so that difference become a force for cohesion rather than division (Sandercock 2003). Also, the nature of the contemporary challenge to multiculturalism as a policy project must be subject to scrutiny (e.g. Kymlicka 1995), along with the implications of that challenge to late modern framings of the normative citizen and of citizenship from the perspective of urban linguistic diversity.

These various developments raise a critical issue in planning strategy for those who seek to defend a language community. In a globalising world, where power is mediated through flows and networks, the historical hegemony of the nation-state is being steadily eroded. Language communities concerned with the continuity of the languages they speak, and their representatives, must find new ways of challenging those powers that are inimical to their interests. But contemporary forms of cultural resistance to globalisation are vulnerable to a self-destructive introspection, for example:

> The meaninglessness of places, the powerlessness of political institutions are resented and resisted, individually and collectively by a variety of social actors. People have affirmed their cultural identity, often in territorial terms, mobilizing to achieve their demands, organizing their communities, and staking out their places to preserve meaning, to restore...control...in the midst of abstraction of the new historical landscape...Faced with the variable geometry of the space of flows, grassroots mobilisations tend to be defensive, protective, territorially bounded, or so culturally specific that their codes of self-recognizing identity become non-communicable, with societies tending to fragment themselves into tribes, easily prone to fundamentalist affirmation of identity. (Castells 1989: 349–50)

Avoiding this descent into tribalism requires a strategy that operates on three levels – cultural, political and economic. Local government rather than the traditional nation-state holds the key in the operation of strategy. This is because the critical issue for the global economy is the possibility of adaptation to the forces of globalisation 'in each specific location as it relates to a given locality'. In the nation-state, government is too remote from the local and exercises no control over the global. Local government, in partnership with others – the city in particular – has the greater potential to respond effectively:

> [I]f innovative social projects, represented and implemented by renewed local governments, are able to master formidable forces unleashed by the revolution in information technologies, then a new socio-spatial structure could emerge made up of a network of local communes controlling and shaping a network of productive flows. Maybe then our historical time and our social space would converge towards the reintegration of knowledge and meaning into a new Informational City. (Castells 1989: 353)

In a globalising world of wired communities, virtual states and city polities the actions of those whose aim is to sustain threatened languages should be local, networked and urban.

Acknowledgement

The author is grateful to Routledge for permission to use material from Mac Giolla Chríost, D. (2003) *Language, Identity and Conflict*. London and New York: Routledge.

References

Aitchison, J. and Carter, H. (2000) *Language, Economy and Society: The Changing Geography of the Welsh Language in the 20th Century*. Cardiff: University of Wales Press.

Aitchison, J. and Carter, H. (1994) *A Geography of the Welsh Language, 1961–1991*. Cardiff: University of Wales Press.

Aitchison, J. and Carter, H. (1987) 'The Welsh Language in Cardiff: A Quiet Revolution', *Transactions of the Institute of British Geographers*, NS12, 482–92.

Anderson, B. (1983) *Imagined Communities: Reflections on the Origins and Spread of Nationalism*. London: Verso.

Appadurai, A. (1995) 'The Production of Locality', in R. Fardon ed., *Counterworks: Managing the Diversity of Knowledge*. London: Routledge, pp. 204–25.

Bulot, T. (2003) 'La sociolinguistique urbaine: une sociolinguistique de crise? Premières considerations', *Marges Linguistiques*, 3, 8–10.

Calvet, L. -J. (2002) 'La sociolinguistique et la ville; hazard ou nécessité?', *Marges Linguistiques*, 3, 46–53.

Castells, M. (2000a) *The Rise of the Network Society*, 2nd edition. *The Information Age: Economy, Society and Culture*, vol. I, Oxford: Blackwell.

Castells, M. (2000b) 'The Institutions of the New Economy', Paper presented at Delivering the virtual promise? Conference. London, June 19 (http://virtualsociety.sbs.oc.ac.uk/events/castells.htm).

Castells, M. (1997) *The Power of Identity. The Information Age: Economy, Society and Culture*, vol. II, Oxford: Blackwell.

Castells, M. (1989) *The Informational City. Information Technology, Economic Restructuring and the Urban-regional Process*. Oxford: Blackwell.

Christopher, A. (2004) 'Linguistic Segregation in Urban South Africa', *Geoforum*, 35(2), 145–56.

Cochrane, A. (1999) 'Administered Cities', in S. Pile, C. Brook and G. Mooney eds, *Unruly Cities? Order/Disorder (Understanding Cities)*. London: Routledge, pp. 299–344.

Crystal, D. (2001) *Language and the Internet*. Cambridge: Cambridge University Press.

Crystal, D. (1997) *The Cambridge Encyclopaedia of Language*, 2nd edition. Cambridge: Cambridge University Press.

Davies, N. (1997) *Europe: A History*. London: Pimlico.

Dixon, R. (1997) *The Rise and Fall of Languages*. Cambridge: Cambridge University Press.

Eade, J. and Mele, C. eds (2002) *Understanding the City*. Oxford: Blackwell.

Everard, J. (2000) *Virtual states: the Internet and the Boundaries of the Nation-state. Technology and the Global Political Economy*. London: Routledge.

Extra, G. and Yagmur, K. (2004) 'Multilingual Cities Project on Immigrant Minority Languages in Europe', *Babylonia*, 1(4), 32–5 (www.babylonia-ti.ch).

Farr, M. (2003) *Ethnolinguistic Chicago*. Mahwah, NJ: Lawrence Erlbaum Associates.

Fischer, S. (1999) *A History of Language*. London: Reaktion Books.

Fishman, J. (1994) *Reversing Language Shift: The Theoretical and Empirical Foundations of Assistance to Threatened Languages*. Clevedon: Multilingual Matters.

Graham, A. (1997) 'Policies for Participation: Myth, Reality and the Media in Local Initiatives in the UK'. Boulder, Colorado: Paper presented at the Euricom Conference Communication, citizenship and social policy, October 2–5 (http://ucsub.colorado.edu/%Eweinberr/Graham.html).

Guéhenno, J. -M. (1997) 'The Topology of Sovereignty', Paper presented at Virtual diplomacy: The global communications revolution and international conflict management conference. United States Institute of Peace, Washington, DC, April 1.

Guéhenno, J. -M. (1995) *The End of the Nation-state*. Minneapolis: University of Minnesota Press.

Hall, S. (1996) 'Who Needs Identity?', in S. Hall and P. duGay eds, *Questions of Cultural Identity*. London: Sage, pp. 1–17.

Hall, S. (1992) 'The Question of Cultural Identity', in S. Hall, D. Held and T. McGrew eds, *Modernity and its Futures*. Cambridge: Polity Press, pp. 274–325.

Jackson, P. (1989) *Maps of Meaning*. London: Unwin Hyman.

James, C. and Williams, C. (1997) 'Language and Planning in Scotland and Wales', in R. MacDonald and H. Thomas eds, *Nationality and Planning in Scotland and Wales*. Cardiff: University of Wales Press, pp. 264–302.

Kaplan, R. and Baldauf, R. (1997) *Language Planning: From Practice to Theory*. Clevedon: Multilingual Matters.

Karim, K. (1998) *From Ethnic Media to Global Media: Transnational Communication Networks among Diasporic Communities*, WPTC-99-02 (http://www.transcomm.ox.ac.uk).

Kennedy, P. and Roudometof, V. (2001) *Communities across Borders under Globalising Conditions: New Immigrants and Transnational Cultures*, WPTC-01-17 (http://www.transcomm.ox.ac.uk).

Kymlicka, W. (1995) *Multicultural Citizenship: A Liberal Theory of Minority Rights*. Oxford: Clarendon Press.

Laver, J. and Roukens, J. (1996) 'The Global Information Society and Europe's Linguistic and Cultural Heritage', in C. Hoffmann ed., *Language, Culture and Communication in Contemporary Europe*. Clevedon: Multilingual Matters, pp. 1–27.

Le Gales, P. (2005) 'Elusive Urban Policies in Europe', in Y. Kazopov ed., *Cities of Europe*. Oxford: Blackwell, pp. 235–54.

Levine, M. (1990) *The Reconquest of Montreal: Language Policy and Social Change in a Bilingual City*. Philadelphia, PA: Temple University Press.

Loader, B. ed. (1998) *Cyberspace Divide. Equality, Agency and Policy in the Information Age*. London: Routledge.

Mac Giolla Chríost, D. and Aitchison, J. (1998) 'Ethnic Identities and Language in Northern Ireland', *Area*, 30(4), 301–9.

Maxwell, R. (1996) 'Technologies of National Desire', in M. Shapiro and H. Alker eds, *Challenging Boundaries: Global Flows, Territorial Identities*. Minneapolis: University of Minnesota, pp. 327–58.

May, S. (2001) *Language and Minority Rights: Ethnicity, Nationalism and the Politics of Language*. London: Pearson.

Morata, F. (1997) 'The Euro-region and the C-6 Network: The New Politics of Sub-national Co-operation in the Western Mediterranean Area', in M. Keating and J. Loughlin eds, *The Political Economy of Regionalism*. London: Frank Cass, pp. 292–305.

Morley, D. and Robins, K. (1995) *Spaces of Identity: Global Media, Electronic Landscapes and Cultural Boundaries*. London: Routledge.

Nettle, D. and Romaine, S. (2000) *Vanishing Voices: The Extinction of the World's Languages*. Oxford: Oxford University Press.

Newman, P. and Thornley, A. (2005) *Planning World Cities: Globalization and Urban Politics*. Basingstoke: Palgrave Macmillan.

Parekh, B. (2000) *The Future of Multi-Ethnic Britain*. London: Profile Books.

Ricento, T. (2000) 'Historical and Theoretical Perspectives in Language Policy and Planning', *Journal of Sociolinguistics*, 4(2), 196–213.

Rondfeldt, D. (1992) 'Cyberdemocracy Is Coming', *The Information Society*, 8(4), 243–96.

Sandercock, L. (2003) *Cosmopolis II: Mongrel Cities of the Twenty First Century*. London: Continuum.

Sassen, S. (1991) *The Global City*. Princeton, NJ: Princeton University Press.

Scott, A. (2000) 'Globalization and the Rise of City-regions', *Globalization and World Cities Study Group and Network Research Bulletin*, 26 (http://www.lboro.ac.uk/departments/gy/gawc/rb/rb26.html).

Serafin, A. (1998) 'The Kurds Fight Back on Guerrilla TV', *The Independent*, March 9, pp. 5–6.

Skutnabb-Kangas, T. (2000) *Linguistic Genocide in Education – or Worldwide Diversity and Human Rights?* Mahwah, NJ: Lawrence Erlbaum Associates.

Smith, A. (1986) *The Ethnic Origins of Nations*. Oxford: Basil Blackwell.

Solomon, R. (1997) 'The Information Revolution and International Conflict Management', Paper at Virtual diplomacy conference, United States Institute of Peace.

Taylor, P. (1999) 'World Cities and Territorial States under Conditions of Contemporary Globalization'. The 1999 Annual Political Geography Lecture, *Globalization and World Cities Study Group and Network Research Bulletin*, 9 (http://www.lboro.ac.uk/departments/gy/gawc/rb/rb9.html).

Thomas, N. (2000) Editorial, *Contact Bulletin*, 2.

Tsagarousianou, R., Tambini, D. and Bryan, C. eds (1997) *Cyberdemocracy. Technologies, Cities and Networks*. London: Routledge.

Turkle, S. (1996) *Life on the Screen*. London: Weidenfeld and Nicolson.

Wahlbeck, Ö. (1998) 'Transnationalism and Diasporas: The Kurdish Example', Paper presented at the International Sociological Association XIV World Congress of Sociology. Montreal, Canada, July 26 (http://www.transcomm.ox.ac.uk).

Wardhaugh, R. (1992) *Sociolinguistics*. Oxford: Blackwell.

Williams, C. (1994) *Called unto Liberty: On Language and Nationalism*. Clevedon: Multilingual Matters.

Williams, C. and Van der Merwe, I. (1996) 'Mapping the Multilingual City: A Research Agenda for Urban Geolinguistics', *Journal of Multilingual and Multicultural Development*, 17(1), 49–66.

Withers, C. (1991) 'Class, Culture and Migrant Identity: Gaelic Highlanders in Urban Scotland', in G. Kearns and C. Withers eds, *Urbanising Britain. Essays on Class and Community in the 19th Century*. Cambridge: Cambridge University Press, pp. 55–79.

Withers, C. (1984) *Gaelic in Scotland 1698–1981: The Geographical History of a Language*. Edinburgh: John Donald.

Woolgar, S. (2001) 'Reflections on the Virtual Society?', Paper presented at ICUST 2001. Paris, June 12–14.

Woolgar, S. (2000) 'Virtual Society? Beyond the Hype?', *The Source Public Management Journal* (http://www.thesourcepublishing.co.uk/articles/a01070.html).

Wright, S. (2004) *Language Policy and Language Planning: From Nationalism to Globalisation*. Basingstoke: Palgrave Macmillan.

3
Linguistic Human Rights in Education: International Case Studies

Jane Saville

Across the globe, there is a perceptible shift in the analysis of the form, teaching and use of the English language. Against the notion of the 'linguistic imperialism' of British and American English (Phillipson 1992), the development of bilingualism and English as an International Language (EIL), which allows the inclusion of varieties of English and recognises the contribution of non-native speaker teachers, is beginning to form a counteroffensive. In addition, the growth of English has not continued at the predicted pace. The television news channel CNN has failed to reach a mass market and has had to produce different editions of news programmes in different languages because English has not spread as far as the corporation had believed or expected (Morley and Robins 1995). At the same time, there is an increasing acknowledgement of the linguistic and cultural rights of communities. In 1996, the Universal Declaration of Linguistic Rights was approved by 220 people from almost 90 states worldwide. In Article 24, it states that all language communities have the right to decide to what extent their first language is to be used or studied at all levels of their educational system (www.linguistic-declaration.org).

This chapter will explore the relationship between language and culture; how far linguistic and cultural rights have permeated into educational systems and how this may ultimately affect the life chances of individuals, using countries from three continents as examples. The 2004 Human Development Report (United Nations Development Programme – UNDP) entitled *Cultural Liberty in Today's Diverse World* (hdr.undp.org/reports/global/2004/pdf/hdr04_complete.pdf) reminds us that the eradication of poverty and inequality depends on the successful building of inclusive, culturally diverse societies.

The international linguistic and cultural context

Llurda (2004) points out that the perception of English has changed. In the last two decades of the twentieth century it was regarded by some as the 'killer language' (Pakir 1991, Mühlhäusler 1996) and many supported the view that linguistic imperialism was being exercised (Phillipson 1992, Saville 2002, Tollefson 1995) through organisations such as the British Council and the World Bank. The twentieth century closed with concerns about the future dominance and growth of English as a global language despite competition from Mandarin, Spanish, Hindi and Arabic (Graddol 1997). Demographic projections show that by 2050 there will be more speakers of English as a second language rather than as a mother tongue (Graddol 1999), with an increase to 462 million speakers as a second language. Consequently, although few doubt whether English is still a desirable language to acquire, language teachers and researchers are increasingly questioning whether the attainment of native-speaker models of English is necessary and whether non-native speakers of English should have a say in the development and assessment of EIL. The concept of 'World English' or 'English as a Lingua Franca' as it is called by other writers would acknowledge the many varieties of English which are used across the globe for different purposes.

Brutt-Griffler (2002) identifies four features which occur along with the internationalisation of a language: (1) its development as a product of a world 'econocultural' system, a global economy and a global, scientific, cultural and intellectual life; (2) its accommodation with local languages in multilingual contexts composed of bilingual speakers; (3) its acquisition by various levels of society (and not just the elite); and (4) its acquisition by many individuals desiring to free themselves from former bonds such as colonialism and to engage with internationalisation.

While the first and second features above are true of the development of EIL, it does not appear to be the case that all individuals in a society have the opportunity to acquire English. To perform well in a language, one often needs more than the limited tuition that state school offers, if it offers any at all. English is still an elite *lingua franca* in many countries or to poorer parts of the world population (McKay 2002, Saville 2002). Tollefson's claim that state schooling, or lack of it, can create social inequalities in the access to learning English is still an unfortunate reality for many as 'state policies play a decisive role in determining who has access to the institutions of the modern market and therefore to political power. This shift to school-based language learning is a worldwide phenomenon, and so language policy plays an important role in the structure of power and inequality in countries through the world' (Tollefson 1991: 6).

McKay (2002) also emphasises that the development of EIL necessitates an examination of the assumptions which underlie the relationship between language and culture and the teaching and learning methods employed in the classroom. Duranti (1997: 336–7) states that culture is a complex phenomenon but all theories of culture 'form a broad mandate for the analysis of language as a conceptual and social tool that is both a product and an instrument of culture' and claims that language is more than a means of expressing how we make sense of our experiences: 'Language also entertains metonymic relations with our society and culture'. As Harry Hoijer (1953) insisted, 'one should think of language *in* culture and not just of language *and* culture' (Cited in Duranti 1997: 336). Duranti explains that as language connects us to our past, present and future, it becomes our past, present and future and it is through language that we assert our rights, express our identity and sanction those who try to oppress us. 'Language is… the prototypical tool for interacting with the world and speaking is the prototypical mediating activity. Control over linguistic means often translates into control over our relationship with the world just as the acceptance of linguistic forms and the rules for their use forces us to accept and reproduce particular ways of being in the world' (ibid.: 49).

It has long been thought that to successfully learn another language one must learn about the culture associated with it: the culture provides the context for the language and thus enhances and clarifies meaning and helps appropriate a natural usage. Teachers of English as a Foreign Language have thus included lessons on culture in their curriculum but it is now proposed that to teach EIL, the learners' own culture and the students' own language should be introduced into the classroom. This would have an empowering effect and would improve the artificiality of the monolingual and monocultural setting in which students are forced to communicate only in English and about the cultures of English-speaking societies, and to pretend that it is their reality. The vast majority of learners of English will only use English in their own country to translate or interpret information they have already processed in another language (Dendrinos 2001).

However, the incorporation of learner culture and relevant English into EIL classrooms is problematic. For example, whose learning culture should be used in the classrooms? Whose discourse rules should apply? Should native speakers' standards be set? Should local teachers assess student competence? To be considered an international language, a language must not be linked to any one country or culture and must belong to those who use it. Widdowson believes that language authenticity is not merely native-speaker usage. 'The language that is authentic for native speaker users cannot possibly be authentic for learners' (1998: 711).

Another important development in the approach to language planning and curriculum development is notion of language ecology. Moving towards a classroom where non-native teachers use materials relevant not only to international issues but also to learners' local lives, culture and language needs fit into Mühlhäusler's view of local context and ecological thinking in linguistics (2000: 308), which has several distinct features. In addition to a language system's internal factors, it considers the wider environmental issues reflecting the context within which language operates; an awareness of the dangers of monolingualism and the loss of diversity; a perception of the limitations of both natural and human resources; long-term vision and a knowledge of the factors which sustain healthy ecologies.

Languages are not isolated systems but interact with other systems beyond linguistics: such as culture, environment and politics and language planning impacts on all parts of the interlinked system. A good example of language ecology in action comes from Colombia which Katarina Tomaševski, as Special Rapporteur on education for the United Nations High Commission for Human Rights (UNHCHR), visited in 2002. In her report (2004: paragraph 38:14), she explains that Ethno-education, a concept provided for under Act No. 115 of the Colombian government of 1994, is aimed at groups or communities 'that have their own native culture, languages, traditions and certain laws' and requires a differentiated approach to education. She welcomes the scheme for an educational forum proposed by local people in Chocó, the poorest region in Colombia, to 'draw up an educational curriculum with the involvement of all bearers of the right to education, whether individual or collective'. Ethno-education is described in the Colombian Constitution as education for ethnic groups which must be in accordance with their aspirations.

Mühlhäusler points to situations where language maintenance programmes have led to language loss because the activities planned have badly affected the language ecology. Language diversity is seen in the same way as biodiversity, and the growth of dominant languages is seen as dangerous for the stability of ecologies. He believes that languages with small numbers of speakers can survive in an ecology which uses intercommunity and interregional *lingua francas* for wider communication but allow the preservation of identity through mother-tongue use where appropriate. In ecological linguistics and Mühlhäusler's view, linguistic diversity is not the cause of poverty and social problems, but social problems and poverty are seen as one of the causes of the loss of this diversity.

Most of the proposed solutions to inequities in societies have urged the necessity to improve the economies of those countries. Another common solution propounded is to improve both the numbers of children attending school and the educational achievement of those pupils. One reason for the poor performance of many children is the lack of education offered in their mother tongue if it is a minority language. Stroud (2001: 342) argues that many proposed solutions to the educational predicament of minority languages in education reinforce global trends to see everything in economic terms. For example, solutions to a lack of materials in indigenous languages suggest streamlining and simplifying teaching manuals and reducing the number of subjects offered in those languages in order to increase the markets for the products. In addition, curriculum reform may retain elitist content, oriented towards metropolitan values and forms of knowledge. However, according to Mühlhäusler, language planning is not a matter of economics. In fact, healthy ecologies are mostly self-regulating and 'maintenance of single languages requires constant interference and management – restoring language ecologies will minimize management need over time' (2000: 358–9). If this is the case, this debunks the myth that language diversity produces increased costs.

The United Nations Environmental Program (UNEP) acknowledges the connection between biological resources and human resources: 'For the maintenance of linguistic and cultural diversity on our planet and the development of languages, educational language rights are not merely vital but the most important linguistic human right' (Skutnabb-Kangas 1999: 190). This is in order to maintain or increase the use of a group's language within a community. With the increase in children attending school, the language can be learnt either as a medium of instruction or as a subject in the curriculum. However, if parents are not given a choice of alternatives, they are usually unaware of the consequences or long-term aims of such a policy, one of which may be linguistic genocide. Skutnabb-Kangas sees this as a reaction to the insecurity of our 'post-modern' age, where there is a need to simplify everything, for example, one economic system (capitalism), one world language (English), one political ideology ('free-market'). Referring to education, she asks, 'How can decentralized education correspond to local needs when the "distance educators" who pull the financial and ideological strings know neither local cultures nor local languages?' (ibid.: 195). This is especially galling in the face of the seemingly intransigent monolingualism of the United States and Britain. Development and aid packages have been seen as detrimental to human rights, and non-governmental organisations have documented this.

The response of the human rights system to a free-market system is, according to human rights lawyer Katarina Tomaševski, to act as 'correctives to the free market' and she claims that 'the purpose of international human rights law is...to overrule the law of supply and demand and remove price-tags from people and from necessities for their survival' (Tomaševski 1996: 104). These necessities include the basics for a dignified life, such as civil, political and cultural rights. Education is part of these necessities: it helps to form our identity and well-being and is a prerequisite for security and freedom. Governments have the responsibility to make sure that this is offered to all people, or, in case individual governments fail, to the international community (Skutnabb-Kangas 1999: 198).

The problem is that global human rights policies rarely cover economic and social rights, and in global economic policies, human rights are hardly mentioned except when used as a political tool. In fact, it is not the case that all language rights are acknowledged as linguistic human rights which are protected by international law. Furthermore, Rannut (1999: 110) tells us that international law does not deal with languages directly but as 'markers of identity and dignity...of persons belonging to a specific group...expressed in various language functional domains' and that although international law recognises collective rights, all the linguistic rights are attached to individuals. Explicit reference to the collective aspect would give minority language speakers more protection.

There are two main linguistic human rights in education: to learn the standard form of an official language in the country of residence and to learn and use your mother tongue (Skutnabb-kangas and Phillipson 1994: 71). Kontra (Kontra et al. 1999: 10–15) describes three ways in which language-in-education rights can be restricted. First, a state can restrict the age groups and the range of subjects for which minority-medium education is provided. This usually applies to national minorities. The second way is to limit the number of languages or language varieties through which minority education in general is made available and the third method of restriction is to reduce the number of people entitled to minority-medium education by making or allowing it to remain unclear who the beneficiaries should be.

De Varennes emphasises that moral and political desires to allow or move towards the use of minority languages are not the same as the weight of the law in enforcing this right (1999: 117–46). This is acknowledged as a challenge, especially in education, where it often depends on the benevolence of the state. De Varennes outlines how international law relates to the use of minority or non-official languages in public education. In brief, in order not to be charged with a breach of the right to non-discrimination, a state has to provide an 'appropriate degree' of the use of a minority language as a medium of instruction in public schools. This degree will vary according to three criteria to be applied to each context – reasonability, appropriateness and practicality – and these cover issues such as the extent of demand for this instruction, the level of use of the minority language as a medium of instruction and the level of resources a state can offer.

A state can be seen as discriminating against individuals speaking a minority language or non-official language as a mother tongue if it provides education only in an official language in public education, and that this creates disadvantage for these people compared to others, which is considered unreasonable in that context (Article 4 of the Declaration on the Rights of Persons belonging to National or Ethnic, Religious and Linguistic Minorities; Article 14 of the Framework Convention for the Protection of National Minorities). It is equally important that the official language is taught to all pupils, in order that they may attain a good level of fluency. Failure to provide this tuition would, under existing international human rights, be deemed discriminatory if these linguistic minorities were excluded from employment or educational opportunities (ibid.: 130–2). Clearly the language of these articles is very tentative and non-specific, and the outcome is determined by many different and locally specific criteria.

Linguistic human rights in education: Three case studies

The current United Nations' Special Rapporteur on the right to education, Vernor Muñoz Villalobos (2005), says that while he cannot outline all the factors impeding the right to education in the short section entitled 'Education and Development' (Sec. C, paragraph 39:8) he highlights 'international economic policies that ignore social costs and the imposition of a uniform political and socio-economic model based rigidly on economic liberalism'. He calls for more awareness of the need for 'more flexible, human-rights-sensitive development models' and quotes Raff Carmen (2004: 83), who notes that 'the expressions "education *for* development" and "education *in* development" reflect an ideology that perceives education and development as quantifiable economic factors that can be manipulated by planners'.

Villalobos says that the ideal solution is to invest in education not only to help economic development but, more importantly, 'to build values and knowledge aimed at developing human dignity and proactive citizenship committed to the rights of the individual' (paragraph 46:8). He says that 'pressure to entrench the use of one language for all people.... is a sign of intolerance' (paragraph 72:14) and claims that the right to education 'includes the practice of people being allowed and encouraged to express their own views, appreciate the freedom to think for themselves and respect the views of others' (paragraph 117:22). He calls this 'practice of liberty'. However, he does not specifically call for these to be done through the medium of the mother tongue, the language in which all human beings can best express themselves. An examination of the use of mother tongue in education and the use of English in South Africa, the Philippines and Peru will reveal whether the 'practice of liberty' is being freely allowed and promoted.

Birgit Brock-Utne paints a depressing picture of the strengthening of ex-colonial languages in education policies across most of Africa, aided and abetted by agencies such as the British Council and the Alliançe Française, bilateral and multilateral donors, Western scholars and the African elites. The World Bank is also criticised and seems to pay lip service to the idea of the importance of African languages, seeing them as a stepping stone to the mastery of European languages while at the same time cutting subsidies to education in beleaguered countries (2000: 242).

In South Africa, however, the status of the Pan South African Language Board (PanSALB) is seen by many as a reflection of how fundamentally important linguistic human rights are viewed. PanSALB was established as an agency which, along with the government, is responsible for implementing the language provisions set out in South Africa's Constitution of 1995. While the government is charged with regulating and monitoring the language provisions, PanSALB is responsible for promoting and creating conditions for the development and use of all 12 official languages, the Khoe, Nama and San languages and South African Sign Language and to ensure respect for these. Their website outlines the objectives of 'Language in Education', which include the promotion of the use of indigenous languages as languages of learning and teaching at all levels of education. "Language in Education is pivotal to the **promotion** and **development** of the South African languages especially those languages that were previously marginalised" (Bold in the original) and 'Research conducted so far, lay [*sic*] emphasis on the value of mother tongue/home language as a language of learning and teaching (LoLT) for cognitive development…this creates a solid foundation in the learning process' (www.pansalb.org.za).

However, Heugh is one of several critics of the inability of the government of South Africa to plan and implement policies which would result in success for the majority of school children (2000: 234). Neville Alexander (2000: 172) is also negative about language policy and explains that 'the social-psychological effects of the hegemony of English in the South African and the broader African context are no less than astonishing'. In 1997, 53 per cent of all the students who took the school-leaving exam failed and Alexander suggests it is due to the poor teaching of English, the medium of instruction. What is required is what Ngũgĩ wa Thiong'o, who was imprisoned in Kenya for writing in his mother tongue, Gĩkũyũ, calls the 'decolonialisation of the mind', and he appeals to the African leaders to reverse the underestimation of their own languages. He tells us that very few people have understood the economic, cultural and political import of the language question. 'The concrete task consists of confronting the active and tacit resistance and opportunism of middle-class politicians and to inspire a new generation of African social activists to tackle the real issues of democratic transformation' (ibid.: 173).

In higher education, Webb (2002) explores whether using a second language as a medium of instruction, in this case, English, is detrimental to the learning, academic development and assessment of students at university, especially if they do not have the 'expected proficiency' in that language. He says that 'since language is an emotional and a politicised issue in South Africa, it is essential to approach it in an informed, rational and systematic manner…within the framework of strategic planning' (2002: 58–9).

Webb identifies several areas which need clarification in such an approach, including research into the language attitudes and language-based stereotypes which govern the behaviour of both staff and students; the vision of the university with regard to being locally relevant and nationally and internationally competitive; the mission of the university to undertake the development of students' academic potential and community service through academic expertise, part of which involves the maintenance and promotion of community languages as part of national and cultural development (2002: 59). He calls for the implementation of a reliable, valid, diagnostic language skills assessment for not only Afrikaans and English but also Bantu languages as 'they may provide a better indication of students' cognitive skills'. Finally, he believes that students need guidance 'to enable them to make sociolinguistically justifiable decisions regarding their academic working language, bearing in mind that knowledge and skills are not language-bound and are transferable from language to language, provided one knows the target languages involved well enough' (2002: 60). Webb believes it is more important to use resources to assess master's and doctorate level students as their work will have a greater impact on their communities: 'In this way the university can make a more significant contribution to the general level of knowledge and skills development in South Africa.'

As in most countries worldwide, the development of technology is seen as a step forward by the government, which went into partnership with Microsoft to develop software in isiZulu and Afrikaans in 2003. At the time, Andile Ngcaba; Director-general in the Department of Communications, said the government was attempting to communicate with the public in their own spoken languages – English and Afrikaans, despite the fact that these are two formerly imposed languages for most people. In 2005 it was announced that all South Africans would, by the end of that year, have a choice of language when using their home computers as Translate.org.za, a non-profit organisation, would offer support for all eleven of the official languages of the country through its OpenOffice.org 2 suite, which is a community effort between various operating system providers and independent contributors. Furthermore, the first isiZulu news website was launched carrying the same content as Isolezwe, the leading isiZulu newspaper, though it is accessed by subscription only and the editor of the newspaper admits the site targets 'the emerging, urban-based, aspirational and knowledgeable Zulu market' (2 July 2005). Indeed, all of these developments have a limited application to the everyday lives of the majority of South Africans, most of whom have no access to this technology, especially at home (www.southafrica.info).

On 17 June 2005 the Minister of Education, Naledi Pandor, announced a number of reforms which included making the learning of an indigenous language compulsory. It is hoped that this will give indigenous languages equal status with English and Afrikaans, although the Minister emphasised that this was not an intention to downgrade the importance of learning English, which, she said, would be 'foolhardy' (www.southafrica.info). This may be so, but until the majority of South

Africa's citizens receive good quality education in a language which is comprehensible to them and enables them to fully participate in society at all levels, the focus on English is premature and misguided.

Filipino–English bilingualism has been a policy in the Philippines since the early 1970s. Nevertheless, its success, which is a constantly debated issue, centres around three issues: the dominance of English; the imposition of Filipino, the designated national language which was engineered in the 1980s and the status and use of indigenous languages such as Cebuano. Arcelo (1990) concluded that the type of bilingualism that occurs depends on the socio-economic situation of the speakers: where manual workers will switch between their vernacular and Filipino. Philippinos working in the professions rely mostly on English and the government uses English as its principle means of written and oral communication.

With regard to education, although successive governments have implemented the Bilingual Education Policy (BEP), the curriculum which promotes bilingualism, they have failed to take into account the development of the vernaculars of the people whose first language is neither English nor Tagalog, the language on which Filipino is largely based. There is an acknowledgement of the need to use 'regional' languages as an auxiliary media of instruction and an initial language for literacy where necessary, but this is submerged within the heavy focus on the increase of, initially, Filipino and, more recently, English at all levels of education.

The latest studies of the use of language in Philippine education (Brigham and Castillo 1999) found several flaws in the implementation of the curriculum (http://www.deped.gv.ph): it did not allow for creativity or good communication; there was inadequate preparation and low proficiency levels of language teachers in schools and a fair degree of resistance to the policy, especially in the southern islands where an English-only policy for instruction is preferred. Sibayan (2000: 253) has said that the BEP has produced 'semilinguals', with an inadequate command of both English and Filipino and an inadequate knowledge of subject matter in both languages. Those who have dropped out of basic education; those who have completed secondary and college education and many current teachers are included in this group. Smolicz and Secombe (2000: 169) claim that the neglect of indigenous languages other than Tagalog is a form of linguistic imperialism which, as Phillipson (1998: 104) points out, is a 'sub-type of cultural imperialism, along with media, educational and scientific imperialism'. Tupas (2001 cited in Bernardo 2004: 26) repeats the observation that economic advantages gained with English proficiency are restricted to those who are already privileged, comprising the 'top' 5 per cent of the population who attend excellent schools in Metro Manila or other urban centres.

Bernardo (2004) identifies both the practical problems of moving away from the use of English and the current damaging effects of English on learning, rather than learning in one's mother tongue. If the poor do manage to complete secondary education, they enter the poorest quality colleges, end up speaking imperfect English, risk failing the professional licensure examinations, which are in English, and end up with low-paying, low-level jobs if they find employment at all. Bernardo concludes that the changes in the role and status of English in the Philippines hardly ever occur out of pedagogic considerations. 'The short history of English in Philippine education clearly shows that political, ideological and other socio-economic considerations will always strongly bear on this issue' and that it is vital that planners of educational language policy do not consider English as a 'neutral' language. 'Education, after all, is not simply about acquiring skills and knowledge. More importantly, education is about developing perspectives and tools of analysis with which people can come to understand and engage the problems in their personal and social environments' (2004: 29).

Those who support the Filipino and English bilingual education policy believe that, by eliminating all but one indigenous language for all educational and official functions and, in effect, relegating most of their speakers to illiteracy in their first language, they are preventing English from dominating. In reality, the opposite is occurring, as educated young people (the elite of other Philippine language groups) are turning towards English in preference to Filipino, which they perceive as representing the core values of other people and as less useful for advancement in an increasingly globalised society (Smolicz and Nical 1997). Those children will attend extra-curricular English language classes, or even attend private schools where English is the medium of instruction. They see English as an economic resource and, conversely, the promotion of their national language, Filipino, as holding back economic development. Therefore, those who are unable to receive their education in their native tongue, and are unable to receive effective tuition in English, are still disenfranchised. At elementary level, the children of the rural poor have to learn two completely new languages, English and Filipino, and yet still only achieve a 'halting' level of fluency in both while, at the same time, not acquiring adequate literacy in their mother tongue (Gonzales 1996: 43). Since most people are unable to acquire English fluently, and over a third of the population does not speak Tagalog as a first language, they are stuck with poorly paid, marginal employment with little hope of advancement. Although there have, as Tollefson (1991) predicted, been recent signs of awakening language consciousness in the form of advocacy of Cebuano in the Cebuano-speaking provinces to replace Tagalog as the official language, it is paradoxical that in order to gain influence with the government to change policy in favour of the majority, the pressure groups have to be competent users of English or Filipino and become participants in a society which does not serve their interests. Thus, it is clear that language policies requiring widespread second language acquisition may help to maintain a system in which language is a key indicator of socio-economic class and power. English was sold as the 'great equaliser' and Filipino is sold as the 'unifier', but in reality the ability to use either fluently depends on your status in society or your first language.

There is no indication that this is about to be reversed: a memorandum from the Department of Education, dated 19th June 2003, encloses a copy of Executive Order No. 210 (17 May 2003), (http://www.deped.gv.ph) entitled *Establishing the Policy to Strengthen the Use of the English Language as a Medium of Instruction in the Educational System*. This advocates that English is to be taught as a second language starting at first grade of primary school. English is to be used as the medium of instruction for Mathematics and Science from at least third grade and is to be used as the primary medium of education, in both state and private schools, at secondary and tertiary levels. The main reason given is 'to develop the aptitude, competence and proficiency of all students in the use of the English language to make them better prepared for the job opportunities emerging in the new, technology-driven sectors of the economy'.

The commitment to the continued development of Filipino is also repeated. However, an examination of the basic educational achievement statistics for the years 1998–2004 at primary and secondary levels shows less than 50 per cent for both levels in particular grades: 49.92 per cent in English for grade four at primary level in 2003–2004 and 41.48 per cent after a year at secondary level in the same year (http://www.deped.gv.ph). While it does not offer reasons for the poor performance of students, it can be assumed that language proficiency may well play a part. In fact, the Department of Education has announced plans for remedial classes in English, Science and Maths to improve the achievement rates (*Education Post*, 40(11), 2005). It is to be hoped that strengthening the use of English and improving teacher-training will help Philippine children to achieve better grades and take part in a more equitable society but at what cost to the local ecology and those speakers of indigenous languages other than Tagalog?

In Peru, there are 93 living languages and all languages are official (www.ethnologue.com). Spanish is spoken by 80.3 per cent of the population, Quechua by 16.2 per cent and other indigenous languages are spoken by 3 per cent (www.peru.gob.pe). However, despite the official status of all languages and existing legislation which recognises the linguistic and cultural rights of all Peruvians, there has been discrimination against speakers of indigenous languages for years. In order to improve the situation, the Office for the Coordination of Educational Rural Development (OER), the Ministry of Education and the National Office of Intercultural Bilingual Education (DINEBI) presented a proposal for a new law (Ley de Lenguas) to specify linguistic and cultural rights in order to make them easier to guarantee and implement and to attempt to halt the marginalisation and exclusion of speakers of indigenous languages in Peruvian society. The law would extend the legal framework of the legitimacy of intercultural bilingual education, with Article 20 offering intercultural bilingual (mother-tongue–Spanish) education at all levels (www.minedu.gob.pe). The consultation process with various groups of users, academics and so on began in December 2002 and the proposal was presented to the Congress of the Republic. However, although it became law in November 2003, its content was amended, resulting in a much weaker format whereby the state's commitments to implement linguistic rights are couched in vague terms and the law is renamed: the recognition, preservation, promotion and spread of indigenous languages. This has resulted in disappointment and disillusionment among indigenous language speakers (www.aymara.org).

With regard to the use of English, the government specifies that the learning of internationally used languages should not be the privilege of a few and that all children should have access to 'the new world order' (DINEBI 2002: 2:4). However, the research of Mercedes Niño-Murcia shows that these aspirations to achieve equity are likely to remain mere aspirations. She conducts research in three different socio-economic areas in Peru in order to examine attitudes towards studying English and concludes that the widely held idea that mastery of English will lead to greater social and economic opportunities is 'an example of overgeneralised globalist analysis' which ignores geographic, social, cultural and local differences (2003: 139). The notion that globalisation is inevitable and that everyone will speak English is, she says, 'dubious...but irresistible'. The reality for Peruvians is that unless one can enter highly expensive, well-resourced English–Spanish bilingual schools in cities such as Lima, or travel and study abroad, one will never attain proficiency in English. Despite the fact that learning English is part of the national school curriculum, and English language courses abound for children and adults alike, these classes are equipped with obsolete materials and taught through rote learning by individuals who are themselves unfamiliar with the target language (ibid.: 130). Unfortunately, in education, there is an increasing imbalance between requirements and resources in Peru. There is a lack of infrastructure, materials and equipment and poor quality of services delivered. For example, in 2001, 613 000 girls either repeated or abandoned state primary school, and expenditure on state education in 2003 was only $90 per person (PNUD Peru 2005: 144–5).

Interestingly, the resulting debate in Peru is not focused on the inequality of this situation for the majority of Peru's citizens, but is more inclined towards criticism of those who use English in an informal, and what is seen as inappropriate, way by those of lower social classes. Mastery of English is seen as the right and privilege of the upper social classes only (2003: 139). It thus appears that the inequality for the majority of Peruvians in both minority language and English language education is unlikely to be reversed in the foreseeable future.

Globalisation and multilingualism

The 2004 Human Development Report (UNDP), entitled *Cultural Liberty in Today's Diverse World*, examines the growing demands for inclusion in society with respect to people's ethnicity, religion and language and argues that the development of any society requires more than democracy and equitable growth. Multicultural policies that recognise differences, champion diversity and promote cultural freedoms so that all people can choose to speak their language, practise their religion and participate in shaping their culture are also needed for a sustainable approach. 'If the world is to reach the Millennium Development Goals and ultimately eradicate poverty, it must first successfully confront the challenge of how to build inclusive, culturally diverse societies' (Malloch Brown, foreword, HD report 2004, www.hdr.undp.org).

The report contends that claims for recognition and equality by diverse groups comprise one of the most urgent issues affecting international stability and human development in the twenty-first century. The Minorities at Risk project at the University of Maryland has identified more than 5000 different ethnic groups living in roughly 200 countries at present and claims that a seventh of the world's population face some form of discrimination because of their ethnic, religious or racial identities. Being in a minority due to your mother tongue is an everyday reality for many people and limitations on people using their native language can exclude people from education, political life and access to justice. In Sub-Saharan Africa, where more than 2600 languages exist, in more than 30 countries the official language is different from the one most commonly used and only 13 per cent of children who receive primary education do so in their native tongue (Human Development Report 2004: 33). Bilingual language policies are heavily recommended to give local languages equal or superior status, which reduces the high dropout rates and number of repetitions and builds human skills (HD Report 2004: 63).

However, as the Human Development Report recognises, the question about the right to receive one's education in one's native tongue is complex and though there is evidence to demonstrate that a child learns better in this language, it may become a handicap later in his/her school career if it is at the expense of learning a more widely spoken language necessary to avail himself/herself of employment opportunities. This fear is reflected in the language policies of the Philippines, where the continued increase of the use of English in preference to Filipino, which is rejected as a national language by many as the core values of other people, is not only a direct response to the imposition of Filipino on non-Tagalog peoples but also a result of the apparent requirement to participate in a globalised economy. English is seen as more useful and, in fact, an absolute requirement among the young, educated groups of the middle and upper parts of society who have access to better teaching and resources. Thus, English can be seen as perpetuating social and structural inequalities. Mühlhäusler (2000: 327) says that the processes that made English the official language of the Philippines are an example of a deliberate, artificial intervention in language ecology.

In Peru, proficiency in English is also an example of how different groups have different access to different forms of cultural capital (Niño-Murcia 2003: 138) but this also demonstrates how the overgeneralisation of the impact of globalisation can be misleading. In fact, Niño-Murcia suggests that we use the term 'globalisations' to better describe the variety and unevenness of the ever-changing social relations which may result in some cultural domains becoming relegated from the global to the local space. In the same way that Spanish–European language (preferably English) bilingualism is considered an elite attribute and

Spanish–Amerindian bilingualism is considered the 'essence of radicalised low status', the appropriation of English by those who have not learnt it 'properly' at a bilingual school, along with the manners considered necessary for international exchanges, is also stigmatised (ibid.: 125–6). English has become an asset, a prized linguistic currency, a form of cultural capital (Bourdieu 1991). Most of all, English is seen as a requirement imposed by globalisation and a global market. Learning English has become a component of an 'imagined global citizenship', one of the many ways of 'imagining globalisation'. It has also been transformed into an object of consumption rather than as a tool for learning (Niño-Murcia 2003: 121–2). This generates tension, conflict and inequality.

One of the proposed solutions to this conflict worldwide is to include linguistic ecology in government planning. It is believed that local languages are necessary to solve local problems, manage local environments and be used for locally appropriate political, cultural and economic purposes. 'Language policy must reconcile these dimensions of language ecology with the pressures of globalisation and supranationalisation that are propelling English forward' (Kontra et al. 1999: 9). For example, although in Africa 90 per cent of the population speaks only an African language and in India only 3–5 per cent speaks English, there is a constant drive for more English speakers. Mühlhäusler believes that 'by planning for ecological quality and social justice an equality can be created which can accommodate diversity' (2000: 354), and Stroud takes this further, suggesting that issues of language policy and programmes are, in fact, questions of social and economic equity and that economic solutions to minority languages do not tackle the underlying structural problems (2001).

With specific reference to African Mother-tongue (MT) programmes, Stroud says the problems are not about education in a 'narrow' sense but 'are about the nature of institutional structures that work to disempower their clients, by reinforcing tendencies to marginality of [*sic*] minority languages and speakers already prevalent in outside society … problems that centre on the distribution of power and economy in society, and ultimately turn on issues of democracy, equity and access to political voice for speakers of indigenous languages' (ibid.). Stroud also calls for greater participation of communities in the writing and development of MT programmes and questions how marginal linguistic groups can exert political influence to make legitimate claims for a bigger share of the resources necessary for successful MT programmes. Tomaševski and Zygmunt Bauman also believe that their acquisition will not improve until there is a more equal distribution of resources for implementing them and that this cannot be done under the current free-market system (Skutnabb-Kangas 1999: 201).

Though the application of linguistic human rights has been hailed as a means whereby minority language speakers can acquire greater public acknowledgement and greater political legitimacy, Stroud concludes that, in relation to Africa, there is no recognition of sociolinguistic realities and that when social and economic issues are debated in relation to language, they continue to deal with the rights to acquire a former colonial language and only refer to formal, official arenas (2001: 346–50). Thus he presents his notion of 'linguistic citizenship', which, he believes, is often overlooked though it has the potential to promote greater social change and will provide greater long-term benefits to minority language groups than the promotion of linguistic human rights (2001: 345–6). 'Linguistic citizenship addresses the very real materiality of language in minority politics by attending to the fact that linguistic minorities suffer from both structural and valuational discrimination' (2001: 351). It includes equal rights in employment, access to social welfare provision and education, and equal protection of the law. It is linguistic citizenship which 'criticises the legitimacy of mainstream, majority speaking, official-language society to delimit and characterise language practices solely in terms of formal and public spheres', embodies 'commonality *of* action and commonality *in* action' and encourages broad language coalitions. He shows how it would remedy the problems he outlines with the application of human rights (348–50).

It does appear that the current situation in South Africa needs a new direction. Language rights in Africa are based on the individual human rights of equality for all and non-discrimination against any person wishing to access their rights. A leaflet, entitled *Know Your Language Rights*, tells South African nationals that multilingualism is a reality in their country and that the Constitution contains a bill of rights to ensure parity and non-discrimination for all. PanSALB is legally obliged to investigate all written complaints regarding alleged discrimination on the basis of language and has the power to make findings. However, the investigation would be 'informal' and 'PanSALB *may* (my italics) be in a position to assist' an individual in cases of discrimination (www.pansalb.org.za). This is then, in fact, not a powerful agency to protect the language rights of speakers of indigenous languages, many of whom are not achieving at school where their education is in a language which is not their mother tongue and is not taught sufficiently well.

With regard to native-speaker varieties of English, it can be argued that organisations such as the World Bank and countries like the United States have, in the past, all tried to 'manage' the growth and dominance of British and American English. In many countries, such as South Africa, British English is still pre-eminent as an official language and as a medium of education, especially in higher education, even when its use does not lead to greater achievement by students or contribute obviously to the development of society as a whole. The British Council, which claims to be teaching English to 495 000 students in 57 countries at present, has responded to the charges, holding seminars titled 'Globalisation and the English Language' in February 2003 and 'Minding the Gap: Intercultural Approaches to ELT' in March 2005, and has developed websites such as 'Connecting Futures' where young people can share experiences and ideas with the aim of building understanding and respect between people with different cultural backgrounds. In addition, the websites of both the British Council and the BBC have pages for non-native speaker teachers of English which include articles on intercultural awareness, socio-cultural issues and using the learners' mother tongue in the classroom (www.britishcouncil.org/bbc.co.uk). Both organisations bear a great responsibility.

Lifestyles, languages and values are fluid in all societies. With the increasing popularity of English as an International Language, English is becoming more relevant to learners and is thus more likely to succeed. McKay (2002) states that local teacher standards, competence, assessment and local learning culture should be used in EIL in classrooms. McKay sees culture learning as a social process and thus 'in reference to EIL, understanding one's own culture in relation to that of others is paramount' (2002: 81). If one accepts Byram's distinction between biculturalism – accepting another culture – and interculturalism – learning about but not accepting another culture – it can be concluded that the acquisition of an international language does not require biculturalism (Byram 1998). Llurda calls for EIL to become a 'stabilised variety' whereby changes caused by the international nature of the language should be learned by native speakers rather than the other way round and says that 'English can be used as a tool for linguistic unity without compromising cultural, historical, or ideological diversity' and that this may save minority cultures from 'cultural obscurity' (2004: 321).

Cultural and linguistic diversity is increasingly becoming 'recognised' as a political and judicial necessity. As stated in the first Article of the UNESCO, Universal Declaration on Cultural Diversity, 'cultural diversity is as necessary for humankind as biodiversity is for nature. In this sense, it is the common heritage of humanity and should be recognised and affirmed for the benefit of present and future generations' (UNESCO 2002 in HD Report 2004: 89). However, the reality in all three countries examined above shows that the attitudes in society resulting from the conflict between the use of English and indigenous languages, which is heavily linked to economic globalisation, is currently problematic and could prevent many individuals from benefiting from the development of their own countries. Instead of obsessing about a globalised economy, we should affirm global culture and linguistic diversity which is about 'universal ethics based on universal human rights and respect for the freedom, equality and dignity of all individuals' (HD Report 2004: 90). Maintaining linguistic diversity means respecting local ecologies. As Niño-Murcia states, 'The interface between the global and the local discourses can no longer be ignored' (2003: 123).

References

Alexander, N. (2000) 'Language Policy and Planning in South Africa: Some Insights', in R. Phillipson ed. *Rights to Language: Equity, Power and Education.* New Jersey: Lawrence Erlbaum Associates Inc., pp. 170–3.

Arcelo, A. A. (1990) 'The Role of Language in Philippine Society', *Philippine Journal of Linguistics*, 21(1), pp. 51–5.

Bernardo, A. B. I. (2004) 'McKinley's Questionable Bequest: over 100 Years of English in Philippine Education', *World Englishes*, 23 (1), pp. 17–31.

Bourdieu, P. (1991) *Language and Symbolic Power.* Oxford: Polity Press with Blackwell Publishers Ltd.

Brigham and Castillo (1999) *Language Policy Formulation in the Philippines: Technical Background Paper*, 6. Philippine Manila: Educational Sector Study, Asian Development Bank.

Brock-Utne, B. (2000) 'Education for All–In Whose Language?', in R. Phillipson ed. *Rights to Language: Equity, Power and Education.* New Jersey: Lawrence Erlbaum Associates Inc., pp. 239–42.

Brutt-Griffler, J. (2002) *World English: A Study of Its Development.* Clevedon: Multilingual Matters.

Byram, M. (1998) 'Cultural Identities in Multilingual Classrooms', in J. and F. Genesee eds, *Beyond Bilingualism.* Clevedon: Multilingual Matters, pp. 96–116.

Carmen, R. (2004) *Desarrollo Autónomo.* Heredia: EUNA.

Dendrinos, B. (2001) 'The Pedagogic Discourse of EFL and the Discoursive Construction of the NS's Professional Value'. Paper Presented at the International Conference on Non-Native Speaking Teachers in Foreign Language Teaching, Lleida, Catalonia, Spain.

de Varennes, F. (1999) 'The Existing Rights of Minorities in International Law', in M. Kontra, R. Phillipson, T. Skutnabb-Kangas and T. Várady eds, *Language: A Right and a Resource.* Budapest: Central European Press, pp. 117–46.

Dirección Nacional de Educación Bilingüe Intercultural (DINEBI) (2002) *Programa Nacional de Lenguas y Culturas en la Educación.* Lima: Ministerio de Educación.

Duranti, A. (1997) *Linguistic Anthropology*. Cambridge: Cambridge University Press.

Gonzales, A. (1996) 'Bilingual Communities: National/Regional Profiles and Urban Repertoires', in Bautista, M. ed., *Readings in Philippine Sociolinguistics*. Manila: De La Salle University Press, pp. 38–62.

Graddol, D. (1997) *The Future of English? A Guide to Forecasting the Popularity of the English Language in the 21st Century*. London: The British Council.

Graddol, D. (1999) 'The Decline of the Native Speaker', *AILA Review*, 13, pp. 57–68.

Heugh, K. (2000) 'Giving Good Weight to Multilingualism in South Africa', in R. Phillipson ed., *Rights to Language: Equity, Power and Education*. New Jersey: Lawrence Erlbaum Associates Inc., pp. 234–8.

Hoijer, H. (1953) 'The Relation of Language to Culture', in A. Kroeber ed., *Anthropology Today*. Chicago: University of Chicago Press, pp. 554–73.

Kontra, M., Phillipson, R., Skutnabb-Kangas, T. and Várady, T. (1999) 'Conceptualising and Implementing Linguistic Human Rights', in M. Kontra, R. Phillipson, T. Skutnabb-Kangas and T. Várady eds, *Language: A Right and a Resource*. Budapest: Central European Press, pp. 1–21.

Llurda, E. (2004) 'Non-native Speaker Teachers and English as an International Language', *International Journal of Applied Linguistics*, 14(3), 314–23.

McKay Lee, S. (2002) *Teaching English as an International Language: Rethinking Goals and Approaches*. Oxford: Oxford University Press.

Morley, D. and Robins, K. (1995) *Spaces of Identity: Global Media, Electronic Landscapes and Cultural Boundaries*. London: Routledge.

Mühlhäusler, P. (1996) *Linguistic Ecology: Language Change and Linguistic Imperialism in the Pacific Rim*. London: Routledge.

Mühlhäusler, P. (2000) Language Planning and Language Ecology, *Current Issues in Language Planning*, 1(3), 306–67.

Muñoz Villalobos, V. (2005) *Annual Report 2005*. UN Economic and Social Council.

Niño-Murcia, M. (2003) ' "English is like the Dollar": Hard Currency Ideology and the Status of English in Peru', *World Englishes*, 22(2), 121–42.

Pakir, A. (1991) 'The Range and Depth of English-Knowing Bilinguals in Singapore', in *World Englishes*, 10, 167–79.

Phillipson, R. (1998) 'Globalising English: Are Linguistic Human Rights an Alternative to Linguistic Imperialism?', in P. Benson, P. Grundy, and T. Skutnabb-Kangas eds, *Language Sciences*, 20(1), 101–12.

Phillipson, R. (1992) *Linguistic Imperialism*. Oxford: Oxford University Press.

PNUD Peru (Programa de las Naciones Unidas para el Desarrollo [in English: UNDP]) (2005) *Hagamos de la Competitividad una Oportunidad para Todos*. Lima: PNUD.

Rannut, M. (1999) 'The Common Language Problem', in M. Kontra, R. Phillipson, T. Skutnabb-Kangas and T. Várady eds, *Language: A Right and a Resource*. Budapest: Central European Press, pp. 99–117.

Saville, J. (2002) 'Language and Equity: A Development Perspective', in U. Kockel ed., *Culture and Economy: Contemporary Perspectives*. Aldershot: Ashgate Publishing Ltd.

Sibayan, B. (2000) 'Resulting Patterns of Sociolinguistic, Socioeconomic and Cultural Practice and Behavior After More than Four Hundred Years of Language Policy and Practice in the Philippines', in M. Bautista, T. Llamzon and B. Sibayan eds, *Parangal can Brother Andrew: Festschrift for Andrew Gonzales on his Sixtieth Birthday*. Manila: Linguistic Society of the Phillipines, pp. 247–61.

Skutnabb-Kangas, T. (1999) 'Linguistic Diversity, Human Rights and the "Free" Market', in M. Kontra, R. Phillipson, T. Skutnabb-Kangas and T. Várady eds, *Language: A Right and a Resource*. Budapest: Central European Press, pp. 187–222.

Skutnabb-Kangas, T. and Phillipson, R. eds (1994) *Linguistic Human Rights: Overcoming Linguistic Discrimination*. Berlin: Mouton de Gruyter.

Smolicz, J. and Nical, I. (1997) 'Exporting the European Idea of National Language: Some Educational Implications of the Use of English and Indigenous Languages in the Philippines', *International Review of Education*, 43(5–6), 1–21.

Smolicz, J. and Secombe, M. (2000) 'Language Resilience and Educational Empowerment', in R. Phillipson ed., *Rights to Language. Equity, Power and Education*. New Jersey: Lawrence Erlbaum Associates Inc., pp. 164–9.

Stroud, C. (2001) 'African Mother-tongue Programmes and the Politics of Language: Linguistic Citizenship Versus Linguistic Human Rights', *Journal of Multilingual and Multicultural Development*, 22(4), 339–55.

Tollefson, J. (1991) *Planning Language, Planning Inequality*. London: Longman.

Tollefson, J. (1995) *Power and Inequality in Language Education*. Cambridge: Cambridge University Press.

Tomaševski, K. (1996) 'International Prospects for the Future of the Welfare State', in *Reconceptualising the Welfare State*. Copenhagen: The Danish Centre for Human Rights, pp. 100–17.

Tomaševski, K. (2004) *Economic, Social and Cultural Rights. The Right to Education. Mission to Colombia*, 1–10 October 2003. UN Economic and Social Council, Reports.

Tupas, T. (2001) 'Linguistic Imperialism in the Philippines: Reflections of an English Language Teacher of Filipino Overseas Workers', *The Asia-Pacific Education Researcher*, 10(1), 1–40.

United Nations Development Board (2004) *Human Development Report. Cultural Liberty in Today's Diverse World*. Oxford: Oxford University Press.

Webb, V. (2002) 'English as a Second Language in South Africa's Tertiary Institutions: A Case Study at the University of Pretoria', *World Englishes*, 21(1), 49–61.

Widdowson, H. (1998) 'Context, Community, and Authentic Language', *TESOL Quarterly*, 32(4), 705–16.

Websites

Aymara language organisation – http://www.aymara.org
BBC – http://www.bbc.co.uk
British Council – http://www.britishcouncil.org
Ethnologue: Languages of the World – http://www.ethnologue.com
Government of Peru – http://www.peru.gob.pe/
Ministry of Education, Peru – http://www.minedu.gob.pe
Official Domain Registry, Republic of the Philippines – http://www.deped.gv.ph
Pan South African Language Board – http://www.pansalb.org.za
South Africa's Official Gateway – http://www.southafrica.info/
UNDP, Human Development Report, Peru – http://www.pnud.org.pe
Universal Declaration of Linguistic Rights – http://www.linguistic-declaration.org

4
English in Europe: Threat or Promise?

Robert Phillipson

> Did you know that you have to start at the age of six and you have to stick at it until you're twelve at least (…) And from the very first day you go, you'll not hear one word of Irish spoken. You'll be taught to speak English and every subject will be taught through English and everyone'll end up as cute as the Buncrana people. (Friel 1984: 395)

> The study of the deeds of our ancestors is thus more than an antiquarian pastime, it is an immunological precaution. (Eco 1997: 316)

> The only true voyage of discovery, the only really rejuvenating experience, would be not to visit strange lands but to possess other eyes.…(Proust 1982: 260)

How can English be seen as a threat to the other languages of Europe if the European Union's institutions ensure the equality of the languages of the member states? Moreover, the EU is committed to maintaining linguistic diversity and member states are under an obligation to 'respect cultural, religious and linguistic diversity' in The Charter of Fundamental Rights (Article 22), agreed on by heads of state and incorporated into the Draft Constitutional Treaty (currently on hold as a result of the French and Dutch referenda).

There are in fact many reasons for concern. History, as dramatised above by Brian Friel (1984), shows that language oppression has been the norm in nation-states, whether monarchic Britain, republican France or fascist Spain. In analysing language policy we therefore need, as Eco suggests, to be aware of the deeds of our ancestors, and to learn from them. We should also be prepared, following Proust, to be sceptical of appearances and to approach the territory of the languages of Europe with a critical eye.

This chapter considers the operation of multilingualism in Europe, and suggests that there are several forms of linguistic apartheid in EU institutions. The second section documents some of the Englishisation processes under way in continental Europe, and measures that are being taken nationally and in the EU to promote diversity. The third section warns against the uncritical advocacy of English and the risks of conceptual muddle in the field of language policy, and ends by tabulating the many factors that militate against the formulation of equitable language policies.

The pro-English pressures of the European linguistic market

Some would like to see English replacing other languages. The US ambassador to Denmark, Mr Elton, was rash enough to state in 1997 that 'the most serious problem for the European Union is that it has so many languages, this preventing real integration and development of the Union'.[1] This fits with US foreign policy, because although the EU is at root a Franco-German project, the integration of Europe has been US geostrategic and economic policy since 1945. This reflects the belief that, in the words of George W. Bush when campaigning for the presidency in 2000, 'Our nation is chosen by God and commissioned by history to be a model to the world.' Condoleezza Rice, Foreign Secretary in Bush's second term, is also on record as stating, 'the rest of the world is best served by the USA pursuing its own interests because American values are universal'. The US plans for global dominance have been in formation since 1990 and been implemented vigorously since Bush took office (Armstrong 2005). Globalisation can be seen as synonymous with Americanisation (Bourdieu 2001) and all the more effective because it is not merely a conspiracy but a much more complex process permeating all aspects of our lives, and involving many push and pull factors.

The American empire agenda requires the dominance of English globally. An article frankly entitled 'In praise of cultural imperialism?' in the establishment journal *Foreign Policy* (Rothkopf 1997: 45) proclaims,

It is in the economic and political interest of the United States to ensure that if the world is moving toward a common language, it be English; that if the world is moving toward common telecommunications, safety, and quality standards, they be American; and that if common values are being developed, they be values with which Americans are comfortable. These are not idle aspirations. English is linking the world…Americans should not deny the fact that of all the nations in the history of the world, theirs is the most just, the most tolerant, the most willing to constantly reassess and improve itself, and the best model for the future.

In the second half of the twentieth century, French and German declined as major international languages, leaving English in effect unchallenged. When Romani Prodi, shortly before retiring as President of the EU Commission, was asked by a journalist from *Newsweek* (31 May 2004) about a unified Europe in which English, as it turns out, is the universal language, he replied, 'It will be broken English, but it will be English.'

Quite how this should be interpreted is anybody's guess, but Prodi was then responsible for maintaining linguistic diversity in the EU. Two legitimate inferences follow. One is that Prodi had experience of a great deal of incorrect English being used in the internal workings of the EU. This is a well-known problem, and an Editing Service has been established to ensure that texts written by Eurocrats for whom English or French is a foreign language are improved linguistically before they are translated into other languages[2]. A second inference is that English has acquired a privileged status in the EU system, which some interpret as meaning that it has become *de facto* a *lingua franca*, a prospect that Prodi appears to welcome. Unfortunately terms like *lingua franca* and 'universal language' are open to multiple interpretations, some of which will be explored below. But clearly language is power, and a choice of one language invariably serves some interests better than others. Why should the British and French (and to a lesser extent other EU states) otherwise so energetically promote their languages internationally (Phillipson 1992, 2003)?

A further semantic fuzziness occurs when there is talk of 'European' languages. Does this mean the languages used in Europe or only those languages that have been upgraded to the supranational EU level? These are a small proportion of the languages that have been present on European soil for centuries (marginalised languages are known in Eurospeak as autochthonous, regional, minority or Lesser Used languages). The languages that have the legal right to function as EU official and working languages are those which are acknowledged as having succeeded in dominating nationally in member states. They are the products of nationalist ideology, and the one-nation/one-state/one-language mythology that has prevailed for the past two centuries, both in countries with an ethnolinguistic founding myth (*Blut und Boden*) like Germany and Denmark (given voice by Herder and Grundtvig respectively) and in those in the republican citizenship tradition like France, in which 'equality' was to be created through a single language to which superior attributes are ascribed. Belgium and Finland are the exception in having more than one official EU language for their nationals.

Enlargement in 2004 meant that the EU expanded from 15-member states and 11 languages with equal rights as official and working languages to a Union of 25 states and 20 languages. Enlargement has seen a massive upgrading of the infrastructure for both translation and interpretation for languages which are demographically small, such as Estonian and Latvian. The EU also fully respects the right of the Maltese to claim equivalent rights for their language. The Irish language has had the status of a treaty language since Ireland joined the EU, but from 2007 Irish will also be an official language[3]. In addition, at the request of the Spanish government, languages which are official in specific regions of the country, Basque, Catalan, Valencian and Galician, have been granted certain rights to translation and interpretation services, but the costs are to be borne not by the EU but by Spain[4].

Whatever the EU says about wishing to be in dialogue with its citizens, and even if modest funding is provided for strengthening minority languages, the EU has no wish to expand its repertoire of official languages. Its communication problems and inability to win the confidence, let alone the loyalty of EU citizens, are popularly referred to as the EU's 'democratic deficit'. This is in essence due to the Commission, the EU's administrative apparatus, being perceived as remote, unaccountable, and generally inefficient (a valid analysis, to judge by my own experience), and to the European Parliament not being taken seriously (as the low numbers choosing to exercise their right to vote for it show). Chris Patten, soon after stepping down as a Commissioner, wrote that the European Parliament

> cannot avoid giving the impression that it is a virtual parliament, debating in the virtual languages of interpretation, representing a virtual electorate, organized in virtual ideological groups and disconnected from the political world at home. There are some things about which it can do very little. It cannot create a European electorate; there is none. Europe's demos is fractured. Goods may know no boundaries in Europe, but politics are locked firmly in national

cultures, stereotypes, histories and institutions and in national languages, few of which serve widespread international language functions. (Patten 2005: 131)

The EU language policy issue is so sensitive that it has been described as 'explosive' by the chair of the group of French members of the European Parliament, Pierre Lequiller, at a meeting called on 11 June 2003 to discuss a *Rapport sur la diversité linguistique au sein de l'Union européenne*, prepared by Michel Herbillon. Part of this combustion is due to the French endorsement of multilingualism abroad, while clinging rigidly to monolingualism at home, a policy that has, however, changed significantly in recent years[5]. There is also always the suspicion that French pleading of the cause of multilingualism in the EU is mostly intended to strengthen the position of French. Evidence of this French strategic foreign policy goal can be seen in the substantial investment by the French government since 2003, in partnership with 'Francophonie' countries, and in teaching French to representatives of the enlargement states[6].

English linguistic hegemony means that choice of language is not merely a matter for the individual language user, since we are all constrained by wider structural and ideological forces. An incident in the European Parliament exemplifies this. Members of the European Parliament (MEPs) have a paramount right to use their own language. But *Le Monde* reported on 17 February 2004 that three French MEPs tabled a motion on a financial topic not in French but in English: 'We had to shift to English in order to be heard.' Specifically the issue was the words 'standard' (in French = normal) and 'normal'. 'The problem could only be solved by resorting to English.' If even speakers of French cannot always use their mother tongue, one can imagine what the pressure is like on the speakers of the other EU languages. A lot of information about the EU is publicised on its website, but whereas all texts are available in English, and nearly all in French, there is remarkably little in any other languages, apart from the 'legal acts', the laws and directives that have the force of law in member states. The Commission declared in 2005 an intention to make its website more multilingual.

The fact that minority language users are not entitled to use their languages in EU affairs reflects the parlous state of many regional languages and all immigrant languages in Europe. Those who have national citizenship have also had European citizenship since the Maastricht Treaty of 1991, but millions of immigrants and refugees have neither. The French social scientist Étienne Balibar sees this as symptomatic of a democratic deficit internally in each state:

> European citizenship, within the limits of the currently existing union, is not conceived as a recognition of the rights and contributions of *all* the communities present upon European soil, but as a postcolonial isolation of 'native' and 'non-native' populations…a true *European apartheid*, advancing concurrently with the formal institutions of European citizenship and, in the long term, constituting an essential element of the *blockage* of European unification as a democratic construction. (Balibar 2004: 170, italics in the original)

The uprisings in French suburbs in the autumn of 2005 are the most visible manifestation of the reality of this European apartheid, even for those born in the country and who may have citizenship. The national 'democratic deficit' in each country dovetails with an international democratic deficit that characterises relations between most citizens and the anonymous, remote, elite bureaucratic apparatus in Brussels and the European Parliament.

One can therefore argue that there is now European linguistic apartheid of three types:

- the exclusion of minority mother tongues from schools, public services and recognition;
- the *de facto* hierarchy of languages in the EU system, in internal and external communication;
- inequality between native speakers, particularly of English, and other Europeans, in international communication and especially in EU institutions.

As a result of Americanisation and Europeanisation, what we are experiencing is the erosion of the monopoly of a unifying and stratifying national language in each state. Globalisation impacts on language policy overtly and covertly. In much of Europe, competence in English is becoming a prerequisite for access to higher education and employment, in tandem with preferred forms of communication in a national language. The European monolingual nation-state, always more of a myth and project than a reality, is also under pressure from wider acceptance of the legitimate claims for minority language rights (Skutnabb-Kangas 2000). What is not at all clear is to what extent states are deciding on national language policy, or whether the initiative has already passed to EU institutions, the boardrooms of transnational corporations, and English-using gatekeepers or trendsetters in countless domains. This diversity of influences and actors explains why defensive measures to stem the tide of Anglicism in continental languages (like the Loi Toubon in France) may well be tackling symptoms rather than causes.

The EU has basically steered clear of directly addressing the issue of national language policies. It has no mandate to do so, but many of its policies do in fact impact on the use and learning of languages in member states and by their representatives in dealings with the EU. It is responsible for organising the functioning of its institutions internally and externally in a selected set of languages. It provides funding for student mobility, and for strengthening language learning. Language issues reach the media headlines occasionally when a government or political leader protests about the workings of linguistic apartheid (see examples in Phillipson 2003). For instance, the Copenhagen summit in December 2002 was primarily concerned with reaching agreement on terms for the accession of new member states. At the press conference with heads of state from the existing and potential states, the banner headline behind the politicians read 'One Europe' in one language only. This prompted the Spanish Foreign Secretary, Ana Palacio, to write in *El País* on 16 December 2002: 'The motto "One Europe", solely in English, requires a reflection. Even though Copenhagen did not face the question of languages, this is one of the pending subjects that sooner rather than later must be debated for the very survival and viability of this project of Europe with a world vocation. Within it, Spanish, one of the official UN languages, spoken by more than 400 million people in more than 20 countries, must take on the place it is entitled to.'

Precisely what this 'place' should be is unclear because the issue of languages at the European level has not been openly addressed. The Convention on the Future of Europe ignored language policy issues, even if recent EU reforms aim at increasing accountability and better communication between EU institutions and citizens. The Convention chose to ignore 'Linguistic proposals for the future of Europe', submitted by the Europa Diversa group[7], which pleads for more active policies to strengthen linguistic diversity, for funding for all autochthonous European languages, for the subsidiarity principle to ensure that power and self-regulation in language affairs should be as decentralised as possible, and for a public debate on reform of the EU system.

English is therefore Janus-faced. It can be seen to open doors to commerce, influence, cosmopolitanism and employment for the individual and a national economy. Simultaneously it represents a threat to national language autonomy and vitality, and a closed door for those not proficient in it. Linguistic apartheid operates at the level of both the individual and the group, and is all the more insidious because native speakers appear to be unaware of the operation of linguistic hierarchies. The existence of these has been normalised and internalised as a natural state of affairs – even when it may be 'broken English'.

Push and pull factors in Englishisation

There is an increasing use of English in continental Europe in business, science, the military, education (as the first foreign language and as the medium for teaching in tertiary education and occasionally at the secondary level), in media, youth culture, networking, and so on. This is an ongoing, dynamic scene, but there are various types of document-ation of Englishisation:

- There has been a paradigm shift from a concern in several countries with an invasion of loan words (Étiemble 1964) to the broader sociolinguistic picture, with books appearing bearing titles like *L'Europe parlera-t-elle anglais demain?* (Chaudenson 2001), *Globalization and the Future of German* (Gardt and Hüppauf 2004), and *English-only Europe? Challenging Language Policy* (Phillipson 2003).
- There are studies of the Englishisation of academia in several countries (Phillipson and Skutnabb-Kangas 1999, Wilson 2002, on Ammon 2001 see Phillipson 2002) and of the reception of English at all levels of society in Denmark (Preisler 1999).
- A study of the key Swedish national journal *Ekonomisk Tidskrift*, renamed in 1965 as the *Swedish Journal of Economics* and in 1976 as the *Scandinavian Journal of Economics* (with Blackwell since 1986), documents a fundamental shift in authorship: 90 per cent Swedish in the 1960s, under 20 per cent since 1990 (and 30+ percent US authorship) (Sandelin and Ranki 1997). Related studies show that databases used for 'international' comparisons are biased, since continental Europeans also publish in other languages (Sandelin and Sarafogkou 2004). The expectation that continental academics publish in English influences topics, paradigms, first-language competence, and careers.
- A study of Nordic medical doctors reading an article either in English or in a translation into Danish, Swedish, or Norwegian revealed that doctors reading the text (from the *Journal of Trauma!*), whether in a paper version or on a screen, took in more when reading in

their mother tongue. Open-ended questions testing comprehension revealed that 25 per cent more information was grasped in one's first language (Höglin 2002: 32). This data calls into question whether the way English is expanding in northern Europe is effective or desirable.

- Researchers tend to read one foreign language, rather than several. Figures for translation show that in Sweden a century ago an approximately equal number of titles were translated from French, German, and English. Now most translation is from English (Melander 2001).
- There is a general perception of English being adopted as the dominant corporate language in large companies throughout continental Europe, but while this may well be the case at the higher management level, and in external relations, there is often a bilingual policy in practice.
- A Danish researcher (Hjarvad 2004) analyses medialects, the new variants of language and cultural form – computer games, email and Internet interaction, SMS text messaging, television programmes (whether transmitted in the original language or the local one), advertising, etc. – which are creatively adapted from Anglo-American origins in continental Europe. The medialects consolidate the position of English, while excluding other international languages, and open up for 'linguistic differentiation and innovation'. Englishisation affects the form and content of other languages.
- The increased use of English in EU institutions and practices has been analysed (Phillipson 2003).
- Surveys in all the Nordic countries of the increasing use of English in scholarship and technology, in higher education, the business world and media, suggest that there are strong risks of domain loss in local languages (Höglin 2002), leading to less efficiency in thought, expression, and communication as well as lower prestige for the national language (Melander 2001). 'Domain loss' is an unfortunate term if it obscures agency, and these processes of language shift are preferably seen as entailing linguistic capital accumulation by dispossession (Phillipson 2006).

Recent developments in the Nordic countries deserve special mention, since they document a trend away from a concern with English as a threat towards the articulation of policies for endorsing diversity. The Swedish government established a parliamentary commission to evaluate whether Swedish was under threat from English and to elaborate an action plan to ensure that Swedish remains a 'complete' language, learned and used well by its first- and second-language speakers, and retains its full rights as an EU official and working language. The plan also aims to ensure that Swedes are equipped to function well in foreign languages, particularly English, and that Swedes from a minority language background enjoy language rights. A massive national consultation process was then implemented, and designed to lead to legislation that will strengthen infrastructure for language policy. Unfortunately the government seems to be dragging its feet at this point, but this nation-state seems to be shifting from monolingualism to a differentiated spectrum of multilingualism.

Norway and Finland are also investing substantially in multilingualism, whereas Denmark is expecting its higher education institutions to become bilingual in English and Danish, for teaching and research purposes, without providing any of the additional funding that would be needed for in-service training or professional upgrading. Danish university principals published an analysis of internationalisation in 2004, with many recommendations[8]. There are three main policy thrusts: 1) to retain and attract the best students in competition with foreign universities, a clear nod in the direction of the Bologna process, in which 'internationalisation' is largely regarded as synonymous with English-medium higher education (Phillipson 2006: 2) to persuade government to provide universities with better conditions for internationalisation, a legitimate complaint that funding is being cut back at a time when more is expected of universities, for instance Danes being able to function equally well in English; and 3) to strike a balance between the role of universities as Danish research and teaching institutions, using Danish for these purposes, and the need to strengthen international collaboration in research and teaching, which requires competence in foreign languages, particularly English. Specifically on language policy, universities are encouraged to consider:

- the choice of languages of instruction for specific degrees;
- the languages of teaching materials;
- quality control when English is used by non-native speakers, and in-service training;
- Danish for foreign students;
- the languages of university publicity and regulations; proficiency requirements for university employees dealing with foreign students, teachers and researchers;
- the language competence of new students, and teaching and research staff, including access to Danish;

- strengthening the foreign language and intercultural competence of all students; and
- the languages of publication by researchers.

The Nordic governments circulated a draft 'Declaration of the Language Rights of Nordic residents' in a public consultation process in 2005, as a step towards governmental approval by Ministers of Culture and Education. The language rights of each resident (i.e. all those legally present, and not only for citizens) are of four types:

- to learn the language of society as a whole (Danish, Swedish, etc.);
- comprehension of other Scandinavian languages;
- languages of international utility, such as English, Spanish and French;
- maintaining and developing the mother tongue.

A fairly elaborate document sets some goals for each category and for various types of multilingualism and plurilingualism[9]. It endorses the idea of elites in many sectors of society developing 'parallel competence' in the national language and English (an intuitively appealing idea, but a somewhat fuzzy and probably unrealistic target).

All these Nordic measures represent serious efforts to benefit from the promise that (the learning and use of) English holds out, while addressing the fact that its advance can represent a threat to other languages. The commitment to bilingualism or multilingualism is also in the spirit of the EU Commission's *Promoting Language Learning and Linguistic Diversity: an Action Plan 2004–2006* (24 July 2003) (http://europa.eu.int/comm/language/policies/lang/policy/index). It seeks to promote a 'language-friendly environment' and to diversify the range of languages for learning: it recommends the learning of 'smaller' languages as well as 'larger' ones, regional, minority and migrant languages as well as those with 'national' status, and the languages of major trading partners throughout the world. The document attacks the hegemony of English as the most widely learned foreign language, and warns about the risks of domain loss: 'learning one *lingua franca* alone is not enough […] English alone is not enough […] in non-Anglophone countries recent trends to provide teaching in English may have unforeseen consequences on the vitality of the national language.' Whether domain 'loss' or 'dispossession' is in fact occurring has not yet been adequately explored for any conclusions to be drawn. Likewise, it remains to be seen whether the goal of all European school-leavers having a command of three languages is realistic, or merely a prescription for elites who are consciously or unconsciously committed to English as a hegemonic language.

The Dutch Language Union, *de Nederlandse Taalunie* (http:// taalunieversum.org) (which brings together the Netherlands, the Flemish Belgian community, and Surinam), is on record as believing that national efforts need to be supplemented by supranational ones. The Union is keen to ensure that the Dutch language can remain a 'full-scale' language [...] The first and foremost challenge...is to see that Dutch can remain a language of instruction in higher education', they also note that 'national language policy cannot do all the work – the framework is European – we need to convince governments and the European institutions of the necessity of a real European language policy.'[10] There is as yet not much indication that this has been achieved.

Phillipson (2003) attempts to provide a basis for exploring these issues. After exploring some topical issues in language policy, a historical analysis of the linguistic map of Europe (including showing why to call English the Latin of contemporary Europe is false), how global trends impact on European language policy in commerce, science, culture, and education, and the EU language system, it sets out a number of criteria for facilitating equitable communication. It also presents best – and worst – case scenarios, and makes a large set of specific recommendations for action on language policies. The underlying assumptions are that language policies should not be left to the workings of the market, and would benefit by being made explicit in relation to agreed sociopolitical and cultural goals. This would result in there being a healthy balance between an increased use of English (realising its promise) and the maintenance and promotion of all other languages (reducing its threat).

The need for conceptual rigour, scepticism, and forward planning

There is currently a considerable degree of fluidity in language policy in Europe, due to

- an unresolved tension between linguistic nationalism (monolingualism) and EU institutional multilingualism;
- competing agendas at the European, state (national), and sub-statal levels;

- an increase of grassroots and elite bilingualism, and an official rhetoric exhorting all citizens to become multilingual (an ideal that British educational planning tends to ignore); and
- a rhetoric of language rights, and some national and supranational implementation (for instance in the Celtic parts of the United Kingdom), while linguistic hierarchies largely remain unchallenged.

There is also a largely uncritical adoption of Englishisation, and not enough effort to examine how this interlocks with processes of globalisation, Europeanisation, Americanisation, and what many now see as neo-imperialism (e.g. Harvey 2005a, b).

A major effort is needed to counteract the falsity of much of the legitimation of the current pre-eminence of English. There is much self-deception in the marketing of English as the solution to all of Europe's communication problems:

- In political discourse: 'English is the world's *lingua franca*', Lord Renton, House of Lords, 14.10.2002 (since three-quarters of humanity have no command of this language, they are evidently not regarded as needing a *lingua franca*).
- In academic discourse: 'English is the lingua franca of the European Union', Abram de Swaan (2001: 174), a political scientist who cannot be unaware that there are many *lingua francas* in the EU; 'the language of the proto-European state', Laitin and Reich (2003: 98), two US political scientists specialising in language policy (for critique of this 'liberal' position, see Skutnabb-Kangas 2003).
- In international cultural diplomacy: 'English no longer belongs to the English-speaking nations but to everyone', a recurrent British Council mantra, a claim that conveniently ignores British benefits, political, economic and cultural, when its language also happens to be the language of the only super-power in the contemporary world.[11]
- In applied linguistics: 'the ascendancy of English is merely the outcome of the coincidence of accidental forces', Bob Kaplan of the United States (2001: 19), a prolific author.

When we consider the declaration of the Director of the British Council in Germany (cited in the *Frankfurter Allgemeine Zeitung* of 26 February 2002) that English should be the sole official language of the European Union, this smacks of traditional linguistic imperialism and incredible ignorance of how the EU operates.

All the more reason for us to work to create conceptual clarity and ensure that the terms we use are unambiguous. *Lingua franca* is a slippery concept: it is a misleading term for what is often asymmetrical communication between first-language and foreign/second-language speakers. There also seems to be an underlying assumption that a *lingua franca* is culturally neutral, and detached from dominant global or regional forces and their 'special purposes'. The term derives from the Arabic *lisan alfiranj* referring to the language of the Franks, who were seen as representing the crusaders from all over Europe who set out to recover Jerusalem and wipe Islam off the face of the known earth. There is a depressing historical continuity here, since English is now the *lingua franca* of the modern crusaders with a mission of 'freedom, democracy, and market liberalisation'. The American dog also has a flag-waving British tail: in post-communist countries in the 1990s, English was energetically marketed in tandem with the 'free' market and human rights by the British government.

I would suggest that in whatever specific contexts we meet the term *lingua franca*, we ask whether it might be more appropriately labelled as a

- lingua economica (the globalisation imperative);
- lingua cultura (the specific values and norms of a society, country, group, or class, needing exploration in foreign language teaching);
- lingua academica (an instrument for international collaboration in higher education);
- lingua emotiva (the pull of Hollywood, the global advertising and PR giants, pop culture, and how such grassroots identification with English ties in with top–down promotion of the language);
- lingua tyrannosaura (the language that gobbles up others, linguistic cannibalism) (Swales 1997);
- lingua bellica (the language of military conquest).

There is, alas, abundant evidence of lack of proficiency in understanding American English having fatal consequences in Iraq. This raises serious questions for the citizens of the United States and for others whose governments have joined the 'coalition of the willing', and not least the United Kingdom, Denmark, Italy, and Poland.

Language is integral to Britain's international standing. The ambivalence of English in the EU is connected to US agendas that in theory are not part of the ongoing 'construction' of Europe that has been in top gear since 1992, but came to (temporary?) grief in 2005. The pause for reflection on the entire Europeanisation process should be used to explore how language policies can be made more democratic and accountable, and how linguistic apartheid can be counteracted nationally and internationally.

Unfortunately, there are many obstacles to supranational, Europe-wide language policy formation. They can be enumerated in outline. Each of them impinges on English as both threat and promise. The length of the list makes it abundantly clear that the tension between English as threat and promise is not straightforward. What is unclear is what the outcomes of the present trends will be:

- European history has led to different cosmologies in national linguistic cultures, making cross-cultural dialogue treacherous.
- There are collisions of terminology (e.g. *'lingua franca'*, 'multilingualism', 'working language') in discourse (politics, media, business, etc.), and in distinct academic disciplines, as well as in different countries.
- Overall responsibility for language policy in the EU is fragmented (Council of Ministers, Directorates for Education and Culture, Translation, etc.), and is ultimately an inter-governmental responsibility.
- There is a poor infrastructure nationally (except in Finland and Catalonia, perhaps in Sweden after legislation) and supranationally for addressing language policy issues, including a weak infrastructure in research.
- International co-ordination among national language bodies is in its infancy, and the processes for dialogue between scholars, interest groups, and policy-makers are fragile.
- Language policy is politically untouchable at inter-governmental level.
- The EU institutions are inconsistent in living up to ideals of multilingual equality (website, communications with member states) and in effect practise linguistic apartheid.
- The EU translation and interpretation services are impressive in many respects, but are detached from international research, and subject to an economic rationale, seeing themselves as a service function rather than policy making (Phillipson 2003: Chapter 4).
- The language of EU written texts is increasingly under attack (Koskinen 2000, Lundquist and Gabrielsen 2005, Tosi 2005), even if the translation industry and translation technology are of increasing importance (Cronin 2003).

- The rhetoric of EU multilingualism and linguistic equality is seen as a charade by many.
- Linguistic human rights are a recent development in international law, and do not constrain 'international' languages.
- Criteria for guiding equitable supranational language policy are under-explored.
- Journalistic coverage of language issues tends to be ill-informed.
- Alternatives to market forces (the comparative advantage of English in the European linguistic market) and linguistic nationalism (e.g. Esperanto) are unexplored.

Ultimately, language policy is a matter of power politics, linguistic nationalism, and economics.

Endnotes

1. Stated at a Luncheon, University of Roskilde, March 1997.
2. Press Communiqé, MEMO/05/269 of 20/07/05, DG Translation. Translation in the Commission: Frequently asked questions (FAQ) on the strategy to match supply and demand.
3. Decision of the Council of the EU, 30 May 2005, and approved by Foreign Ministers on 13 June 2005.
4. Note introductive 9506/1/05 de la Présidence à COREPER, Conseil de l'Union Européenne, CAB 19, JUR 221.
5. See 'Rapport au Parlement sur l'emploi de la langue française', published by the Délégation générale à la langue française et aux langues de France, Paris, 2005. The Delegation forms part of the Ministry of Culture and Communication (www.dglf.culture.gouv.fr). The report includes statistics for the use of regional languages in school education, in teacher training, and in the media.
6. Details of this are provided in the report identified in the previous endnote.
7. Fourth draft, 1 July 2002, approved by an international conference convened by five Catalan bodies in Barcelona, May 31–June 1.
8. Rektorkollegiet, *Internationalisering af de danske universiteter, vilkår og virkemidler*, 2004. The website also exists in part in English (www. rektorkollegiet.dk).
9. This pair of concepts is being marketed by the Council of Europe in its many instruments to strengthen language learning and language policy formation. They distinguish between plurilingualism as individual competence in more than one language, generally at varying levels, and wish multilingualism to refer to societies characterised by more than one language.
10. Speech by Johan van Voorde to the Stockholm meeting, 2003, of the European Federation of National Language Institutes, EFNIL (www.eurfedling.org).
11. The UK economy benefits by £11 billion p.a. directly, and a further £12 billion indirectly, from international education. The goal is 8 per cent

annual growth across the sector, and to double the present number of 35,000 research graduates contributing to the United Kingdom's knowledge economy by 2020. In addition at least 500,000 attend language learning courses p.a. (www.britishcouncil.org/mediacentre/apr04/vision_2020_press_notice.doc).

References

Ammon, U. ed. (2001) *The Dominance of English as a Language of Science: Effects on Other Languages and Language Communities*. Berlin and New York: Mouton de Gruyter.

Armstrong, D. (2005) 'Drafting a Plan for Global Dominance', in J. Pilger ed., *Tell me no Lies. Investigative Journalism and its Triumphs*. London: Verso, pp. 516–30.

Balibar, É. (2004) *We, the People of Europe? Reflections on Transnational Citizenship*. Princeton: Princeton University Press.

Bourdieu, P. (2001) *Contre-feux 2. Pour un mouvement social européen*. Paris: Raisons d'agir.

Chaudenson, R. ed. (2001) *L'Europe parlera-t-elle anglais demain?* Paris: Institut de la Francophonie/L'Harmattan.

Cronin, M. (2003) *Translation and Globalization*. London: Routledge.

De Swaan, A. (2001) *Words of the World: The Global Language System*. Cambridge: Polity Press.

Eco, U. (1997) *The Search for the Perfect Language*. London: Fontana.

Étiemble, R. (1964) *Parlez-vous franglais?* Paris: Gallimard.

Friel, B. (1984) *Selected Plays*. London: Faber and Faber.

Gardt, A. and Hüppauf, B. eds (2004) *Globalization and the Future of German*. Berlin: Mouton de Gruyter.

Harvey, D. (2005a) *The New Imperialism*, 1st edition. Oxford: Oxford University Press (2003).

Harvey, D. (2005b) *Neoliberalism*. Oxford: Oxford University Press.

Hjarvad, S. (2004) 'The Globalization of Language. How the Media Contribute to the Spread of English and the Emergence of Medialects', *Nordicom Information*, 2, 75–97.

Höglin, R. (2002) *Engelska språket som hot och tillgång i Norden*. Copenhagen: Nordiska Ministerrådet.

Kaplan, R. (2001) 'English – the Accidental Language of Science?', in U. Ammon ed., *The dominance of English as a Language of Science. Effects on Other Languages and Language Communities*. Berlin and New York: Mouton de Gruyter, pp. 3–26.

Koskinen, K. (2000) 'Institutional Illusions: Translating in the EU Commission', *The Translator*, 6(1), 49–65.

Laitin, D. and Reich, R. (2003) 'A Liberal Democratic Approach to Language Justice', in W. Kymlicka and A. Patten eds, *Language Rights and Political Theory*. Oxford: Oxford University Press, pp. 80–104.

Lundquist, L. and Gabrielsen, G. (2005) 'EU – fortolkningsfællesskab eller fortolkningsfællesskaber?', in H. Kock and A. Lise Kjær eds, *Europæisk retskultur – på dansk*. Copenhagen: Thomson/Gadjura, pp. 123–65.

Melander, B. (2001) 'Swedish, English and the European Union', in S. Boyd and L. Huss eds, *Managing Multilingualism in a European Nation-state: Challenges for Sweden*. Clevedon: Multilingual Matters, pp. 13–31.

Patten, C. (2005) *Not Quite the Diplomat. Home Truths about World Affairs.* London: Allen Lane.

Phillipson, R. (1992) *Linguistic Imperialism.* Oxford: Oxford University Press.

Phillipson, R. (2002) 'Review of Ammon, U. ed. (2001)', *Journal of Language, Identity, and Education,* 1(2), 163–9.

Phillipson, R. (2003) *English-only Europe? Challenging Language Policy.* London: Routledge.

Phillipson, R. (2006) 'English, a Cuckoo in the European Higher Education Nest of Languages?', *European Journal of English Studies,* 10(1), 13–32.

Phillipson, R. and Skutnabb-Kangas. T. (1999) 'Englishisation: one Dimension of Globalization, English in a Changing World', *AILA Review,* 13, 17–36.

Preisler, B. (1999) 'Functions and Forms of English in a European EFL Country', in T. Bex and R. Watts eds, *Standard English: The Widening Debate.* London: Routledge, pp. 239–67.

Proust, M. (1982) *Remembrance of Things Past,* Vol. 3, translated by C. Scott-Moncrieff. New York: Vintage Books.

Rothkopf, D. (1997) 'In Praise of Cultural Imperialism?', *Foreign Policy,* 107, 38–53.

Sandelin, B. and Ranki, S. (1997) 'Internationalization or Americanization of Swedish Economics?', *The European Journal of the History of Economic Thought,* 4(2), 284–98.

Sandelin, B. and Sarafogkou, N. (2004) 'Language and Scientific Publication Statistics', *Language Problems and Language Planning,* 28(1), 1–10.

Skutnabb-Kangas, T. (2000) *Linguistic Genocide in Education – or Worldwide Diversity and Human Rights?* Mahwah, NJ: Lawrence Erlbaum.

Skutnabb-Kangas, T. (2003) Lecture at Glendon College, University of York, Toronto, October 14 (www.glendon.yorku.ca/englishstudies/events.html).

Swales, J. (1997) English as 'Tyrannosaurus Rex', *World Englishes,* 16(3), 373–82.

Tosi, A. (2005) 'The Devil in the Kaleidoscope. Can Europe Speak with a Single Voice in Many Languages?', in C. Leung and J. Jenkins eds, *Reconfiguring Europe: The Contribution of Applied Linguistics.* London: Equinox.

Wilson, D. (2002) *The Englishisation of Academe: A Finnish Perspective.* Jyväskylä: University of Jyväskylä Language Centre.

Websites

British Council – http://www.BritishCouncil.org

De Nederlandse Taalunie – http://taalunieversum.org

European Commission – http://europa.eu.int/comm/language/policies/lang/policy/index

European Federation of National Institutions for Language – http://www.eurfedling.org/

La Délégation Générale à la Langue Française et aux Langues de France – www.dglf.culture.gouv.fr.

The Charter of Fundamental Rights (Article 22) – http://ec.europa.eu/justice_home/unit/charte/index_en.html

The Danish Rectors' Conference – www.rektorkollegiet.dk

5
Minority Protection and Lesser-Used Language Promotion: The Convention on the Future of the European Union

Markus Warasin

The purpose of the Convention on the Future of the European Union was to propose a new framework and structures for the EU, paving the way for a serious reform of the European Union. The proceedings of the Convention comprised three phases: a listening phase in order to identify the expectations and needs of the Member States, their Governments and Parliaments, and those of the European society; a deliberating phase to compare the various opinions put forward and assessment of their implications and consequences; and finally, a proposing phase with a synthesis and a draft of proposals for the Intergovernmental Conference in 2004.

Since the Convention started its work on 28 February 2002 under the presidency of ex-French Prime Minister Valéry Giscard d'Estaing, minority protection or the promotion of lesser-used languages has never been on the agenda. Nevertheless, questions related to minorities in general and to regional or minority languages in particular in the context of the future of the European Union have been part of several debates, conferences and round tables outside the Convention. Several organisations working in the field of minority protection have wholeheartedly promoted an open dialogue about these questions, to which not only European institutions, academics, think-tanks or non-governmental organisations (NGOs) actively participated, but several members of the European Convention itself as well. Although the result of the Convention could therefore surely not be a 'Minority Charter', the Convention offered opportunities and clear perspectives for a potentially significant step forward in the standard setting of European minority protection and lesser-used language promotion. This chapter tries to outline the most important aspects of this potential.

Initiatives for the promotion of lesser-used languages

With 6 resolutions in the last 20 years, the European Parliament supported on a regular basis the activities promoting lesser-used languages. Despite this rather strong political and financial support, legal problems arose in 1998. Following the Court of Justice Judgement C-106/96 of 12 May 1998, the EU-budget-line for the promotion of lesser-used languages was suspended since it lacked a legal basis. Financial support was subsequently allocated for preparatory measures for a multi-annual programme in support of regional and minority languages and cultures, while in 2001 support for lesser-used languages was granted in the context of the European Year of Languages.

When in 1999 a so-called Convention was charged to draft a Fundamental Rights Charter for the European Union, several language activists and minority organisations tried to take advantage of this opportunity and to influence the draft text. Although the Convention did not include any article on minority rights nor on the promotion of regional or minority languages in its final proposal, it adopted two articles (Articles 21 and 22) promoting linguistic diversity and therefore of significance for lesser-used language communities.

The new key word for those promoting lesser-used languages thus became 'linguistic diversity'. This concept was in line with the view of the European Commission, which – after several unsuccessful efforts – made attempts to promote an innovative and new 'inclusive approach' towards minority languages. Moreover, it was in line with the views of the Council of the European Union, on which any cultural policy depends and which are expressed in the Council Resolution on the Promotion of Linguistic Diversity and Language Learning in the Framework of the Implementation of the Objectives of the European Year of Languages 2001, 14 February 2002. In this Resolution the Council emphasises that 'all European languages are equal in value and dignity from the cultural point of view and form an integral part of European culture and civilisation' (European Commission 2002).

But still, neither the Fundamental Rights Charter nor the Commission's and Council's viewpoints could substitute the missing legal basis. The main purpose for the lesser-used languages lobby within the second Convention therefore was to promote an article on linguistic diversity for the new Constitutional Treaty, which could possibly be interpreted as the right framework in which a legal basis could be created. Many of the participating cultural and linguistic organisations believed that the Convention together with the debate about the future of the

European Union would be a unique opportunity for Europe's linguistic and cultural diversity.

During the 16 months of the Convention's work several organisations, academic think-tanks and other institutions have tried to promote the role of lesser-used languages in the future of the European Union. Most of them have been integrated in the proposals submitted to the EU-Convention by the European Bureau for Lesser Used Languages (EBLUL) or are part of the suggestions presented to the Convention by the Europa Diversa Group.

The EBLUL, as an independent NGO working for languages and linguistic diversity, participated in the debate about the future of the European Union from its beginning with several resolutions and statements (www.eblul.org). At the same time the Bureau worked intensively together with several organisations, thus functioning as a network for linguistic diversity. The EBLUL tried to organise and to structure its contributions as efficiently and transparently as possible, taking the time-schedule of the Convention as an example and structuring its own debate in a similar way.

In its first contribution to the Debate about the Future of the European Union, the General Assembly of the European Bureau adopted the Charleroi-Declaration on 13 October (EBLUL 2001). The document proposed that linguistic and identity-related issues should be taken into account at all levels of government and in all stages of cultural policy-making. This would guarantee that the above-mentioned Article 22 of the Charter of Fundamental Rights of the European Union should get full consideration. Once more, the Charleroi-Declaration was clear on the commitment of lesser-used language communities towards Europe:

> Europe's lesser-used language communities want to be close partners in building Europe. United, they are deeply committed to fostering Europe's cultural and linguistic diversity. They share a common vision of a European community of law where citizens and demo-cratic institutions at local, regional, Member State and European levels are closely connected. (www.eblul.org)

In its second contribution, the Palma-Declaration (9 February 2002), EBLUL's General Assembly welcomed the decision to open a Forum in order to involve citizens and civil society in the proceedings of the Convention (EBLUL 2002a). It also called on the Convention to intro-duce an article on the promotion of linguistic diversity in its final document based on Article 22 of the Nice Charter of Fundamental Rights and including European regional or minority languages.

In its third contribution, the General Assembly launched three proposals for linguistic diversity for the Convention on the Future of the European Union. Furthermore, the Ljouwert-Declaration (15 June 2002) included some references to a multi-annual programme on linguistic diversity as well as the role of civil society in the future of linguistic diversity in the European Union (EBLUL 2002b). Additional contributions followed in Helsinki and Bozen, 12 October 2002 and 25 May 2003 respectively.

Besides these five contributions, the EBLUL organised and participated in several meetings and round-table conferences on linguistic diversity, language learning and lesser-used languages. The most important was a seminar hosted by the Basque Government in Bilbao (23 February 2002), where the Package for Linguistic Diversity was considered by a senior group of independent experts with long-term minority policy experience in the United Nations, the Council of Europe and the Organisation for Security and Co-operation in Europe (OSCE) (EBLUL 2002c). In short, EBLUL suggested the following amendments to the Treaty establishing the European Community (EC). It advocated the introduction of a specific article on linguistic diversity building on Article 22 of the European Charter of Fundamental Rights and the inclusion of language as a basis of discrimination in Article 13 EC on Non-discrimination. It also proposed a change from unanimity to qualified majority voting by the Council of Ministers in Article 151 EC on Cultural Policies.

In fact, the Bilbao Seminar, held during the Spanish Presidency, can be regarded as the prelude to EBLUL's preparation of the realistic and widely welcomed proposals in favour of linguistic diversity. For the preparation of the Package for Linguistic Diversity, the Annual Colloquy with the European Commission in Brussels (October 2001), the International Conference on Regional and Minority Languages in Noordwijkerhout (The Netherlands, November/December 2001) organised by the Council of Europe and the Dutch Government as well as EBLUL's Partnership for Diversity Forum II in Palma de Mallorca (February 2002) proved to be extremely useful. The follow-up of EBLUL's package was on the other hand very much influenced by the Europa Diversa experts' meeting in Barcelona (May/June 2002) and by the round-table conference in Ljouwert/Leeuwarden (June 2002), which were both particularly constructive and valuable.

The EBLUL has thus been in permanent contact with more than 20 NGOs and think-tanks as well as with local and regional authorities and governments working in the field of linguistic diversity, language learning and human rights, and was able to further develop the proposals for the Convention on the Future of the European Union. Since the Bureau at that time was considered an actor of utmost importance in European networking in the field of language promotion, EBLUL was chosen at the meeting of the Convention's Contact Group 'Culture' (12 June 2002) to represent civil society on language and minority issues at the Convention hearing on 24 and 25 June 2002.

The Europa Diversa Group also proved to be an excellent initiative for the promotion of linguistic diversity (http://www.europadiversa.org). The Group, constituted by the Fundació Jaume Bofill, the Department of Humanities and Philology of the Universitat Oberta de Catalunya, the Institut Europeu de la Mediterrània, Intercultura – Centre pel Diàleg Intercultural de Catalunya and the Linguapax Institute of Centre Unesco de Catalunya, organised an experts meeting in Barcelona on 31 May and 1 June 2002, in the framework of the *Eurocongrés* 2002, and with the support of the *Patronat Català pro Europa*, in order to discuss 'Linguistic Proposals For The Future of Europe'. The outcome of this meeting was one of the most comprehensive and well-prepared documents for the EU-Convention concerning the future of linguistic diversity and lesser-used languages in the European Union. In addition to EBLUL's suggestions, the Europa Diversa Group asked for

- a multi-annual Community action programme to support and promote linguistic diversity;
- the extension of all current EC language programmes, or actions that are language-specific, in order to cover all autochthonous European languages;
- a public debate to reform the rules governing the languages of the institutions of the Community and enshrining the general provisions in an Article of the Treaty, so as to ensure efficiency and a substantial redistribution of the very large budget of the present arrangement;
- ensuring that the principle of subsidiarity is reflected in matters of language policy, so that all tiers of government work together, with sufficient resources, in order to safeguard linguistic diversity.

In the autumn of 2002, important consultation events took place, for example in Helsinki (Finland) and in Brugge (Belgium), where several high level experts and politicians participated, such as Viviane Reding, Commissioner for Culture and Education, Finnish Prime Minister Paavo Lipponen, Martti Ahtisaari, former President of Finland, Giuliano Amato and Jean-Lue Dehaene, both Vice-Chairmen of the European Convention. At the European Cultural and Educational Forum in Brugge in November 2002 Giuliano Amato stated, 'While becoming more and more multicultural and multi-religious, we are more and more frightened by diversity. We want to preserve our own diversity but not those of others' (http://217.136.252.147/webpub/eurolang/pajenn.asp?ID=3964).

Amending legislation

As shortly mentioned above, a variety of proposals were submitted to the EU-Convention. The main purpose of these proposals was to consider Article 22 of the Charter of Fundamental Rights of the European Union of 7 December 2000, which declared that 'The European Union shall respect cultural, religious and linguistic diversity.' At the same time, the proposals addressed the interpretation of the words 'linguistic diversity' and 'respect' and argued that the concept of 'linguistic diversity' is based on Europe's cultural and linguistic heritage and is a vital and dynamic element of European identity. Linguistic diversity contributes to cultural wealth, social development and economic prosperity. It is part of the wider concept of 'cultural diversity', as specified in Article 151 of the Treaty establishing the European Community (Conseil de L'Union Européene) and therefore is characterised with a European dimension (Scheidhauer 2001). The concept of linguistic diversity does not distinguish between official or state languages on the one hand, and regional or minority languages on the other, this co-relates with both the Commission's and the Council's inclusive approach.

The concept of respect on the other hand includes non-discrimination in the sense of Article 13 of the same Treaty (European Commission 2002). Presumably this includes affirmative as well as non-discriminatory actions. To respect linguistic diversity implies the recognition of the equality of all European languages, whether they are widely-used or lesser-used. Respect implies the freedom and opportunity of choice and expression in all languages and it contributes to intercultural understanding and a culture of peace.

How could the new Constitutional Treaty best serve this purpose? Different solutions were considered, and EBLUL proposed the introduction of a specific article on linguistic diversity building on Article 22 of the European Charter of Fundamental Rights. Other proposals included the specific mention in Article 13 EC on Non-discrimination of 'language' as a basis for discrimination. A paragraph on positive discrimination was also proposed. Another suggestion was a change from unanimity to qualified majority voting by the Council of Ministers in Article 151 EC on Cultural policies.

While there was certainly some support in the Convention for a proper article on cultural and linguistic diversity, this Chapter does not deal with the first proposal, since it can be regarded as the maximum request presented to the EU-Convention for the promotion of linguistic diversity including lesser-used languages and therefore rather unrealistic. Instead it focuses on the developments concerning the other two proposals.

Article 13 of the Treaty establishing the European Community states:

> Without prejudice to the other provisions of this Treaty and within the limits of the powers conferred by it upon the Community, the Council, acting unanimously on a proposal from the Commission and after consulting the European Parliament, may take appropriate action to combat discrimination based on sex, racial or ethnic origin, religion or belief, disability, age or sexual orientation. (http://www. europa.eu.int/eur-lex/en/treaties/dat/ec-cons-treaty-en-pdf)

While ethnic origin generally includes languages, some individuals and communities define themselves in linguistic terms only. In this case, the absence of specific language protection could lead to indirect discrimination. Article 22 of the Charter of Fundamental Rights of the European Union, however, implies at least the absence of discrimination based on language. Therefore, the proposal put forward by representatives of the Civil Society consisted of including the word 'language' after 'ethnic origin', in order to introduce greater consistency with other international standards, accepted by all the EU Member States.

Moreover, the proposal was not just grounded on intellectual arguments and reasonable thinking, but based on experiences. In 2001 EBLUL tried to participate in a call for proposals to support umbrella European NGOs representing and defending the rights of people exposed to discrimination. A civil servant of the European Commission told EBLUL's General Secretariat that the call for proposals 'would certainly not comprise minority languages. What is at stake is not the official recognition of minority languages in Member States but the fact that people are treated unfairly just because they are black or of Asian origin etc' (Personal communication from D4 Unit, 23 November 2001).

The EBLUL promptly replied to the European Community showing its astonishment and contacted Members of the European Parliament (MEPs) from the Intergroup for Regional and Minority Languages in order to find political support. Commission President Romano Prodi and the Commissioner for Culture and Education Viviane Reding were contacted; in addition Michl Ebner MEP forwarded a written question to the Commissioner for Employment and Social Affairs, Anna Diamantopoulou (Ebner 2002). Nevertheless, the answer given by Ms Diamantopoulou on behalf of the Commission was defending the viewpoint of the European Community with legal arguments (Diamantopoulou 2002).

Members of the European Parliament (EP) as well as language activists therefore shared the opinion, that the European Union should not remain below the minimum international standards but should, on the contrary, respond to new developments of international standards, for example Protocol 12 to the European Convention of Human Rights, which provides for a general prohibition of discrimination in the enjoyment of any right set forth by law. Therefore, the promotion of an amendment to Article 13 TEC during the work of the EU-Convention was envisaged.

Convinced that including the word 'language' into Article 13 TEC would provide better consistency with the EU Charter of Fundamental Rights of the European Union in general and with Article 21 on Non-discrimination of the same Charter in particular, EBLUL, together with the MEPs, contacted several Convention Members in order to raise awareness of the possible inconsistency in EU-law. Michl Ebner MEP for instance sent a letter to the Convention to draw the attention of its Members to this fact (letter dated 8 October 2002).

However, it soon became evident that a significant number of key figures at the Convention did not share this view. Amongst others, Commissioner António Vitorino wrote in a letter to Michl Ebner MEP: 'I would like to stress that while Article 21 of the Charter establishes the principle of non-discrimination, Article 13 of the EC Treaty creates a competence to act.' He continued that the 'proposal [to put Article 13 in phase with Article 21] has therefore the consequence that it will extend the competences of the European Community related to Article 13 of the Treaty' (letter dated 11 November 2002).

Obviously the Convention was not dealing with new competencies for the EC/EU but rather with structuring the current ones in a more comprehensive and transparent manner. Nevertheless, the question remained, for what reasons a political system – like the European Union – might embrace a general principle of human rights without seeking a specific competence for positive action in the very same field in order to defend the principle. Under such circumstances the Fundamental Rights Charter of the European Union resembled more tokenism than a real tool or mechanism for the protection and the promotion of human rights.

Some prominent individuals were sensitive to the issues involved. From outside the Convention, the High Commissioner on National Minorities from the OSCE, Mr Rolph Ekeus, in a speech delivered at the Danish Parliament on 5 November 2002 on the topic 'From the Copenhagen Criteria to the Copenhagen Summit: The Protection of National Minorities in an Enlarging Europe', highlighted the challenge of Article 13 as follows:

> Take, for example, language issues. In an enlarged Europe, there will be a number of official EU languages more or less corresponding to the titular majority of Member States. But what will be the status of languages spoken by EU citizens who do not speak one of the State languages as their mother tongue? Languages like Catalan, Romani and Russian will be spoken by millions of Europeans. These are hardly so-called 'lesser used languages'. And yet it is worth noting that Article 13 of the EC Treaty (which prohibits discrimination) does not include 'language' among its grounds. This conspicuous shortcoming needs to be addressed to ensure that, in a transformed Union, all Europeans will enjoy full equality and that Europe will maintain the full extent of its rich linguistic diversity which is both an essential part of European identity and a tremendous human resource.
>
> Regrettably, the concern I hold in this regard is not merely abstract. There are worrying signs that discrimination, racism, intolerance and xenophobia not only persist across Europe, but in some cases are gaining strength. It is also clear that such ideas remain powerful mobilizing agents for populists, and that EU membership provides no immunity in this regard. In particular, religious intolerance – especially anti-Semitism and Islamaphobia – have not abated and could open fissures within our societies. These are issues that Europe must address in order to prevent intra-State cleavages from cracking the bigger inter-State project. (Ekeus 2002)

At the Convention plenary session on Monday 21 January 2002, Giscard d'Estaing announced that all in all there were currently 414 treaty articles. Of those, around 205 would remain entirely unchanged, some changes were required in a further 136, and approximately 73 would need to be rewritten. In order to draw the Convention President's attention to Article 13, the EBLUL contacted him one more time on

15 January 2002, submitting a proposal in line with previous attempts (letter, dated 15 January 2002).

The content of the EBLUL's proposal to the Convention on the Future of the European Union was supported in written form among others by Rolph Ekeus, High Commissioner on National Minorities from the OSCE (personal letter, dated 28 March 2003), by Patrick Thornberry, UN rapporteur of the Committee on the Elimination of Racial Discrimination (CERD), and by Fèlix Martí, from UNESCO's Linguapax Institute. These examples show that intergovernmental organisations as well as NGOs shared EBLUL's proposals regarding the inclusion of linguistic diversity into the future constitutional treaty of the European Union. It was clear that Article 13 of the Treaty establishing the European Community did not sufficiently cover positive actions in order to combat discrimination on the basis of language. This fact seemed to be acknowledged outside and inside the Convention. The question remained, whether there would be sufficient political will among Convention Members to amend Article 13.

For several years, Article 151 of the Treaty establishing the European Communities had been posing a difficult challenge to the promotion of linguistic diversity including lesser-used regional or minority languages. Decisions based on Article 151 require unanimity in the Council of Ministers, which for questions about minority languages can hardly be achieved. Thus, a multi-annual programme promoting lesser-used languages was never put to vote, since the veto of at least one of the fifteen Member States was highly probable. Therefore, one of the proposals put forward to the Convention consisted in replacing the required unanimity vote of the Council of Ministers by a qualified majority vote. This would facilitate the promotion of cultural heritage as a general European interest, with full respect for Member States' competencies in the field of cultural policy.

The developments in this field seemed rather positive. To look at issues more closely, the Convention decided to set up Working Groups on specific subjects, which were difficult to debate during plenary sessions. From the ten Working Groups established, two were particularly interesting regarding Article 151: Working Group V on Complementary Competencies chaired by Christophersen, representing the Danish government, and Working Group IX on Simplification chaired by Vice-President, Giuliano Amato. The Working Group defined 'complementary competencies' or 'supporting measures' (also 'supportive actions') as 'Union measures in fields where Member States are fully competent'. According to the Group, to ensure legal precision each article related to supporting measures should expressly ensure that only supporting measures could be adopted.

Furthermore the Working Group proposed to incorporate languages as 'core responsibilities of the Member States' and as 'essential elements of the national identity' in the future Constitution. This Working Group was especially important concerning the introduction of qualified majority voting into Article 151 (Culture), replacing the existing unanimity requirement. It argues that exceptional cases notwithstanding the Council would act by a qualified majority. These exceptional cases where the Council still acts unanimously are social security measures for Community migrant workers (Article 42), the co-ordination of the provisions laid down by law, regulation or administrative action in Member States concerning the taking up and pursuit of activities as self-employed persons, and the co-ordination of the existing principles laid down by law governing the professions with respect to training and conditions of access for natural persons (Article 47) and incentive measures in the area of culture (Article 151). Already during the work of the working groups it became very likely that Article 151 would have a good chance to pass from unanimity to majority voting.

In the meantime the Convention had produced the first 16 articles for a future European constitution. Presenting the articles to delegates on 6 February 2003, Convention President Valéry Giscard d'Estaing spoke of the 'political and symbolic importance of the first articles'. From his perspective, they deal with some of the most important issues for a future EU: the values, objectives and divisions of competences between Member States and the European Union.

On 11 February 2003, the European Parliament's Intergroup for Regional and Minority Languages met in Strasbourg. The then EC Commissioner for Education and Culture, Mrs Viviane Reding spoke at the event, outlining the Commission's Action Plan on Language Learning and Linguistic Diversity. She stressed the importance of safeguarding and promoting linguistic diversity including lesser-used languages in the European Union. 'All languages are equal, no matter if they are big or small', she argued once more. Following from this, an important subject of debate at the meeting was the work of the Convention. The Intergroup concluded that the first draft Constitutional Treaty articles do not adequately cover linguistic diversity. The EBLUL therefore proposed an amendment to draft Article 3.3 by including 'and languages' in the concept of diversity. The proposed amendment reads as follows: 'The Union shall constitute an area of freedom, security and justice, in which its shared values are developed and the richness of its cultural *and linguistic* diversity is respected' (letter to Professor Sir Neil MacCormick, dated 14 February 2003). According to EBLUL, this amendment was justified since the EU Charter of Fundamental Rights, as an integral part of the new Constitutional Treaty, includes the respect for cultural and linguistic diversity in Article 22.

The European Bureau contacted all Intergroup Members with the request to forward the proposal to their colleagues in the Convention. Hereafter, a variety of Members of the Convention, some of which had already been very active on previous occasions, submitted amendments to Article 3.3. Several amendments called not only for respect for different cultures of Europe but also for its languages.

On 28 and 29 March 2003, a conference was organised in a joint initiative by Michl Ebner MEP, the European Academy of Bozen, the EBLUL and the press-agency Eurolang in Bozen, and sponsored by the north Italian region of Trentino-Südtirol. Participants agreed that minority rights as well as linguistic rights should be included into the new Constitutional Treaty. Attending regional, national and European politicians, all stressed the importance of linguistic diversity, including lesser-used languages or the rights of minorities. Thus, it seemed that inside and outside the Convention there was an unmistakable and unequivocal support for the introduction of the promotion of linguistic diversity into the new EU-Treaty.

After 16 months of tough debate and bargaining, on Friday, 13 June 2003, the Convention on the Future of Europe adopted the first Draft Constitution for an enlarged European Union. Hereafter, the Intergovernmental Conference followed, which could contribute to a significant improvement of the draft presented by the Convention; namely that the rights of persons belonging to minorities could be explicitly included in the Union's values. Under the Irish Presidency the Intergovernmental Conference reached a final agreement on 18 June 2004. Finally, the Heads of State or Government and the Ministers for Foreign Affairs of the 25 Member States of the European Union signed the Treaty establishing a Constitution for Europe in Rome on 29 October 2004.

Implications of the new context

The new text signified a variety of achievements. In particular, the preamble describes Europe as 'united in its diversity' while Articles I-2 and I-3 on the Union's values and objectives state that the Union 'shall respect its rich cultural and linguistic diversity, and shall ensure that Europe's cultural heritage is guarded and enhanced'. For the first time in the EC/EU's history, linguistic diversity has found a place in the treaties. But more advancements could be registered.

More significantly, Article I-10 referred to the right of EU citizens to address the institutions and advisory bodies of the Union in any of the Constitution's languages and to obtain a reply in the same language: It noted that

> Citizens of the Union shall enjoy the rights and be subject to the duties provided for in the Constitution. They shall have: [...] the right to petition the European Parliament, to apply to the European Ombudsman, and to address the institutions and advisory bodies of the Union in any of the Constitution's languages and to obtain a reply in the same language.

A logical consequence of these provisions could well be that the European Union, enjoying legal personality, would sign not only the European Convention for the Protection of Human Rights and Fundamental Freedoms, but possibly other similar conventions of the Council of Europe as well, for example the European Charter for Regional and Minority Languages.

The second part of the Draft Constitution includes the Fundamental Rights Charter of the European Union. The already known Articles 21 and 22 were renumbered and became Article II-81 and Article II-82 respectively: They read as follows:

> Article II-81: Non-discrimination
> 1. Any discrimination based on any ground such as sex, race, colour, ethnic or social origin, genetic features, language, religion or belief, political or any other opinion, membership of a national minority, property, birth, disability, age or sexual orientation shall be prohibited. [...]
> Article II-82: Cultural, religious and linguistic diversity
> The Union shall respect cultural, religious and linguistic diversity.

The third part of the Draft Constitution no longer dealt with general principles but with concrete instruments which permitted the European Union to apply EU-law. And there were some inconsistencies although Article II-81 on non-discrimination had included language as an important issue. Neither Article III-118 nor Article III-124 referred to discrimination based on language or on membership of a national minority. Although the European Union does in principle forbid discrimination on the basis of language, in practice no affirmative actions against possible or real discrimination are allowed, since Article III-5.1 does not explicitly allow the European Union to become active in this field.

Under the Irish Presidency further provision for minority languages was introduced. As already indicated, Article I-10 gave the right of EU citizens to address the institutions and advisory bodies of the Union in any of the Constitution's languages and to obtain a reply in the same language. Moreover, heads of states and governments had to include a provision on the languages to which this Article would apply. Significantly the second paragraph gave a concrete place for Regional and Minority Languages. It suggested that apart from the official languages of the European Union, the treaty could 'also be translated into any other languages as determined by Member States among those which, in accordance with their constitutional order, enjoy official status in all or part of their territory', and required that 'a certified copy of such translations shall be provided by the Member States concerned to be deposited in the archives of the Council'.

In recent decades the European Union had made a huge effort to emphasize its multilingual nature. Being an international organisation, the European Union and its institutions have always promoted multilingualism. No other international organisation has so many official languages. Moreover, despite enlargement, the European Union remains committed to multilingualism. However, the Union has not adopted an entirely inclusive approach to multilingualism. While it is prepared to promote language learning of official languages, it ignores lesser-used, regional or autochthonous minority languages. This occurs because the European Union lacks the competence to act in this field. The discussion about the missing legal basis and the controversy over the anti-discrimination article are the most apparent and evident symptoms of the gap between an inclusive and an exclusive language policy.

From the beginning, it was questionable whether the Convention on the Future of the European Union would be able to change this situation, since its main task did not consist in providing new competencies to the European Union. Therefore, no specific article in the new Constitutional Treaty of the European Union was designed to support minority rights. There was no specific article for the promotion of lesser-used languages and no article for the promotion of linguistic diversity in general including lesser-used languages. Finally, the Convention did not amend the anti-discrimination article and introduce the word 'language' as a possible ground of discrimination.

However, changing ex-Article 151 on Culture from unanimity voting to qualified majority voting did fall within the tasks of the Convention and this change will significantly simplify the EU decision-making process. Although the amended Article III-280 (ex-Article 151) will not have an immediate impact, lesser-used language communities might profit from the amendment in the long term since future EC proposals to the Council regarding language policy no longer require unanimous voting.

The Draft Constitutional Treaty has been very clear on language issues. Its principles are based on Human Rights and Linguistic Diversity. Members States will continue to remain primarily responsible for the language policy of the European Union. But as the definition of 'minority' changes substantially from state to state, so does the definition of minority languages and state policies towards them. This makes a European terminology and a European understanding of the topic difficult, although not impossible. Some of the most important attempts have been undertaken by the OSCE, the Council of Europe and the European Union. Notwithstanding the importance of an accepted definition, the different policies of states have an important influence on the relationship between individuals belonging to lesser-used language communities as well as on the interactions between linguistic minorities and majorities. Therefore, a European approach, setting minimal standards in minority rights and the promotion of lesser-used languages, seems so important.

Although the European Union is a very important European organisation, it has not yet provided a legal framework for the protection of minority rights and the promotion of minority languages. In this regard it does not compare favourably with the Council of Europe, or the High Commissioner, or National Minorities of the OSCE. Nevertheless, project funding for lesser-used languages within the European Union's cultural policy dates back to 1983. In this context it is astonishing that while the Council of Europe's 'Charter for Regional or Minority Languages' entered into force in 1998, the European Union was confronted with legal problems regarding its lesser-used languages project funding.

Lesser-used language communities will face many challenges in the future. The role of the High Commissioner for National Minorities is likely to lose influence in shaping minority policies in the context of an enlarged European Union. This represents the loss of an important reference point for speakers of regional or minority languages. The suspension of the budget ensures no more support from the European Commission for measures to promote and safeguard regional and minority languages and cultures. While there are European funding possibilities for lesser-used language projects within the European Union, it is questionable if the new mainstreaming approach, as set out on 24 July 2003 in the *Action Plan 2004–2006*, will produce the expected positive results.

The Council of Europe on the contrary has acquired an important instrument with the European Charter for Regional or Minority Languages, which is ratified by more and more countries. From this perspective it would have been eminently sensible to discuss the issue within the European Convention. Although it is understandable that the Convention had to deal with a variety of different topics, it can certainly be regarded as a missed opportunity. It is regrettable that the EU-Convention did not pay any attention to the protection of minority rights in general or to the promotion of linguistic diversity including lesser-used languages in particular. Surely the EC-Action Plan on Language Learning and Linguistic Diversity offers some hope, but ultimately support for linguistic diversity can only be successful when a real programme for linguistic diversity allowing clearly targeted funding possibilities is implemented.

One would hardly suggest a single strategy model for all linguistic situations. Minorities differ in their history, in their size, in their relations with the majority and in their legal, political and economic possibilities. Lesser-used language communities often differ from each other in their linguistic competences, in the opportunities to use their languages as well as in their desire to do so. Sometimes, they are not even socially and psychologically empowered to do so. While these differences cannot be neglected, there is a common factor. All European languages, whether more or less widely spoken, are part of Europe's cultural heritage and merit appropriate support and promotion.

For minority communities Europe symbolises an important 'ally' in the struggle to safeguard their language. The concept of Europe implies variety and presents an ideal of unity and community in diversity. The European integration process is not thinkable without the will for co-operation between states, which historically may have been hostile towards one another. Today, the citizens of different Member States respect each other's cultures, languages and traditions, and all are citizens of the European Union. Within the Member States however, this mutual respect is not clearly developed. State languages are usually privileged in ways that do not apply to non-state, regional or minority languages.

Majority language speakers are seldom confronted in their daily lives with a feeling of 'linguistic inferiority'. They rarely experience communication problems, unless they travel. They hear their language spoken in schools, on radio stations and TV channels. They are accustomed to street signs in their mother tongue and to the fact that public administration answers to them in their language. Moreover, they are unaccustomed to the fact that their language might be instrumentalised for political purposes. They therefore seldom might notice the nexus between language and identity. Speakers of minority languages are confronted with it every day and often the struggle to preserve the language is closely related to the preservation of their identity. For them, national borders are not identical with cultural and linguistic borders.

We commonly think of culture in terms of an implicit equation between ethnic and cultural identity, in a homogenous cultural unit, in a larger homogeneous society. We are not surprised by the mutual failure of these cultures to understand one another. Nevertheless, the European ideal suggests just the opposite: it symbolises trans-culturality, internal differentiation and cross-border co-operation. The achievement of the EU-Convention as well as the policy put forward by the EU-Action Plan could signal a first step in the right direction. The promotion of lesser-used languages now depends on the political support and will. The years to come will show if Europe will be able to fulfil the expectations of and promises to lesser-used language communities and if it will be capable of meeting its own ideal.

References

Conseil de L'Union Européene (2000) 'Article 21 *Charte des Droits Fondamentaux de l'Union Européene*', *Journal Officiel des Communautés Européennes*, C364, 18/12, pp. 1–22, 3.

Conseil de L'Union Européene (2002) 'Version Consolidée du Traité Instituant La Communauté Européennes', *Journal Officiel des Communautés Européennes*, C325/33.

Ebner, M. (2002) 'Parliamentary Questions: Written Questions, combating Discrimination', E-3479/01, *Europarl* (http://www2.europarl.eu.int/omk/OM-Europarl?PROG=WQ& . . . /EN&LEVEL—3&NAV).

Diamantopoulou, A. (2002) 'Parliamentary Questions, Written Question E-3479/01 by Michl Ebner (PPE-DE) to the Commission, answers given by Ms Diamantopoulou on Behalf of the Commission', 1 Feb, *Europarl* (http://www2.europarl.eu.int/omk/OM-Eur . . . /EN&LEVEL=4&NAV=S&SAME_LEVEL=).

Ekeus, R. (2002) 'From the Copenhagen Criteria to the Copenhagen Summit: The Protection of National Minorities in an Enlarging Europe' (http://www.osce.org/henm/documents/speeches/2002/henmspeech2002-6-pdf).

European Bureau for Lesser Used Languages (2001) *Resolution, First Contribution by EBLUL to the Debate on the Future of the European Union*, The Council in Charleroi, 13 October (see www.eblul.org).

European Bureau for Lesser Used Languages (2002a) *Final Document in the Later European Council and the Future of the European Union*, adopted by the Council of EBLUL in Palma de Mallorca, 9 February (see www.eblul.org).
European Bureau for Lesser Used Languages (2002b) *Final Document, Declaration on Linguistic Diversity and the Future of the European Union*, adopted by the Council of EBLUL in Ljouwert/Leeuwarden on 15 June (see www.eblul.org).
European Bureau for Lesser Used Languages (2002c) *Package for Linguistic Diversity: 3 Proposals to the Convention on the Future of the European Union*, Elaborated by a high level of independent experts with long-term minority policy experience in the United Nations, the Council of Europe and the Organisation for Security and Co-operation in Europe, in a Seminar Hosted by the Basque Government.
European Commission ed. (2002) *Official Journal of the European Communities*, C 50/1, 23/02/2002.
European Commission (2002) 'Article 13: Charter of Fundamental Rights of the European Union', *Official Journal of the European Communities*, C325/43.
Scheidhauer, C. (2001) 'Comment La Défense des Langues Régionale est Devenue une Politique Européenne', in D. Reynié and B. Cautrès eds, *L'Opinion Européenne*. Paris, Sciences Po Presses, pp. 65–84.
The European Convention (2003) Draft Treaty Establishing a Constitution for Europe. Luxembourg: Office for Official Publications of the European Communities.

Websites

European Bureau for Lesser Used Languages – http://www.eblul.org
European Union – http://www.europa.eu.int/eur-lex/en/treaties/dat/ec_cons_treaty_en.pdf
High Commissioner on National Minorities of the OSCE – http://www.osce.org/hcnm/documents/speeches/2002/hcnmspeech2002-6.pdf
Press agency Eurolang – http://217.136.252.147/webpub/eurolang/pajenn.asp?ID=3964

6
Broadcasting for Minorities: The Case of the Celtic Languages

Philip McDermott

The Celtic languages are a group of Indo-European languages that are still spoken on the periphery of Western Europe. Welsh, Irish, Scots Gaelic, Cornish and Manx are indigenous to the British Isles, and Breton is still spoken in Brittany on France's west coast. In the past one hundred years the Celtic languages have witnessed a dramatic fall in the number of speakers. In Ireland the percentage of the population that spoke Irish had halved between 1861 and 1926 (Central Statistics Office 2005). In Wales the number of Welsh speakers had fallen from 54 per cent of the population in 1891 to fewer than 30 per cent by 1951 [National Statistics Online (2004)]. In Scotland the situation has proved even more precarious, where recent figures suggest that there are now fewer than 60,000 speakers of Scots Gaelic (McKinnion 2004). In Brittany there has also been a serious decline in the number of speakers throughout the twentieth century. However, determining the size of the Breton-speaking community is problematic because there is no question on the language in the French census. One study conducted by a private company in 1991 suggested that there were around 320,000 speakers of Breton (Research Centre of Wales 1996).

Native speakers, supporters and enthusiasts of the Celtic languages have had a huge role to play in a recent upturn in fortunes which has included slight increases in the number of speakers of both Welsh and Irish. Minority-language speakers have long argued that access to public services is a vital part in the recognition, maintenance and promotion of their languages. One area where such attempts have been made has been the establishment of broadcasting infrastructures, particularly those funded by the government. This chapter attempts to chart and analyse the development of Celtic language broadcasting and highlights some of the debates surrounding the use of the media in relation to minority languages. Particular emphasis will be placed on radio and television production and broadcasting in Welsh, Scots Gaelic, Irish and Breton.

Language and national identity

The concept of language has been inherently linked to issues of power and identity. In the nineteenth century, under the influence of the Romantic Movement, language was regarded as an important element of nation-building. This was particularly significant in the creation of European states such as Italy and Germany, where language was used to invoke a sense of nationhood where it may not have previously existed. After the unification of Italy a prominent statesman declared, 'we have made Italy, now we have to make Italians' (Hobsbawm 1990: 44). This comment was partly in reference to the need for the creation of a stand-ardised version of Italian. In Germany, writers such as Jacob Grimm (1848) emphasised the importance of a peasant language and literature in order to create a sense of national solidarity and philosophers such as Fichte (1922) and Herder (see Barnard 1965) emphasised the idea of a common language as a natural unitary factor in the notion of a nation-state.

More contemporary theorists such as Benedict Anderson (1991) also point to the use of language in the creation of nation-states. Anderson argues that nations have been constructed in a manner that creates a sense of belonging even though each individual member will never actually meet the majority of their fellow citizens and this was partly achieved through the promotion of a national language. As a consequence the issue of national language seems to be taken for granted and it is very often assumed that national languages have always existed. However, despite these assumptions there exist alternative cultures and languages which have survived such nation-building processes. In contemporary Europe there have been a number of differing responses from governments, two of which are significant in the context of this Chapter. One reaction has been to continue to ignore the existence of some languages within the nation-state and primarily recognise only the majority language. Another response has been to offer a form of regional status to the minority language in question yet at the same time maintaining an overall sense of national identity.

The recognition of such national minorities has proved to be a hugely controversial topic not simply because of cost but also because of the problems that it poses to notions of equal citizenship. Some commentators have argued that advocating group rights is problematic in many nation-states because offering extra rights to people is contradictory to the notions of citizenship that afford rights on a purely individual level. For instance, in such states everyone is equal and has access to the same opportunities such as the right to education, the right to employment, the right to healthcare and so forth. Affording extra rights to individuals on the basis of group membership is seen by some to be inherently opposed to this notion of equality.

Will Kymlicka (1995) has made some interesting and valid counter-arguments in this regard. Kymlicka argues that in order to equally participate in a society one must have access to societal cultures, 'that is a culture which provides its members with meaningful ways of life across the wide range of human activities, including social, educational, religious, recreational, and economic life, encompassing both public and private spheres' (1995: 76). Kymlicka goes on to argue that the use of a language is a form of societal culture and that providing access to such cultures is important because 'of the role it plays in enabling meaningful individual choice and in supporting self identity' (ibid.: 105). Providing such group rights have been regarded as being constructive in allowing full participation in society and is therefore 'not only consistent with liberal values, but is actually promoting them' (ibid.: 106). The provision of media in a minority language then can be seen as a way in which certain groups can access their societal culture.

The development of the European Union and its focus on 'unity in diversity' has meant that these issues have come to the fore in the second half of the twentieth century. As a collective entity, Europe seems to be in favour of the protection of the cultures of minority groups and in particular languages. In 1992 the Council of Europe drafted the European Charter for Regional or Minority Languages, which aims to 'protect and promote regional and minority languages as a threatened aspect of Europe's cultural heritage and on the other hand to enable speakers of a regional or minority language to use it in private and public life. Its overriding purpose is cultural. It covers regional and minority languages, non-territorial languages and less widely used official languages' (Council of Europe 1992).

As a state which has ratified the treaty, the United Kingdom has pledged its support to the provision of certain services for speakers of Welsh, Scots Gaelic, and Irish and to a lesser extent for speakers of Scots, Ulster-Scots and Cornish. The Republic of Ireland and France have signed but not ratified the treaty, meaning that they have merely recognised the importance of linguistic diversity but have not yet committed themselves to establishing frameworks for better provision which would be expected from ratification of the treaty. The Republic of Ireland has not ratified the treaty because Irish is the first official language of the state, and therefore is not regarded as a minority language. The French government was expected to ratify the Charter but after an officially commissioned report which suggested that there were 75 indigenous languages spoken in the region, it refused to do so (Cerquiglini 1999). It seems that although the French were willing to recognise that there was linguistic diversity the current interpretation of citizenship would prevent them from actually offering support to the various minority groups within the state.

The Charter and indeed supporters of minority language groups have identified the broadcast media in particular as important in the promotion of minority languages. This is partly because the media have the capacity not only to provide services for native speakers but also to introduce the language to non-speakers. Commentators such as Joshua Fishman claim that this is not entirely the case and there is a general overemphasis on the power of the media which detracts from the effectiveness of other means of restoring a minority language, such as the role of education and the family (Fishman 1991: 473). However, this is not to negate the fact that the media can serve to complement the role of education and the family for a minority-language speaker. This has not gone unnoticed within academia, and the European Commission and the University of Wales have set up the *Mercator* network, which aims to increase the profile and self-confidence of minority-language speakers in Europe by focusing its research on overlapping issues such as education, legislation and the broadcast media.

In addition to this the scope of the broadcast media has radically changed in recent years with digital television and the Internet beginning to play a role in broadcasting minority cultures and identities to wider audiences. Critics may have argued in the past that minority cultures would have suffered in an era of globalisation and would be gradually phased out. However, minority communities can actually use globalisation to their own advantage. This has been termed as 'Glocalisation' by Roland Robertson (1994). Robertson argues that 'Glocalisation' allows for the 'tailoring and advertising of goods and services on a global or near-global basis to increasingly differentiated local and particular markets (1994: 36). So in practice one could argue that the broadcast media and in particular the Internet can be used to promote local cultures, languages and identities to a much wider audience. In effect, Celtic languages are no longer restricted to their own local regions but can avail of advances in technologies to promote the language to diaspora communities abroad.

Broadcasting, national identity and minority rights

Most critics agree that the concept of Public Service Broadcasting originated in the United Kingdom when the British Broadcasting Corporation (BBC) under the Directorship of Sir John Reith voiced its intention to educate, entertain and inform the nation. Since its foundation in the 1920s the BBC has remained a public organisation funded solely by way of a licence fee paid by the general public. The role of Public Service Broadcasters has been to provide for the diverse array of interests and tastes that are represented within the nation. Negrine adequately concluded that the role of Public Service Broadcasting has been to 'cater for minorities' yet at the same time maintaining a 'concern for national identity and community' (Negrine 1998: 226).

However, this role can prove to be both problematic and contradictory for a number of reasons. First, there is no real measure as to what constitutes proper provision for each individual taste. Also, the concept is flawed in deciding which cultures, tastes and minorities are representative of the nation-state. At present it seems that only cultures and values that do not challenge the legitimacy of the nation-state have been an acceptable part of public broadcasting. For example, Welsh, Scottish and, to a certain extent, Northern Irish cultures have been regarded as culturally representative of the United Kingdom and as a result these cultures have been given a certain degree of provision. Each had their own dedicated radio service and by the 1960s television broadcasts were being made from all of these regions. However, other cultures have not been offered similar recognition even though their numbers may be large enough to justify such a position. For instance, the arrival of immigrants from the Caribbean in the late 1940s and early 1950s challenged the notion as to what constituted Britishness. Bhiku Parekh in his report *The Future of Multi-Ethnic Britain* has argued that such immigrant communities have been perceived since their arrival to be 'bounded homogonous groupings each fixedly attached to its ethnicity and traditions' (Parekh 2002: 26) and that such views and opinions still permeate various aspects of public life.

In regard to the issue of the Celtic languages, Welsh and Scots Gaelic have benefited from such a position as they are regarded as indigenous or regional languages to the island of Britain and for that reason they seem to fit more comfortably into the notion of regional British identities than both the Irish language and the languages of the various minority ethnic communities. There have been recent examples of how programming in both Scotland and Wales has been used to fit into the wider remit of the BBC with programmes focusing on issues of national importance such as the commemoration of those who died in both world wars. For instance, the Welsh language series *Cerdded Y Llinell* (Walking the Line) charted the experiences of Welsh soldiers during the First World War at Messines and Ypres. Similarly the Gaelic radio series *Strì gu Sìth* (From Strife to Peace) charted the experiences of Gaelic speakers during the Second World War. Also Gaelic and Welsh were prominent in the BBC's 'voices' project, which explored 'the way we speak around the UK' (BBC Voices Project 2005). Although at times provision for Welsh and Gaelic has proved to be a controversial topic, both still receive superior financial support to that of Irish in Northern Ireland. For example in 2001–2002, £53 was spent on each Welsh speaker and £64 was spent on each Gaelic speaker. The equivalent spend on each speaker in Northern Ireland was just £3 per annum (ULTACH Trust 2005).

In Scotland the first Gaelic language broadcast actually took place in 1923 when a 15-minute religious programme was aired on the BBC's Radio Scotland; this was the first broadcast in a Celtic language by the BBC. Throughout the 1920s a number of programmes were broadcast intermittently in the Gaelic language and these normally focused on music and folklore. Provision for Welsh did not begin until 1935, when the BBC broadcast a radio programme from Bangor in North Wales. In 1937 a home service for the Welsh region was established thereby facilitating more regular broadcasts in the language.

Developments were also continuing in Scotland, where there was the establishment of a separate dedicated department for Scots Gaelic in 1935. These developments allowed for a wider more diverse range of programming to be transmitted. In the 1950s and 1960s the BBC established two local radio stations for Gaelic speakers. Radio Nan Eilean served the Outer Hebrides, and Radio na Gaidhealtachd broadcast to the Highland region. In 1962 the first television programme in Gaelic *Ceol nan Gaidheal* (Music of the Gaels) was broadcast. In this period, a greater scope was developed for programming in other areas such as light entertainment. By the 1970s a current affairs programme, *Bonn Comhraidh* (Basic Comprehension) was produced and an emphasis was beginning to be placed on programmes for learners, with the first programmes for schools on both television and radio.

The first television broadcast in Welsh was transmitted on St David's day in 1953; this was a religious service from Cardiff. By 1964 the BBC had established the regional BBC Wales television service, which had the facility to opt out of the national network at various times so as to broadcast programmes with a local focus. This allowed such Welsh language programmes to be broadcast as *Heddiw* (Today), the religious series *Dechrau Canu, Dechrau Canmol* (Begin Singing, Begin Praising) and the most successful of all the Welsh language soap opera *Pobol Y Cwm* (People of the Valley). In 1977 the BBC established a dedicated Welsh language radio service, Radio Cymru.

Although the Public Service ethos originated in the United Kingdom, many other regions particularly in Europe have adopted similar models of broadcasting. The model of Public Service Broadcasting in the Republic of Ireland has followed the 'educate, entertain and inform' concept as used by the BBC. The major differences in terms of the Celtic languages in both regions was that in Britain, Welsh and Scots Gaelic constituted forms of regional identity, whereas in the Republic of Ireland the Irish language was inherent to the notion, construction and main-tenance of a national identity. In the early years of broadcasting, the media were closely linked to the development of a national character. Broadcasting was 'expected not merely to reflect every aspect of national activity, but to create activities which did not exist' (cited in McLoone 1991: 4). This meant that programming in Irish would become a staple part of the newly formed Raidió Éireann's schedules. In particular the station focused on learners programmes with quite a degree of success. The *Listen and Learn* series, which was aimed at those with a basic comprehension of the language, gained very high viewing figures when it was broadcast in the 1950s. However, although programmes aimed at learners were successful, low listenerships for other programmes such as drama, light entertainment and music resulted in Irish gradually losing its privileged position within the schedules.

With the introduction of television, the 1960 Broadcasting Act declared that the public service broadcasters, Raidió Teilifís Éireann (RTÉ), would 'bear constantly in mind the national aims of restoring the Irish language and preserving and developing the national culture' (Government of Ireland 1960). This has proved difficult as RTÉ is funded jointly by a licence fee paid by the public and by the revenue gener-ated through advertising. This conflict between public service broad-casting and commercialism has resulted in lower viewing figures for Irish rather than English language programmes. In consequence, Irish language productions have gradually lost their place within the televi-sion schedules. This is unfortunate as there have been some successful examples of Irish language programming. For instance, the pilot episode of the Irish language soap opera, *Rós na Rún*, was broadcast on RTÉ in 1993 and gained 360,000 viewers (Foley 1996). The factual documentary series *Léargas* (Insight) has achieved similarly high viewing figures. This proves that Irish programmes have indeed been appealing if placed in a suitable time slot, marketed in the proper manner and presented with high production values.

In terms of radio provision there had been discontent since the late 1960s, particularly in the Irish-speaking *Gaeltacht* regions when an organisation known as *Gluaiseacht ar son Cearta Sibhialta na Gaeltachta* (Gaelteacht Civil Rights Movement) called on the government to provide better provisions for native speakers of the Irish language. One of their demands was the creation of a separate Irish language radio station. The movement went as far as establishing their own illegal radio station Saor Raidió Chonamara, which was eventually closed down by the authorities (Watson 2002: 743). The demands of the movement were met in 1972 when RTÉ established Raidió na Gaeltachta. The establishment of the station was the first major step to be taken in the creation of a dedicated Irish medium broadcast infrastructure. The major debate within the station had been its total ban on the use of the English language which in turn was blamed for the low interest among younger speakers of Irish in the station. This debate has also been prevalent in Scotland and Wales. Radio Cymru in Wales had a similar ban which has now been lifted, and a restructuring of the service has taken place so that English language pop music can now be played in order to attract a younger listenership.

In its first two decades of transmission Radio Cymru followed the model set by its predecessor Radio 4 and tended to primarily offer 'a number of short, often pre-recorded programmes, linked by a continuity announcer' (Ellis 2000: 191). However, by 1995 the station, despite opposition from some Welsh language activists, had opted to attract younger Welsh speakers and the decision was taken in 1995 to broadcast English language pop music on Radio Cymru. From 1995 the number of listeners aged below 34 increased by over 40 per cent. Similarly in Scotland Radio nan Gaidheal also features a programme aimed at young people called *Rapal* which also features music in English. In 2005 Raidió na Gaeltachta established a similar night-time schedule called *Anocht FM* (Tonight FM) aimed at younger listeners and also featuring English music. Some concerns were raised in all regions as to the implications of this for young native speakers.

In recent years the total reliance on Public Service Broadcasters for the provision of minority language media has been challenged. Often sufficient airspace cannot be found to broadcast programmes to a minority audience. This has generated considerable dissatisfaction, and alternative ways have been sought to create a better broadcasting infrastructure, particularly in regard to television. From the 1970s, Welsh and Irish language supporters began to lobby for the creation of separate television stations for their respective languages.

Throughout the 1970s the campaign for a fourth television channel in Wales intensified as the Welsh Language Society set about organising petitions and even public burnings of television licences. In 1975 the British government commissioned the Siberry Report which eventually recommended the establishment of a Welsh language station. By 1979 both the Labour and Conservative parties included the issue of a separate television channel in their political manifestos for the general election. When the Conservatives eventually came to power the issue of a Welsh language television station gradually lost significance again; this was the catalyst for an even more vociferous campaign. Many Welsh speakers and political activists refused to pay their television licences, and the Plaid Cymru MP Gwynfor Evans announced he would go on hunger strike if the channel were not established. In response to this opposition the government compromised and announced that the 1980 Broadcasting Bill would make provisions for the establishment of the fourth channel, which would be responsible for Welsh language broadcasting in Wales. This Bill led to the establishment of Sianel Pedwar Cymru (S4C) in 1982 and since then the channel has been responsible for providing a space for the broadcasting of Welsh language television programmes.

In Scotland a number of developments were made in regard to television; however, these developments have not included the establishment of a dedicated television service. In 2000, Alasdair Milne, a former Director of the BBC and a fluent Gaelic speaker, conducted a report into the viability of a dedicated service. He concluded that 'the creation of a dedicated Gaelic television channel (which would have the potential to carry other material) is both feasible and desirable. We believe that it would – as in Wales and Ireland – unlock creative talent and make a major contribution towards the future well being of the language and culture.' (Milne 2000). Unfortunately the calls for a dedicated channel have not been realised thus far. Despite this there have been developments since the early 1990s which have improved provision on television for Scots Gaelic speakers. For instance, the 1990 Broadcasting Act led to the creation of a Gaelic Boadcasting Fund *Comataidh Craolaidh Gàidhlig* (CCG), which stood at around £12 million per annum. Although CCG has been responsible for sponsoring programmes, its main drawback is that there is no dedicated service to broadcast its programmes and such productions are aired on the terrestrial channels such as BBC Scotland as well as on the various commercial stations available in Scotland. The commercial stations also seem to prefer to broadcast Gaelic language programmes in 'dead time-slots', meaning that Gaelic programming is not broadcast at a time that is suitable to the Gaelic speaker. The creation of the Gaelic Media Service (GMS) in 2003 as a replacement to CCG is a positive step forward in that the additional powers have allowed the GMS to lobby the BBC for the creation of a separate digital channel for Gaelic.

In the Republic of Ireland there was a similar debate to that in Wales over the possible establishment of a dedicated television channel. In 1980 an organisation called Coiste ar son Teilifís Gaeltas (Commission for Irish Language Television) was formed to lobby the government for the creation of a dedicated television channel for native speakers. By the late 1980s the campaign had been restructured under the auspices of *Feachtas Náisiúnta Teilifíse* (National Television Campaign), which was demanding a national as opposed to simply a regional channel for the Irish language. Such pressure was certainly a contributory factor to the establishment of *Teilifís na Gaeilge* (TnaG). *Teilifís na Gaeilge* was renamed *Teilifís Gaeilge 4* (TG4) during a rebranding of the corporate image in 1999.

The TG4 broadcasts an average of 4 hours per day of peak-time programming in the Irish language, whereas S4C broadcast 32 hours per week in the Welsh language (http://www.s4c.co.uk). This averages at around 4.5 hours of Welsh language programming per day. Neither TG4 nor S4C make the programmes themselves but act as bodies which commission productions from a variety of sources. The BBC provides 10 hours per week of programming for S4C while RTÉ also provides a similar amount of programming in Irish. The additional programming comes from independent production companies. This structure is possibly one of the reasons why both TG4 and S4C have succeeded in finding their core audiences. The involvement of already established broadcasters such as the BBC and RTÉ has provided stability and experience, which in turn has meant good quality of programming as well as a degree of familiarity for the audience. For example, the flagship programmes of both S4C (*Pobol Y Cwm*) and TG4 (*Ros na Rún*) had appeared on both BBC and RTÉ prior to their airing on the new channels. A useful contrast with this familiarity has been the involvement of independent broadcasters ensuring opportunities for new and original talent to emerge. The fact that independent production companies were being commissioned has also ensured that a whole production section in the Welsh, Irish and Scottish Gaelic has emerged.

One issue of concern has been the use of on-screen English subtitles for many of the programmes broadcast on TG4, S4C and programming in Scottish Gaelic. TG4 had initially experimented with a system of Teletext subtitling; however, it was decided that all programming in Irish should be subtitled on-screen in English as not all people had access to teletext. In Scotland in particular there has been a policy of open subtitling as programme makers have regarded the use of on-screen subtitles as key to capturing a larger audience. Other critics have pointed out that on-screen subtitles have had the effect of transforming a monolingual programme into essentially a bilingual one where the presence of the English language literally destroys the experience for the native speaker (Mac Dubhghaill 2005). However, a survey by TG4 in 2002 showed that the majority of fluent Irish speakers in the Gaeltacht (56 per cent) have accepted the use of subtitling (cited in Mac Dubhghaill). In Wales this has not been the case and S4C offered subtitles to viewers through the teletext information system and the majority of subtitles were not permanently on-screen as many Welsh speakers had found the use of on-screen subtitles to be intrusive (Jones 2001). The imminent switch-over to digital television will have the potential to resolve this problem as the digital technology allows native or fluent speakers to choose if they do not want to see the on-screen subtitles. Already in Wales the S4C *Digidol* (Digital) service has allowed the viewer the option to have subtitles on-screen if they wish or to view the programme without subtitles. As this technology is introduced in Ireland it should have the potential to resolve this dispute.

In terms of the programming the general consensus in the Republic of Ireland and Wales has been to broaden the range of programming in the Celtic languages. Previously history, traditions, traditional music and folklore had been evident in the schedules. However, contemporary programming has reflected the more modern aspects of these Celtic languages. In Ireland a travel show aimed at a youth audience, *Amu Amigos*, has proved to be one of TG4's major hits. Also, within the small film industry the station has been involved in a number of productions. Its first ever programme, the film, *Draoícht*, dealt with a young boy's relationship with his father as he came back from peacekeeping duties in the Congo. Other alternative views on life in modern day Ireland have also been evident. For example, one short film, 'Yiu Ming is ainm dom', explores the issue of multicultural Ireland through the eyes of an immigrant who is learning the Irish language. Also social issues more associated with the English-speaking world have been explored in the Irish language soap opera *Ros na Rún*. In addition to this there is a nightly news bulletin and since 1996 TG4 has been involved in broadcasting two major series for language learners *Now You're Talking* and *Turas Teanga* (Language Tour).

Similarly in Wales, programming has followed similar patterns with the main flagship programme on S4C being *Pobol y Cwm*; a current affairs programme *Byd Ar Bedwar* (The World on Four) has been on air since the station's inception. Also there is a nightly news programme *Newyddion* (News) produced by the BBC. Programming for learners has also proved popular with 'Talk About Welsh' and 'Welsh in a Week'. Programming in Scotland has also been particularly keen on attracting learners with a major online course *Beag air Bheag* (Little by Little) available worldwide through the Internet. Documentaries and current affairs have been a particularly popular genre, with yet again many of the topics focusing on the traditions of the Gaelic-speaking regions. For example, *Moladh na Maighdinn* (Praise the Morning) looked at the tradition of Scots Gaelic poetry and *Ealtain*, which is a traditional music programme.

Another major target group has been young Gaelic speakers, and a sizeable amount of resources have been dedicated to providing material for this audience. This is possibly a consequence of the fall in numbers of speakers indicated in the 2001 census. Children and younger speakers of the language are key to its future. One study conducted by the *Lèirsinn* research institute found that young Gaelic speakers would prefer to see modern Gaelic language programming that also manage to 'suit their lives as young bilingual Gaels' (Nic Nèill 2001: 105). The flagship programme for young people in Gaelic is a magazine style programme called *De-A-Nis?* (What Now?) and seems to follow this style with young presenters visiting different Gaelic-speaking areas and reporting on events and activities of interest to Gaelic speakers. However, such a focus on simply the local community can prove to be problematic and the development of the language particularly among non-speakers and learners can be curtailed by such an isolationist approach.

The survey also found that young Gaelic speakers preferred to access the 'mainstream, more global culture in their English-language viewing' (ibid.) and that they were opposed to any such programming in Gaelic. May (2003) argues that such a view is problematic as it supposes, 'majority languages are "vehicles" of modernity and minority languages as (merely) "carriers" of identity. And yet it is clear that *all* language(s) embody and accomplish both identity and instrumental functions for those who speak them' (italics original in 2003: 112).

In the cases of both TG4 in Ireland and S4C in Wales, programming has moved away from this notion of minority languages as merely an identity carrier and has offered alternative visions in a minority language. Programming on both stations has focused not simply on local issues but also on more contemporary issues such as current cinema, music, fashion and more wide-ranging current affairs. Programming in Scots Gaelic will have to broaden its remit of services in the future if it is to appeal to a wider audience and it would seem that the possibility of this happening would be increased vastly if a dedicated service in the language were available throughout Scotland.

The S4C in recent years has expanded in response to the onset of digital television. It now has two extra digital channels: S4C digital broadcasts over 80 hours per week of archived programmes as well as repeats and sporting events, entirely in the Welsh language; and S4C 2 broadcasts coverage of the proceedings of the National Assembly for Wales. Both of these digital channels are now accessible throughout the United Kingdom, which has meant that the stations are available to a much wider audience, and it should be noted that broadcasting through digital will offer the opportunity for the programmes in Celtic languages to be broadcast to a wider audience.

Threats to national identity

The case studies so far show that broadcasting in the Celtic languages has in the past been used to represent and maintain national identities in two ways. First, in the case of the Republic of Ireland it has endorsed a national identity, where the Irish language has been regarded as key to the cultural wealth of the nation. In the case of the United Kingdom the Celtic languages have been promoted as elements of regional identities within a multi-nation state. However, there have been instances where the Celtic languages have posed particular problems to this notion of national identity and indeed some instances where they have been perceived as threatening the notion of a national identity. This has been particularly true of two regions: Brittany, which is under the jurisdiction of France; and Northern Ireland, which is under the jurisdiction of the United Kingdom. Such perceptions have had implications on the manner in which Irish in Northern Ireland and Breton in France can be broadcast.

The case of Irish in Northern Ireland has proved to be a hugely controversial topic. The Irish language has been regarded as culturally important to a sizeable number of people in Northern Ireland. The majority of these are mainly, though not exclusively, from the Catholic tradition (McCoy and Ní Bhaoill 2004) and indeed it was Protestant businessmen who had revitalised an interest in the Irish language in the nineteenth century (Blaney 1996, Ó Snodaigh 1995). However, over time and particularly since partition in the 1920s the language has come to be closely associated with solely Irish nationalist politics (Andrews 2000, Mac Póilin 2000). In particular there has been a growing perception that that Irish has been closely linked to the politics of Irish Republicanism. In turn certain elements of the community, particularly unionists, are suspicious of the motivations of Irish speakers. Such controversies have not gone unnoticed within the BBC and as a direct result the organisation has approached the issue of provision in the Irish language rather more tentatively than in Scotland and Wales. In contrast the development of Irish language programming has been fraught with difficulties ranging from an entire ban on the use of the language to more contemporary problems such as programme content, funding and the de-politicisation of the language. This section will attempt to highlight some of the issues surrounding the Irish language media sector in Northern Ireland.

From as early as the 1930s the BBC has been under pressure from Irish language activists to broadcast Irish programmes. On one such occasion in the 1930s, George Marshall, the head of BBC NI, dismissed calls for Irish-medium programmes by pointing out that there would be no programming because 'the number of Gaelic speakers in Northern Ireland is negligible and, as far as schools are concerned, the proportion of those where the Irish language is taught is quite small and is practically confined to secondary schools' (Cited in Bardon 2000: 209). This was typical of the views expressed by the BBC until the early 1980s.

The first Irish language broadcasts by the BBC did not commence until 1981, when a short series of radio programmes for schools were aired. In 1991 the British government included a question on the use of Irish in the census, which concluded that there were 142,000 people in Northern Ireland who could speak some Irish. This represents less than 10 per cent of the population. It is not surprising therefore that the first Irish language television programme on the BBC was also produced in this year. *Dá mbíodh Ruball ar an Éan* (If the Bird had a Tail) was a documentary about the Irish language poet and author Seosamh Mac Grianna. The programme was initially broadcast without subtitles but such was the interest at the time that it was later rebroadcast with English subtitles. Since 1991 the BBC has continued to produce Irish language programmes albeit at an irregular basis. At present Irish has no fixed place in the BBC's television schedules and appears only occasionally. The programming has generally been regarded as being of a very high standard, but some critics have argued that the content focuses too much on the issue of the Irish language community itself and does not deal specifically with other issues of social importance. Recently there have been some innovative changes, not least a magazine programme aimed at younger viewers called *SRL* (Something Else). Also missing in the BBC's schedules has been a news service on either radio or television. Indeed the political sensitivities of Northern Ireland have ensured that current affairs are never dealt with in Irish language programming. This is an issue that should be addressed by the BBC particularly in view of the fact that the BBC provides news and current affairs programming to Welsh and Scots Gaelic speakers in other parts of the United Kingdom.

There have however been a number of major successes, not least the BBC's commitment to producing programming and multimedia tools for learners of the Irish language. In 1995 a highly successful series, *Now You're Talking*, was produced in co-operation with RTÉ. This has been complemented in recent years with an online learners' website which has aimed to appeal to learners of all age groups and standards. The BBC also provides 30 minutes of radio programmes every weekday with an additional 2 hours provided on Saturday. At present the quality of programming is very high, but in a similar vein to television broadcasting there is no provision of news and current affairs and the amount of provision provided is still inadequate considering that the 2001 Northern Ireland census indicated that there were 169,000 people with knowledge of Irish in Northern Ireland. Of this it has been estimated that there are between 40,000 and 60,000 functional Irish speakers in Northern Ireland (Mac Giolla Chríost 2001).

One solution to the poor amount of provision has been to make the Republic of Ireland's Irish language channel TG4 more widely available throughout Northern Ireland (see Mac Póilin 1997). Indeed in the 1998 Good Friday Agreement both the British and the Irish governments pledged to increase the coverage of the Irish language television channel throughout Northern Ireland as well as to increase funding for Irish language productions. So far this has partly been achieved through the use of digital television technology which now allows Irish speakers in Northern Ireland to receive TG4. In addition to this a broadcast fund of £12 million for the period 2005–2009 was established and is currently administered by the Northern Ireland Film and Television Commission (NIFTC).

So far the initiative has been responsible for funding projects not only by the BBC but also by independent broadcasters. For instance, the local Belfast community television station NVTV gained funding to provide a 30-minute weekly series *Scéalta ón Fheursuid* (Stories from the Farsad) on Irish language activities in the city. Also a local community radio station Raidió Fáilte was recently awarded a licence by the UK broadcasting regulator the Office of Communications (OFCOM), meaning that the large Irish-speaking community in Belfast has its own dedicated service. Such developments are encouraging; however, the provision for Irish language programmes in Northern Ireland still lags behind its Celtic counterparts in Scotland and Wales.

In France the concept of Public Service Broadcasting is much more monolithic than in a region such as the United Kingdom where the Public Service concept has allowed for various regional and local identities to be represented in the media. The French system has taken a more rigid approach allowing only minimal expressions of local cultures. Prior to the 1950s the only broadcasts in Breton had occurred during the Nazi occupation. Broadcasts were closely monitored by the Nazi authorities at the time and transmitted by Radio Rennes Bretagne. Roparz Hemon, a native of Brest and a leading figure in the culture and language movement at the time, was employed to organise and produce the Breton language output of the station. Hemon had been involved in the movement since the 1920s and had been an editor of a Breton journal *Gwalarn*. As a result, the programming focused on Breton literature and poetry and had a largely academic and intellectual style. After the war amid claims of collaboration Hemon declared that his programmes were not political but instead attempted 'to promote the Breton language and reveal the treasures of their literature and culture to a people from which these things had been hidden' (Thomas 2001: 108). Some critics have disagreed and have argued that the programming contained racist and anti-Semitic undertones. Nevertheless Hemon was accused of being a collaborator and spent 40 years in exile in Ireland. Such accusations of collaboration were not uncommon against Breton speakers, and such incidents and perceptions undoubtedly influenced the manner in which the language would be treated for years to come.

Despite this, programming in Breton did not cease entirely and broadcasting recommenced only 18 months after the end of the war with sporadic radio programmes resuming in December 1946. In this period greater emphasis was placed on folklore and agriculture rather than the highly intellectual approach followed by the previous administration, but the quantity of programming was drastically reduced. It was a further 20 years before the first broadcast in Breton on publicly funded television was made; this was in 1964 and its length was only 90 seconds. Provision for Breton speakers on publicly funded stations such as *France 3 Ouest* has generally remained poor and has averaged no more than 1 hour and 45 minutes per week, although this varies from area to area within Brittany itself (Moal 2000: 125). Programmes generally focus simply on current affairs and music and there is virtually no production of original drama or indeed other genres. In addition to this many of the programmes produced in Breton at this time were funded by regional bodies within Brittany, meaning that virtually none of the licence fee was being spent on production of Breton language programmes. This manner of provision suggests that the existence of the language is very much something that has been tolerated but not promoted and there is very little evidence of attempts to improve the scope and scale of the current provision among the Public Service broadcasters.

Because of the lack of interest within the public sector many of the developments that have taken place in the Breton language media have occurred within the independent commercial sector. This of course has proved difficult and there have been examples of both successes and failures. The major successes have occurred in the provision of radio services. However, the establishment of a commercial Breton language television station has not been as successful as the publicly funded channels in Ireland and Wales, and has ultimately failed in its aims of providing a television station for Breton speakers.

The development of radio in the region has in comparison been more successful. Radio Kreizh Breizh was set up in 1983 and is a bilingual service that operates in both French and Breton. Despite the fact that this is a commercial broadcaster, it declares among its objectives the promotion of the Breton language and culture in its programming. (Radio Kreizh Breizh, http://radio.stalig.com/Presentation-RKB.html.) Another bilingual service is Radio Bro Gwened, which has a very broad remit, and although it transmits programmes in French, significant space is also given to the Breton language and in particular Breton music. Additionally, in recent years a further two services, Radio Kerne and Arvorig FM, have commenced monolingual services in the language. These two stations focus yet again on music and magazine programmes and broadcast up to 60 hours each of programming per week. They serve two separate areas of Brittany and so they are not commercial competitors. Radio Kerne and Arvorig FM have joined forces and have co-produced a number of programmes so as to reduce their operating costs (Conseil Générale du Finistere Penn-Ar-Bed 2003). Such has been the success of these ventures that the larger stakeholder in the region, Radio Kreizh Breizh, has also decided that it too wishes to become involved in this collaboration. This has ensured that a wider range of programming is available throughout Brittany for Breton speakers. In addition to this, these commercial stations have taken advantage of digital and Internet technology and have commenced broadcasts online. In September 2004 the *Stalig Association* was formed between the local radio stations, meaning that all of the commercial Breton radio services are available on one electronic resource (www.stalig.com). The result of this is that the sizeable Breton diaspora spread throughout France can, if they wish, have access to programming in their language.

The establishment of the new commercial cable channel TV Breizh in 2000 aimed to improve the provision of programming for Breton speakers. One of those behind the creation of TV Breizh, Patrick Le Lay, declared that the station would 'promote European culture by developing Celtic culture' (BBC 2000). Three media tycoons backed the station from the beginning. Rupert Murdoch, Silvio Berlusconi and Le Lay, who was also at that time the head of Europe's largest commercial television station TF1. It is also interesting to note that Le Lay himself is from Brittany and obviously had a vested personal interest in the project; without his support it is fair to say that the station would never have got off the ground.

However, there were a number of factors working against the station. One of these was that it was a subscription channel available on satellite or cable, but not terrestrially. From the outset the channel had a number of strategies which reinforced the role of Brittany not within France itself but within the context of a wider Celtic culture as it was hoped that there would be greater co-operation between the broadcasters in the Celtic regions with co-productions or even the dubbing of documentaries and drama from the other Celtic broadcasters into Breton.

By 2003, TV Breizh had also become embroiled in the bitter rivalry that existed between Patrick LeLay's TF1 and the Canal Satellite company. Canal Satellite broadcasts TV Breizh on its frequency and had switched the frequency of the channel on 5 separate occasions in its first 3 years (Moore 2003). This meant that it was difficult for the station to establish itself with viewers, and ratings, which were so vital to the success of the station, began to suffer. By 2003 the audience share for TV Breizh was just 0.4 per cent of the cable/satellite market and in that year there were also financial losses (ibid.). The low viewing figures have also meant that many of the original investors have backed out of the venture and Patrick Le Lay's TF1 by 2003 had acquired over 50 per cent of the company's shares. This in turn prompted an announcement in September 2003 stating that there would be a reduction in regional programmes on the station. By 2005 the provisions in the Breton language stood at only 5 hours per week, a much-diminished figure on the initial provision (Mercator 2003). The other programming would attempt to attract a more general interest audience as well as aiming to have a more national approach. Therefore, although the station still survives within the TF1 corporate identity, the original essence of the station has been lost and Breton speakers continue to be deprived of a service in their own language.

The issues explored in this chapter confirm the assumption that language and politics have and will continue to be closely influenced by political ideologies. The use of one language in order to create a sense of national identity in many states ensured that minority-language speakers were denied full participation or membership of a political entity. In some cases such opposition still exists and the situation in Brittany and Northern Ireland proves that there are still many challenges facing minority-language speakers. There have been examples where such views have been challenged, and group rights, which had hitherto been dismissed as being unconstitutional, unfair and undemocratic, have begun to be regarded as important in the creation of a sense of commonality in multi-nation states, such as the United Kingdom. Welsh and Scottish Gaelic have begun to see some developments in relation to the media in both regions.

Such developments are by no means perfect but they at least show a degree of commitment on behalf of the Public Service Broadcaster to recognise the linguistic diversity of the United Kingdom. In the Republic of Ireland the establishment of a dedicated radio and television service for a minority group (native Irish speakers) has also functioned so as to promote the Irish language on a national level. The recognition of minority languages has been regarded as a divisive factor; however, when properly managed, proper services for speakers of minority language can create a sense of commonality which had previously been denied.

References

Anderson, B. (1991) *Imagined Communities: Reflections on the Origin and Spread of Nationalism*. London: Verso.

Andrews, L. (2000) 'Northern Nationalists and the Politics of the Irish Language: The Historical Background', in J. Kirk and D. O' Baoill eds, *Language and Politics: Northern Ireland, the Republic of Ireland and Scotland*. Belfast: Queens University Belfast, pp. 45–64.

Bardon, J. (2000) *Beyond the Studio: A History of BBC Northern Ireland*. Belfast: Blackstaff.

Barnard, F. (1965) *Herder's Social and Political Thought*. Oxford: Clarendon.

BBC (2000) *Brittany Joins Celtic TV First* (http://news.bbc.co.uk/1/hi/wales/907000.stm).

Blaney, R. (1996) *Presbyterians and the Irish Language*. Belfast: Ulster Historical Foundation and ULTACH Trust.

Central Statistics Office (2005) *Irish Speakers in Each Province at Each Census since 1861* (http://www.cso.ie/statistics/irishspeakerssince1861.htm).

Cerquiglini, B. (1999) *Les langues de la France: Rapport au Ministre de l'Education Nationale, de la Recherche et de la Technologie*. Paris: Ministères de la Culture et de l'Education Nationale.

Conseil Générale du Finistere Penn-Ar-Bed (2003) *Deux radios uniquement en langue Bretonne* (http://www.cg29.fr/article/articleview/734/1/291/).

Council of Europe (1992) *European Charter for Regional and Minority Languages*. Strasbourg: Council of Europe.

Ellis, G. (2000) 'The Bilingual Sounds of Cool Cymru FM', *International Journal of Cultural Studies*, 3(2), 188–98.

Fichte, J. (1922) *Addresses to the German Nation*. Chicago: University of Chicago.

Fishman, J. (1991) *Reversing Language Shift*. Clevedon: Multilingual Matters.

Foley, M. (1996) 'Programme Quality is Goan's Main Aim', *Irish Times*, October 26.

Grimm, J. (1848) *Geschichte der deutsche sprache*. Leipzig.

Government of Ireland (1960) *Broadcasting Act*. Dublin: Government of Ireland.

Government of the United Kingdom (1981) *Broadcasting Act*. London: Government of the United Kingdom.

Hobsbawm, E. (1990) *Nations and Nationalism Since 1789: Programme, Myth and Reality*. Cambridge: Cambridge University Press.

Jones, G. (2001) 'Linguistic Minorities and Audiovisual Translation', Paper presented at *Lis lenghis tal cine: dopleadure, sottitutazion, difusion/Le lingue nel cinema: doppiaggio, sottotitolatura, diffusione*' (*Languages in the cinema: dubbing, subtitling, distribution*), Udine, Italy; May.

Kymlicka, W. (1995) *Multicultural Citizenship*. Oxford: Oxford University Press.

Mac Dubhghaill, U. (2005) 'Harry Potter and the Wizards of Baile na hAbhann: Translation, Subtitling and Dubbing Policies in Ireland's TG4 from the Start of Broadcasting in 1996 to the Present Day'. Aberystwyth: Paper presented to the IV international Mercator media symposium, University of Wales (http://www.aber.ac.uk/~merwww/Papers/UinsionnMacDubhghaill.doc).

Mac Giolla Chríost, D. (2001) 'Implementing Political Agreement in Northern Ireland: Planning Issues for Irish Language Policy', *Social and Cultural Geography*, 2(3), 307–13.

Mac Póilin, A. (1997) *Irish-medium Television in Northern Ireland*. Belfast: ULTACH Trust.

Mac Póilin, A. (2000) 'Taig Talk', in G. McCoy and M. Scott eds, *Aithne na nGael : Gaelic Identities*. Belfast: Institute of Irish Studies, pp. 88–95.

May, S. (2003) 'Rearticulating the Case for Minority Language Rights', *Current Issues in Language Planning*, 4(2), 95–125.

McCoy, G. and Ní Bhaoill, R. (2004), *Contemporary Protestant Learners of Irish*. Belfast: ULTACH Trust.

McKinnion, K. (2004) 'Reversing Language Shift: Celtic Languages Today', *JceltL*, 8, 133–47.

McLoone, M. ed. (1991) *Culture, Identity and Broadcasting in Ireland: Local Issues, Global Perspectives*. Belfast: Cultural Traditions Group.

Mercator (2003) 'Low Viewing Figures Pose Threat to TV Breizh' (http://www.mercator-central.org/newsletter/newsletter3.htm#).

Milne, A. (2000) *Gaelic Broadcasting Task Force Report*. Edinburgh: Scottish Executive (http://www.scotland.gov.uk/library3/heritage/gbtf-01.asp).

Moal, S. (2000) 'Broadcast Media in Breton: Dawn at last?', *Current Issues in Language and Society*, 7(2), 117–34.

Moore, S. (2003) 'French Broadcast Spat Hurts Station', *The Wall Street Journal*, April 16.

National Statistics Online (2004) *Welsh Language: Welsh Speakers Increase to 21%* (http://www.statistics.gov.uk/CCI/nugget.asp?ID=447).

Negrine, R. (1998) 'Models of Media Institutions: Media Institutions in Europe', in A. Briggs and P. Cobley, *The Media: An Introduction*. Harlow: Longman, pp. 224–37.

Nic Nèill, M. (2001) 'Gaelic Broadcasting: On the Threshold of a New Era', *Mercator Media Forum*, 5(1), 99–106.

Ó Snodaigh, P. (1995) *Hidden Ulster: Protestants and the Irish Language*. Belfast: Lagan Press.

Parekh, B. (2002) *The Future of Multi-ethnic Britain: The Parekh Report*. London: Runnymede Trust.

Research Centre of Wales (1996) *Euromosaic Report: Breton* (http://www.uoc.edu/euromosaic/web/homean/index1.html).

Robertson, R. (1994) 'Globalisation or Glocalisation', *Journal of International Communication*, 1(1), 33–52.

Thomas, N. (2001) 'Two Breton Voices on Radio', *Mercator Media Forum*, 5(1), 107–14.

ULTACH Trust (2005) *Memorandum by the ULTACH Trust*. Belfast: ULTACH Trust (http://www.publications.parliament.uk/pa/ld200506/ldselect/ldbbc/128/5112315.htm).

Watson, I. (2002) 'Irish-language Broadcasting: History, Ideology and Identity', *Media, Culture and Society*, 24(6), 739–57.

Websites

BBC Alba – http://www.bbc.co.uk/scotland/alba/
BBC Cymru – http://www.bbc.co.uk/cymru/
BBC Northern Ireland – http://www.bbc.co.uk/northernireland/irish/
BBC Voices Project 2005 – http://www.bbc.co.uk/voices/
Euromosaic Survey – http://www.uoc.edu/euromosaic/

European Charter for Regional or Minority Languages – http://www.coe.int/T/E/
    Legal_Affairs/Local_and_regional_Democracy/Regional_or_Minority_languages/
Gaelic Media Service – http://www.gms.org.uk/?lang=en
Mercator Network – http://www.mercator-central.org
Raidió na Gaeltachta – http://www.rnag.ie
Raidió Teilifís Éireann – http://www.rte.ie
S4C – http://www.s4c.co.uk/e_index.html
Stalig – http://www.stalig.com
TG4 – http://www.tg4.ie

7
Language, Culture and Identity: The Chinese Community in Northern Ireland

Mary Delargy

Northern Ireland has been part of the United Kingdom since 1921, when it was partitioned from the rest of the island of Ireland. This partition came about as the result of several centuries of conflict between Ireland and, its nearest geographical neighbour, Britain, and this relationship has continued to be turbulent to this day particularly in regard to the Northern Ireland question (see Arthur 2000). There were many reasons for the conflict: England and Scotland sent settlers to claim land in Ireland and there were religious wars since most of the island of Ireland remained Catholic after the Reformation which saw England embrace the Protestant faith. Even after partition there were still difficulties as many Catholics felt no allegiance to the state of Northern Ireland; moreover, the Troubles which began in 1969 were mainly the result of discrimination against the Catholic community by the dominant Protestant population and there is a plethora of academic literature which focuses on this period (Bew et al. 1996; Mc Kittrick and Mc Vea 2000; Coogan 1991).

The situation is not as straightforward as a Catholic/Protestant split. Within the Catholic community there are two main groupings, the Nationalists who support the return to a united Ireland by peaceful means and the Republicans who would have supported the campaign of violence to achieve a united Ireland. However, research by Marianne Elliott (2002) has offered interesting and original perceptions on the diverse nature of this particular section of the community which is very often viewed in a simplistic manner.

Protestants can be roughly divided into Unionists who support the link with Britain and Loyalists who would justify violence as a means of retaining their position within the United Kingdom. Many Unionists despite their loyalty to the British crown have felt that on occasions the British government has betrayed them, particularly over issues of power sharing with Catholics. This has meant that many unionists have regarded themselves as a forgotten people (see Alcock 1994).

The main Republican paramilitary group was the Irish Republican Army, now on permanent ceasefire as its political wing Sinn Féin is involved in negotiations for a permanent peace, and the Ulster Defence Association is the main Loyalist paramilitary organisation. The signing of the Belfast (Good Friday) Agreement in 1998 led to hopes of a lasting peace, although at the time of writing in 2006 negotiations were once again underway for the restoration of its own government to Northern Ireland.

The issue of identity and community has been widely researched by academics such as Anderson (1983). In Northern Ireland, identity and community are strongly linked with religious affiliation. The majority of Catholics would identify themselves as Irish and many embrace the Irish language, traditional Irish music and dance. For members of the Protestant community the choice may be British identity with allegiance to the British crown and sports such as rugby and cricket. The debate on British and Irish identity is one which has been the subject of many conferences and academic writing, particularly works by Nic Craith (2002) and Crozier (1990).

Much less research has been carried out on the minority ethnic communities. Despite a huge increase in the number of people from minority ethnic communities coming to live in Northern Ireland the situation has not changed radically since Irwin and Dunn's (1996) survey noted the lack of research publications on Northern Ireland's ethnic groups, which was a lost opportunity to heighten awareness amongst the majority population of the existence, experiences and cultural heritages of these minorities.

Unlike Great Britain, which has had a Race Relations Act since 1976, Northern Ireland has had legislation relating to race only since the Race Relations (NI) order of 1997. This Order has led to a significant change in the relationship between the host community and the minority ethnic communities in Northern Ireland in the last 10 years. This chapter aims to outline some of the changes which have occurred in the Chinese community since it was first established in the early 1960s.

Context and infrastructure

Estimates as to the size of the Chinese population in Northern Ireland vary greatly. Official figures from the 2001 census give returns of approximately 4000 people (NISRA 2001). This represents less than one per cent of the total population of approximately one and a half million for the whole of Northern Ireland. The number put forward by the Chinese community themselves and by the Multicultural Resource Centre, an agency whose remit is to provide details on ethnic minorities in Northern Ireland, estimate that there are around twice that number.

Even the origins of the community in Northern Ireland are not agreed on, with some claiming that the first Chinese restaurant was opened in Belfast in 1963 while others say the border town of Newry saw the first restaurant in 1962. What is known is that the majority of early immigrants were from the poorer provinces of mainland China and from Hong Kong. Some of those who came to Northern Ireland had previously settled in the major cities of northern England such as Liverpool and Manchester. Discovering that the anticipated business opportunities did not present themselves, they chose to travel further afield to Northern Ireland.

Many of the problems faced by the Chinese community in Northern Ireland are similar to those faced by the communities elsewhere. The first generation of immigrants came from poor rural backgrounds with tightly-knit communities. Languages spoken were Cantonese and Hakka and as most of them had worked as farmers they had little opportunity to learn English before leaving their own country. Additionally, they found that their new lifestyle afforded them few opportunities either to become proficient in English or to integrate with the local community.

Most of the Chinese community based in Northern Ireland were employed in the catering industry, the majority of them having their own takeaway or restaurant and living 'over the shop'. The working day generally began for them at around the time most people were coming home from work and continued into the small hours of the morning. Women spoke of a particularly strong sense of isolation since they not only worked in the business but combined this with bringing up the children, who in the evenings either played on the premises or slept upstairs while their parents worked below. The tradition of working in the catering industry continues today with almost 90 per cent of the community still involved in the restaurant and takeaway business.

In Northern Ireland the two main groupings of Catholics and Prot-estants define their national identity as British or Irish, with the majority of Protestants seeing themselves as British and as part of the United Kingdom while most Catholics would self-define as Irish and as belonging to the island of Ireland. Such definitions are based on a number of factors such as family influences, schools attended and political affiliation. In addition to political and religious beliefs, nationality will influence to a lesser extent the languages learned, sports played and choice of music (Mc Garry and O' Leary 1995).

First-generation immigrants tend to retain their Chinese identity, whereas second- and third-generation members of the Chinese community may choose British and/or Irish identity. Such choices are often influenced by their peers, particularly in teenage years as interviews carried out by this researcher testify. One respondent suggested the following: 'because I think Northern Ireland is part of Britain and some of them if they have lived here for a long time I presume they would think they are British citizens. For the second generation it's very different. If they're born here, they get a bit confused. There's no other word for it.'

Another noted,

> Well when I was younger I always thought of myself as a British citizen. A Chinese British citizen, but when you get older and your company and your influences are Irish people which is where my background is then I'm Irish. I went to a Catholic primary school and Catholic college, I live in a Catholic area. The majority of my friends are Catholic therefore you kind of get swayed, you know, even though I'm not Catholic I'm influenced by Catholics and Irish people.

The issue of identity was discussed extensively in interviews which this researcher (MD) had with members of the Chinese community in Northern Ireland. In the following extracts, one of the interviewees is identified as Chinese male (CM) and the other as Chinese female (CF). Both interviewees are in their mid-twenties and are second-generation members of the Chinese community:

MD: You were talking about the whole question of identity within the Chinese community. Is that something you think should be to the fore?

CM: It's certainly something that I think should be crucial for all communities . . . all groups to get to grips with. You know, especially in Northern Ireland my understanding of conflict is that it is essentially born out of individuals being assured enough in their own identity. If so, you would be able to respect difference and live with identities that are different from yours or opinions and value systems that may be somewhat different than theirs as well.

CM noted the differential experiences of first- and second-generation Chinese in Northern Ireland and the impact of such experiences on issues of identity:

> Obviously growing up in Northern Ireland or arriving in Northern Ireland because you are a minority community you cannot but be aware that you are different. I suppose that most Chinese would grapple with that at different times in their life. And the issues.... you have to generalise in a sense I suppose when you talk about a whole community and the experiences will be different from person to person but from a general point of view, someone who arrives to Northern Ireland who has been brought up elsewhere expects to be treated differently so to some degree they'll almost accept discriminatory treatment. Certainly in the earlier days, back in the 60s and 70s, the general attitude was to keep a low profile and not to draw too much attention to yourself, so there wasn't a sense that you needed to understand what your rights were and fight for those rights whereas the longer you're attached to a place – and we're now into a second... third generation Chinese people in Northern Ireland the longer you have to feel that you belong to a community and that you deserve to be treated equally. So what we've seen over a period of time is a greater sense of your belonging, your right to be here and your rights here and the acting out of making sure your needs are actually met, your individual needs are met and that obviously goes hand in hand with generations that are born here that don't want necessarily to be seen as different.

This respondent emphasised the issue of multiple identities in Northern Ireland and the differential experiences of a sense of belonging in different environments:

> Most people when they're growing up... part of the process of understanding who you are is by wanting to be part of a group, not wanting to be the odd one out. Chances are, Chinese people will identify more with their peers in the classroom or their friends in the area they're living in. Because Northern Ireland has been so segregated and still is in terms of housing and education what you find are Chinese children and young people identifying more with one community or the other – Northern Ireland's two main traditions. In terms of their own Chinese identity while it may be very strong at home both in the language that is spoken and the cultures that are practiced it's

not necessarily something that they want to brag about when they're outside the home because it distinguishes them as being different from their peers.

He noted the mixed emotions that can arise out of being 'pulled in different directions' in terms of one's identity:

> Again this is generalizing – there are some individuals who actually enjoy that or they maintain an area where there are opportunities to mix with other Chinese young people so that would be a major part of their identity being Chinese because there's enough peers to share that with and feel that there's a sense of belonging. But for others there may be a period during their youth where they suppress their Chineseness because they see it as a negative, not a positive thing. I think in adulthood once an individual's identity is formed there's a chance to revisit any aspects of the Chinese culture that they may have suppressed as a young person. And I touch on this from the outset that there is in that younger generation a greater understanding of sectarian issues in Northern Ireland whereas people who are new to Northern Ireland don't see it as their problem. People who are born and brought up and have gone through that sectarian system obviously have a more implicit understanding of it because they're actually being part of it.

However, tensions regarding identity issues among the Chinese community in Northern Ireland were not noticeably different from those of the host communities:

> It's not something that people would talk about a great deal but I also think you won't find a predominant identity – most Chinese people think this – in terms of their identity. In the same way that if you ask someone from Northern Ireland you will get a whole myriad of different answers depending on where they come from, it's the same with Chinese. Now there will be Chinese in there for most, but whenever you start to probe their political opinions and that sort of thing it will very much depend on what school they went to, what area they live in, and Chinese will be part of their whole identity. For some it will be a huge part, for others a much lesser part, the feeling of being Northern Irish or of being Irish or British will be different depending on what area of Northern Ireland that

young Chinese person has been brought up in. (Interview conducted by Delargy September 2005)

The female Chinese interviewee reinforced these points. For her, 'It was difficult being different. I mean when you're younger it's not just the Chinese people, I mean everybody wants to be the same when you're younger at school. But when you grow up it's seen as more of a benefit being from two cultures, bicultural.' She viewed the notion of belonging to two different cultures as distinctly advantageous. 'I think you get the best of both worlds, you get the benefits of Chinese culture, I speak Cantonese well and get to go home to Hong Kong every couple of years and I have the benefit of Irish culture as well here.' When pressed on the point of whether she would give her children English/Irish or Chinese names, she nominated both: 'you would have a Chinese name and a Western name or whatever, Irish name, you know. People use the Irish or English name at school and for some situations, I suppose for some pronunciations it's hard for Irish people so you use your Irish name.' An interesting discussion followed:

MD: So you would have…would you be known by another name in the house?
CF: Yes.
MD: Do you find that difficult, do you feel a bit like two different people?
CF: No, no it's just for Chinese people.
MD: So did you use your Western name before you went to school, would you have used it or would you always have been known by your Chinese name?
CF: Well at home and around relatives I'm known as XXX or sorry, my Chinese name but to the kids in the street and the teachers in the school it's Diana.
MD: So it's always been like.…I suppose maybe if you grow up like that…
CF: You get used to it. (Interview conducted by the researcher, March 2005)

The Chinese community in Northern Ireland is not a homogenous group. Feng (2004) outlines a number of differences between the community from mainland China and those whose place of origin is Hong Kong. People from mainland China began arriving in Northern Ireland in the late 1970s to take up posts in the Province's two universities. Those from mainland China tend to be better educated than people from Hong Kong, and this community puts greater emphasis on education. Interviews which she carried out with adolescents from the Chinese community illustrate that much more emphasis is placed on doing well at school by parents who are from mainland China and who tend to be better educated themselves than parents from Hong Kong.

The grammar school system is retained in Northern Ireland, and these children would be under greater pressure to secure a place at one of the more prestigious schools. Several of the parents make comparisons between the system of education in China and that in Northern Ireland. One suggests that the Chinese education system is more imposing. They force people to learn without caring about children's interest in learning. But here they guide and stimulate children to learn, and pay special attention to their interests. Another says that the educational system here is good, it encourages children to do things and develop their ability to search for knowledge by themselves.

Parents from Hong Kong are more likely to work in the catering trade and have elder children help them in the business (Feng 2004). This tends to have a negative effect on the children's education because they are working long hours after school most days and also for the greater part of the weekend. For that reason, some of the children spent most of their time at school interacting with their friends rather than concentrating on their lessons as they felt this was their only opportunity to do so.

The main emphasis in education for the Hong Kong parents seems to be on learning languages, both Chinese and English. Parents feel that by having a degree of fluency in both these languages their children will have a much wider choice when it comes to employment opportunities, as most parents are reluctant for their children to follow them into the catering trade. The majority of parents were also optimistic that their children would return to Hong Kong eventually and were keen that their children would return to the region with a good grasp of the Chinese language as well as English. Parents felt that understanding Chinese would aid their children in gaining employment in Hong Kong (Feng 2004).

Parents from mainland China were also felt to be much more reluctant for their children to go back to the country of origin and far more likely to have given a negative portrayal of it to their children They tended to emphasise the positive side of life in Northern Ireland such as the good education system and portrayed mainland China as a place where their children would have no opportunity to think for themselves.

Additionally they felt that their children's high standard of education and academic qualifications would stand them in good stead in their search for employment. Any prejudice they felt others might have because of their different racial origin would be offset against having an employee with such high academic qualifications.

The children of these parents were also felt to be influenced by what they felt was the negative portrayal of their country in the British media, particularly on human rights issues. Children of Hong Kong parents took the opposite view. They generally felt that their offspring's best chance was to return to their homeland. Hong Kong with its 24/7 lifestyle would be much more appealing to young people and there would be no problem with racial differences. Those children who spoke both English and Chinese would have no problem in securing a good job for themselves.

The Chinese in Northern Ireland have infrastructures which offer support in terms of language and identity issues. The Chinese Welfare Association (CWA) was formed in 1986 by the Chinese Chamber of Commerce (CCC) in response to the perceived needs of the Chinese community in Northern Ireland (http://www.cwa-ni.org/english/staff.htm). This umbrella organisation has a central office in Belfast and an office in Derry serving the north-west region. A number of groups are located in other parts of Northern Ireland including several women's groups.

The first aim of the CWA is to enable and support the development of community infrastructure. This is achieved through the Chinese Community Forum and through the strengthening of links between the CCC and the CWA. The Chinese Community Forum is made up of 18 different Chinese groups and projects from across Northern Ireland. The main centres of the Chinese community in Northern Ireland are in Belfast, the capital, where approximately one-third of the Chinese population are resident, and Craigavon, a new town in mid-Ulster which was set up in the early 1970s and where the 'Chinese' community is made up of persons from the Chinese mainland, Hong Kong and the Vietnamese Boat people who settled there in the 1970s. The current chairperson Anna Manwah Lo has been in the post since 1997 as its first permanent chairperson and in 1999 received an MBE (Member of the British Empire, an order of chivalry) for services to ethnic minorities.

The CWA also aims to enable children and young people to realise their full potential as active citizens within both the Chinese and the wider community. Several projects aimed specifically at children are organised by CWA. Included among these is the After-Schools Club which takes place five evenings per week. The aims of the After-school-club are to provide English and homework support, to promote deeper understanding of Chinese culture and to maintain their Chinese identity within a multicultural society. The club also provides an opportunity to enhance personal development through recreational and educational activities, to meet socially with other Chinese children, to encourage cross-community links and to learn about local culture and history.

Another support structure for Chinese youth in Northern Ireland is Generation Y, a youth programme which was developed by both the Chinese Welfare Association and the Youth Action Northern Ireland. It grew out of a youth group established by CWA and was formally established in 2001. Its membership is not drawn exclusively from the Chinese community but is also open to members of other communities. Its main aim is to provide a place for young people to meet and socialise, and there is an emphasis on forming links with the wider community.

One of the objectives of Generation Y is to facilitate language support for young people whose first language is not English. Many of the sports activities of this youth programme are aimed at involving Chinese youth in the wider community, including participation in the cross-border Soccer against Racism tournament held in Dublin and a highly successful Kung Fu programme held in Belfast's Indian Community Centre. Indeed many of the youth activities are joint initiatives between the Chinese and the Indian communities in Belfast, including a series of training skills initiatives for those taking part in the Duke of Edinburgh award – a scheme for young people to learn new skills and become more involved in their local community – and sports events for Intercultural Week.

The CWA has also formed a close working relationship with the Northern Ireland Association of Citizens Advice Bureaus (NIACAB). Services include a bilingual leaflet encouraging greater use of the Citizens Advice Bureau by the Chinese community and access by every Citizens Advice Bureau office in Northern Ireland to Language Line, a translation facility. Other initiatives include the delivery of anti-racism and cultural awareness training to the Citizens Advice Bureau by CWA staff. Also contacts and links are forged between regional CWA staff members and CAB staff in Derry, Craigavon, Antrim and Bangor.

A further aim of CWA is to develop greater cultural awareness within both the Chinese and the wider community and to work towards the elimination of racism and discrimination. Cultural awareness and anti-racism training form a larger part of the work of the CWA as can be seen by the diversity of groups to whom the programme was delivered in 2002–2003. They included the Prince's Trust as well as two Irish language primary schools in Belfast. Events such as the Chinese New Year and the Dragon Boat Race have been attended by members of Belfast City Council as well as people from inside and outside the Chinese community. While support for the Chinese in Northern Ireland focuses on youth, there is also an awareness of the special position of the elderly in Chinese society. This is reflected in services provided to the community in Northern Ireland.

A group known as *Hoi Sum* (Happiness and Joyful) was established in Belfast in 1998 to meet the needs of the elderly Chinese, who were most likely to suffer from a sense of isolation and least likely to have sufficient fluency in English, to enable them to communicate easily with their neighbours. It is the result of a partnership between the local health and social services trust and the CWA. The group currently has over 130 members. One of its aims is to identify the health and social needs of the Chinese senior citizens in Belfast and to help further capacity-building within the Chinese Community at local level.

In November 2004, the first purpose-built sheltered accommodation for elderly Chinese was opened in Belfast. Prior to this, elderly members of the Chinese community requiring sheltered accommodation had been forced to travel to areas such as Glasgow and Liverpool to secure such accommodation. Elderly Chinese living in other sheltered housing in the city had found that the language barrier only increased their sense of isolation. The need for local accommodation became apparent and a site was identified in 1999. Funding for the project which cost 9.2 million pounds included a grant of 7.2 million pounds from the Department of Social Development.

Hong Ling (Health and Peace) Gardens accommodates 59 residents and the building's architecture takes account of Chinese culture and traditions (BBC 2004a). For example, the stairs do not face the door as it is believed that will cause the good luck to pass out of the house. Nor are there any flats numbered 4, 13 or 14 as these are believed to be unlucky numbers. Signs are written in Cantonese and English, the lift 'speaks' in both languages and a bilingual warden will live on site. Perhaps the most striking feature in this area of Belfast, which is predominantly rows of red brick built in the late 1980s, is the two stone lions which guard the front entrance. Local people were consulted beforehand to ensure that the project had the support of the local community. The reaction was favourable with the residents association expressing the hope that the Chinese would not see themselves as an ethnic minority but as an important part of the community. They felt that the Chinese shared many cultural values with the local Nationalist community, especially their respect for the elderly.

Language and identity

The Chinese community in Northern Ireland still faces many difficulties due to the language barrier. First-generation members of the Chinese community who arrived in the 1960s suffered severe problems of isolation because they were unable to communicate with the local population. Many of those who came to Northern Ireland had little formal education and could barely write in their own language, let alone learn a new language while working long hours in the catering trade. By the early 1970s, however, the need for language provision became more apparent and the first classes were set up in Rupert Stanley College, a technical institution in Belfast. The classes were attended mainly by younger men who felt themselves in a better position to undertake the difficult task of combining a day's work with learning the new language. Recent attempts by Education and Library boards throughout Northern Ireland to make services more inclusive have involved the production of membership leaflets available in Chinese and having a selection of books and videos in Chinese available in main libraries.

In 1983, the CCC became aware of the need to establish a Chinese school in Belfast, whose aim would be to preserve the Chinese language and culture among the younger generation. Several reasons were put forward for the need to have the school. The main reason for the loss of language was felt to be the fact that a number of Chinese children in Belfast and Derry were fostered by local families. Long working hours meant that parents were unable to look after them and the upbringing of their children was entrusted to neighbours and friends. Additionally, once they started the school, Chinese children found themselves in an English-speaking environment where it became a necessity to learn English as quickly as possible.

Several young Chinese interviewed by this researcher mentioned a language barrier growing up between themselves and their parents, as children found that their skills in whichever Chinese language they spoke extended only to basic conversation about home and their surroundings. Their language for expressing more complex concepts and for expressing emotions was English. Their parents, however, had only a basic vocabulary in English and no means of expressing emotions in the English language. Intergenerational conversations, therefore, tended to be at a most basic level with neither side having the skills to communicate their feelings effectively to the other. Patrick Yu, Chairperson of the Northern Ireland Council for Ethnic Minorities, expresses it thus:

> This (Chinese teenagers in Northern Ireland) is a group which feels even more alienated and confused in this society, because they have not only lost most of their original Chinese culture, but the Western culture which they have adopted in its place is not being easily accepted by their parents. This identity confusion can become the core of family disputes if the importance of communication and understanding is not appreciated. Moreover, with regard to education and open employment, our young people are also facing a certain degree of discrimination. (Yu 1994)

The Chinese Language School was initially housed at the Chamber of Commerce premises close to Queen's University, Belfast. It soon became apparent that these premises were much too small and after a few false starts premises were secured in a local primary school. Initially, only Cantonese was taught at the school as the majority of pupils were from families in which it was the main language, but the need to teach Mandarin was recognised with the growth in trade between Britain and China, and classes were established in 2001. At present, 15 classes per week are held, 15 Cantonese classes for children, 5 Mandarin classes for young people and 1 Mandarin class for adults. The age range among the children is from kindergarten through all primary school classes and right up to General Certificate of Secondary Education (GCSE), the school examination normally taken by 16-year-olds in the United Kingdom.

Mandarin classes were also established in 2001 as part of the Linen Hall Library's Languages of Ulster programme. Although these were initially aimed at making the library more welcoming to members of minority ethnic communities, the majority of those attending the classes were actually drawn from the two main communities. The initial aim had been to encourage a sense of belonging among the minority communities, to give those people from second- and third-generation families an opportunity to learn their parents' language. It was also hoped that these classes would foster a sense of identity and belonging among members of the Chinese community as they would be involved in activities in which the majority community also took part, something which was much less common then than now. It was also felt that the classes would be of use to English speakers such as civil servants, health workers and so on working with the Chinese community; in 2000 there were fewer interpreters than there are now. Of those who attended the classes, the majority gave their reason for wanting to learn as having family connections with China; one woman, for example, explained that her son worked in the British Civil Service and her grandchildren were learning Mandarin, and that she would like the opportunity to communicate with them in both languages. Currently a beginners and an improvers class are offered weekly.

The University of Ulster has forged close links with China in a number of fields including engineering and business studies. Consequently, it was decided that there was a need for some language classes to be offered at the university. Beginning in the autumn of 2004, the university has offered a diploma in Mandarin (University of Ulster 2006).

The Mandarin Speakers' Association, which is based in Belfast, was established in November 2000 and draws its membership from Mandarin speakers from mainland China, Hong Kong, Taiwan, Singapore, Malaysia and Macao. Although it has only one full-time member of staff, its executive committee of 13 members also act as volunteers to undertake all tasks as necessary within the organisation. The Mandarin Speakers' Association defines its main aim as 'to encourage its members to promote cultural and social exchange between the United Kingdom and the Mandarin-speaking groups (http://www.mandarinspeakers.org/asp/programme.html). It has a number of objectives which include the provision of various services such as translation, language training, legal consultancy and so on to its members; involvement in cultural, economic exchange/promotion; helping the Mandarin-speaking group with the maintenance of their cultural heritages; and the promotion of harmony between the Mandarin-speaking groups and the other community groups. The organisation's website also informs us that through provision of information on benefits, housing, cultural activities and so on, approximately 500 people benefit from the Mandarin Speakers' Association every year.

Interpreting services are another key area of language provision in Northern Ireland. Figures from a report in 2003 by the Multicultural Resource Centre, Northern Ireland, indicate that 58 per cent of the Chinese population in Northern Ireland have only basic levels of English. The Chinese community is the only minority ethnic community to have interpreter service level agreements in place in all of the Health Boards. The Regional Interpreting Service for Northern Ireland is a joint initiative by the Department of Health and Social Services, Department of Culture Arts and Leisure, Office of the First and

Deputy First Minister and Department of Education. It ran initially as a pilot project from April 2004 until March 2005. Although not exclusively for the use of the Chinese community, the vast majority of its users are from within this community.

The primary aim of the Project is to significantly improve access to Health and Social Services for members of black and minority ethnic communities in Northern Ireland who do not speak English either as a first or as a competent second language. The project has also created a central register of sessional interpreters and set down codes of practice for Health and Social Services staff such as nurses, doctors and social workers and for interpreters. The project has also engaged with the development of a training programme for Health and Social Services staff and practitioners using interpreters.

Since its establishment, the organisation has held five training sessions to cope with the demand for interpreters. Services provided through this programme are available only for interpreting face to face; however, the CWA offers a further professional interpreting service which includes interpreting over the telephone, the translation of documents and proofreading. Interpreting services for health reasons are paid for by the area Health Board, all other services are charged to the individual.

Relations between the Chinese and the local community

The last 5 to 6 years have seen great changes in the relationship between the Chinese and the local communities in Northern Ireland. On the one hand, there has been a huge rise in the number of reported racist attacks – an increase of 900 per cent between 1997 and 2004 (PSNI). This has led to the widely held perception that 'racism is the new sectarianism'.

Prior to this, Northern Ireland was regarded as a relatively welcoming place in which to live. An added attraction (for the Chinese community) was the perceived lesser racial tension in contrast to the situation in some inner cities in Britain (Mc Knight and Watson 1998). In Northern Ireland everything is seen in the context of Catholic versus Protestant or Republican versus Loyalist. Housing estates are either Catholic or Protestant as are schools and many leisure centres. Certain sports such as rugby and cricket which are 'English' or 'British' would be played by Protestants, while Gaelic (traditional Irish) games such as hurling – a type of hockey – and Gaelic football would have few members of the Protestant community among its players. Even racist attacks fall into this category since one side held itself to be blameless while accusing the other of racism.

Early 2004 saw a spate of racist attacks mainly in Belfast. The majority of attacks took place in a Protestant area of South Belfast and the blame was laid on Loyalist paramilitaries. Chinese families tend to live in Protestant areas, particularly in Belfast, as there is usually more accommodation available for private rental here. Although other ethnic minorities were also targeted, the majority of attacks were against the Chinese community. Ten families were forced out of their homes in the space of a single week. Community leaders were more concerned, however, to learn that at least one estate agent in the area was ordered not to rent homes to members of the Chinese community. The estate agent told reporters:

> I've been told not to rent to Chinese or black people. People I'm letting houses for are very concerned because they have an investment and they could see it going down the river. One house was bought for over £80,000 and it's burnt now. If a Black or a Chinese person tries to rent a property from me I would have to tell them it is not safe. If this goes on, someone is going to be burnt alive or murdered. (BBC 2004b)

The independent regional news service, Ulster Television, runs a website on which readers are invited to comment on local news stories. Comments about the racist attacks included criticism from some sections of the community, but others supported the action citing the usual reasons about taking 'our' jobs and houses alongside claim and counterclaim about whether Catholics or Protestants showed more tolerance towards members of the new communities (UTV 2004).

There was also an incident reported in which a racist leaflet was put into the schoolbag of a Chinese primary school pupil in south Belfast. On investigation it was discovered that hundreds more of the leaflets, entitled 'Yellow Menace' – which outlined the apparent threat of a 'takeover' of the area by the Chinese community – had been distributed in the neighbourhood. Donegall Pass, the area in which most of the leaflets had been distributed, is predominantly Loyalist. It is in an area of the city that is otherwise politically and racially mixed, being close to Queen's University. Although Chinese families have been living there since the 1970s, the increase in their numbers in the area coupled with a decline in the Protestant population in the district was believed to have led to the fears of being 'swamped' by the Chinese population. A copy of the leaflet obtained by the researcher makes disturbing reading:

> Donegall Pass is no longer a Protestant/Loyalist area, it is commonly known as 'Chinatown' throughout our city and the people of the Pass are in the midst of losing the already small stronghold they have in their community forever.
>
> These immigrants occupy a vast amount of our houses, stopping any Protestant families moving in that would be more beneficial for the betterment of our community in all aspects of community life. The Chinese only take from our community and provide nothing for it. These foreign immigrants have no sense of Christian values or decency and have no respect at all for our community. The influx of the yellow people into Donegall Pass has done more damage than 35 years of the IRA's recent campaign of republican propaganda and violence … The forefathers of this community shed their Ulster blood on foreign battlefields to keep their communities free from foreign invasion, while we are now giving our community away to these Chinese immigrants. SHAME ON US. (Anonymous 2004)

Donegall Pass was also the intended site of the sheltered housing for the elderly, but residents refused to have it there, leading to its eventually being sited in the nearby Nationalist Markets area. Plans to build a Chinese community centre on the Stranmillis Road in south Belfast have also been put on hold following objections by local residents. There are, however, many more positive signs. For the last 6 or 7 years, Chinese New Year celebrations have included a meal or similar celebration to which the members of other communities including local elected representatives have been invited. These events and similar ones such as the annual Dragon Boat Race have received extensive coverage in the media, significantly raising awareness of the Chinese community among the local population.

Two events which took place in Derry City Council area are worthy of mention here. One related to the lion figure used in the Lion Dance which is extensively performed at community events in the city, including the St Patrick's Day parade, which is now a multicultural event. In addition to this, Derry City Council provided the funding for a new lion when the old one was worn out. This led to the unusual situation in which the 'Awakening the Lion' ceremony was actually performed by one of the local councillors in place of a member of the Chinese community.

A press release on the event noted that the Mayor gave her support to the celebrations. Mayor Councillor Lynn Fleming noted that she had been told about an old Chinese proverb that existed to explain the background to the Mid-Autumn Moon Festival celebrations – 'When the moon is full, mankind is one', symbolising unity, and this saying was especially significant in the context of Northern Ireland (Derry City Council 2005). The Mayor went on to emphasise that the Sai Pak community had become an integral part of the City's multicultural fabric. With this statement she was attempting to counteract some of the negativity experienced by the members of the Chinese community in the city. The 'Waking the Lion' ceremony is an important part of Chinese culture and identity. It incorporates a blessing of a new Chinese lion head. The ceremony involves painting the lion's eyes before the start of the dance in order to awaken its spirit – through this it has been born into the world. The Lion Dance is a traditional art that dates back thousands of years. The Chinese believe that the dance brings good luck and drives away evil spirits, that is why it forms part of many Chinese festivals and special occasions such as weddings or even the opening of businesses and restaurants.

Other opportunities have been taken to give public expression to Chinese identity in the north-west region of Northern Ireland. As part of the Harvest Moon festival in 2004, a series of events were organised by the Women's Officer at Derry City Council involving women from the Sai Pak Chinese community in Derry and members of Protestant and Catholic women's groups from throughout the city. Interpreters were provided where necessary for the Chinese women, many of whom knew very little English. The events were designed to raise awareness in each community of the cultural symbols of the others.

One such event featured a large black bin liner in which several items had been placed. Each woman in turn had to draw an item from the bag and explain its significance for her. Participants found it interesting to discover how little they really knew about the other cultures; for example, the Chinese community had brought along a variety of musical instruments and board games such as Mah Jong which were unknown to most of the others there. Significantly, community relations officers were interested to find that many cultural symbols from the Protestant and Catholic communities such as Rangers and Celtic football shirts held no significance for the Chinese women. Other events included learning Chinese calligraphy and trying to eat with chopsticks. The emphasis was on enjoyment, but the event had great significance as a first opportunity for most of the women to meet. It concluded with an evening of music and dance open to the general public in which women from all three traditions took part.

As stated at the beginning of this chapter, religion is a pervasive part of life in Northern Ireland. Most of the Chinese community in Northern Ireland, as throughout the United Kingdom, belong to the Taoist or Confucian beliefs and would see religion as a personal affair. There are no external signs such as places of worship in the province. One complaint made, however, was that the only place at which people could be cremated was at Belfast. As a consequence, people from other parts of Northern Ireland had to travel there after someone died.

A significant number, belong to one or other of the two main churches. Belfast Chinese Christian Church (BCCC), a non-denominational evangelical congregation, was established at Easter 1975 when a Northern Irish minister and a local member of the Chinese community began to do some evangelical work among the Chinese community. The community did not really expand, however, until 1987, when a sudden influx of Chinese students at Queen's University began to attend the church on a regular basis. The church has one hundred members and regularly has in excess of two hundred people in attendance, making it one of the largest Chinese congregations in the United Kingdom. Three services are normally held each Sunday, one in English, one in Cantonese and one in Mandarin. Additionally, classes are held one evening per week to allow children from the church to learn Cantonese (See http://www.bccc.co.uk).

Members of the church feel that having a Chinese congregation places it in a unique position. As the BCCC is a 'Chinese' Church, most members of the congregation would be of Chinese origin. The ethnic uniqueness and independence of the BCCC has helped it to foster good relationships with other denominations who hold similar doctrinal views. Indeed, some members of the congregation were members of other denominations, such as the Brethren, Baptist and Elim, before they joined the BCCC. Pastors and Ministers of those churches and other local churches are often invited to speak at the BCCC, and members of BCCC have often been invited to take part in other church services (See Evangelical Contribution on Northern Ireland 2004).

Some members of the Chinese community also belong to the more mainstream Catholic or Presbyterian churches. A few of those interviewed by this researcher cited this as another way in which they were made to feel like outsiders – they were insulted by others because they belonged to the 'wrong' religion. This is particularly a problem for younger people who have mentioned the problems of being the 'wrong' colour as well as belonging to the 'wrong' faith. These remarks came both from the local community and also on a few occasions from within their own community.

Although at an individual level members of the Chinese community have felt their identity threatened, there have been some attempts to address these issues at an institutional level. Section 75 is part of the Northern Ireland Act 1998, relating to Human Rights and Equal Opportunities. In response to this Act, an Equality Coalition has been set up. This is a broad-based alliance of groups committed to the full implementation of the statutory duty to promote equality of opportunity (Government of the United Kingdom 1998). The group is made up of representatives of each of the categories, including the CWA. Under this legislation, CWA is entitled to comment on all new programmes put forward by public authorities and to request changes where it is felt that there is discrimination against one section of the community.

The Act has some important implications for language provision in Northern Ireland. Public authorities must make such documents available in languages other than English if a request is received for them. Documents for the Chinese community are supplied in simplified Chinese rather than Mandarin or Cantonese. There are additional benefits to the Chinese community besides having documents available in their own language.

Because of its membership of the Equality Coalition, CWA is invited to prepare a response on the equality impact of all public authority programmes. This has resulted in them having a voice in public affairs which was previously not available to them. Currently no member of the Chinese community is a public representative either as a local councillor or as a member of the Northern Ireland Assembly. At the time of writing, a new electoral register for Northern Ireland was being compiled. At present, a low percentage of members of the Chinese community are registered to vote. In an attempt to maximise the number voting, the CWA has a bilingual pop-up in English and simplified Chinese on its website encouraging members to register to vote.

At present the District Policing Partnership has no serving members from the Chinese community. Policing is a divisive issue in Northern Ireland, and District Policing Partnerships (DPPs) were set up as a means for the local community to monitor the effectiveness of policing in a specific area. Relations between the police and the Chinese community have not always been good. Although there have been some accusations of racism, the majority of people felt that the police treated them with indifference. Two reasons were given for the fact that there are no members of the Chinese community on the DPPs: first, the hours that are worked in the catering industry leave few people free to sit on such committees; and second, the attitude which many of the Chinese community have towards authority makes them unwilling to serve in such a capacity.

The researcher asked those members of the Chinese community whom she interviewed what they saw as the way forward for the community. The suggestions were varied. One respondent commenting on relations between the Chinese and the local community felt that Chinese integration into the community was hampered by the working conditions. Moreover, the language barrier was a major factor in preventing them from doing so. She welcomed the inclusion of the wider community in Chinese festivals as a positive step and felt that the Chinese community centre would encourage Chinese and local people to mix more easily. She also regarded the Equality Agenda as particularly useful in ensuring that the voice of the Chinese community was held by those in positions of authority.

Another commented on internal divisions within the group. He believed that it had now grown so much that it could no longer be regarded as a single entity. Rather it should be divided into two groups either as Mandarin/Cantonese or according to whether they were permanent residents or migrant workers. In both cases, he felt that the communities were so distinct and had such different needs that these needs could hardly be met by one organisation. Instead, two separate organisations were required to focus on specific needs.

A third person endorsed the CWA both for the support that it offers to the Chinese community here and also for its outreach programme with schools which introduces children mainly in the Belfast area to aspects of Chinese culture. These programmes, she feels, should ensure that the Chinese are no longer regarded as outsiders in Northern Ireland society.

The last 40 years have seen huge changes in what was previously a hidden community in Northern Ireland. While there are negative aspects such as increasing racism and a feeling among some members of the Chinese community that their involvement in community activities amounts to no more than tokenism, there are also those who feel that members of this community, whether they consider themselves as Chinese, British, Irish or some combination of all these identities, have an important part to play in creating a multicultural society in which diversity can be celebrated.

Note from editor

Since this chapter was written, Ms Anna ho of the Chinese Welfare Association has been elected to the Northern Irish Assembly.

References

Alcock, A. (1994) *Understanding Ulster*. Lurgan: Ulster Society.
Anderson, B. (1983) *Imagined Communities: Reflections on the Origin and Spread of Nationalism*. London: Verso.
Anonymous (2004) *Yellow Menace*. Anonymous leaflet.
Arthur, P. (2000) *Special Relationships: Britain, Ireland and the Northern Ireland Problem*. Belfast: Blackstaff.
BBC (2004a) *Special Flats for Chinese Elders* (http://news.bbc.co.uk/1/hi/ northern_ireland/3969981.stm).
BBC (2004b) *UVF Denies Racist Attacks* (http://news.bbc.co.uk/1/hi/northern_ireland/3381675.stm).
Bew, P., Gibbon, P. and Patterson, H. (1996) *Northern Ireland 1921–1996: Political Forces and Social Classes*. London: Serif.
Coogan, T. (1991) *The Troubles: Ireland's Ordeal 1966–1995 and the Search for Peace*. London: Arrow.
Crozier, M. ed. (1990) *Cultural Traditions in Northern Ireland: Varieties of Britishness*. Belfast: Queen's University.
Derry City Council (2005) *Press Release: Mayor Gives her Support to the Sai-pak Mid-autumn Moon Celebrations* (http://www.derrycity.gov.uk/ Press%20Releases/190905-saipak.htm).
Elliott, M. (2002) *The Catholics of Ulster*. New York: Basic Books.
Evangelical Contribution on Northern Ireland (2004) 'The Chinese Church in Northern Ireland', *Lion and Lamb*, 37, 20–1.
Feng, B. (2004) *Ethnicity, Children and Habitus*. Coleraine: Unpublished PhD, University of Ulster.
Government of the United Kingdom (1997) *Race Relations Order*. London: HMSO.
Government of the United Kingdom (1998) *Northern Ireland Act*. London: HMSO.
Irwin, G. and Dunn, S. (1996) *Ethnic Minorities in Northern Ireland*. Coleraine: University of Ulster.
Mc Garry, J. and O'Leary, B. (1995) *Explaining Northern Ireland: Broken Images*. Oxford: Blackwell.
Mc Kittrick, D. and Mc Vea, D. (2000) *Making Sense of the Troubles*. Belfast: Blackstaff.
Mc Knight, E. and Watson, A. (1998) 'Race and Ethnicity in Northern Ireland: The Chinese Community', in P. Hainsworth ed., *Divided Society: Ethnic Minorities in Northern Ireland*. London Pluto Press.
Northern Ireland Statistics and Research Agency (NISRA) (2001) *Northern Ireland Census: 2001*. Belfast: NISRA.
Nic Craith, M. (2002) *Plural Identities, Singular Narratives: The Case of Northern Ireland*. New York: Berghahn.

Ulster Television (2004) *Newsroom: Landlords Fears amid Racist Attacks* (http://www.u.tv/newsroom/indepth.asp?pt=n&id=41206).
Yu, P. (1994) 'From Social Alienation to Social Deprivation – A Response from the Chinese Community', *Racism and Poverty Seminar Report*. Belfast: Northern Ireland Anti-poverty Network.

Websites

Belfast Chinese Christian Church – http://www.bccc.co.uk/
Chinese Welfare Association – http://www.cwa-ni.org/english/staff.htm
Multicultural Resource Centre for Northern Ireland – http://www.mcrc-ni.org
Mandarin Speakers' Association – http://www.mandarinspeakers.org/
Northern Ireland Census 2001 – http://www.nicensus2001.gov.uk/
Race Relations Order – http://www.opsi.gov.uk/si/si1997/70869–k.htm
Regional Interpreting Services – http://www.interpreting.n-i.nhs.uk/

8
Intercultural Communication: Chinese Culture in UK Education

Rebecca Fong

The last 50 years have brought unprecedented changes in knowledge and technology, which have led to developments in business, travel, education and global relations. The face of UK higher education (HE) has changed too, with a dramatic rise in international students in recent years. It is within these complex new 'intercultural spaces' that policy makers, institutions and educators attempt to create conducive conditions for learning to suit the complex world we live in today. But between the necessarily robust policy statements promoting 'internationalisation', the administrative frameworks that support and deliver teaching and learning, and the non-native student's individual expectations and experience, much is inevitably 'lost in translation'.

This chapter will deal first with the trends in the numbers of Chinese students in UK HE, particularly within the field of English as a Foreign Language (EFL) and with old and new views on how Chinese students learn. It will go on to discuss the reasons and methods for addressing 'culture' directly in the curriculum and finally discuss implications for both educators and students, with reference to the benefits in language, power and identity that these could bring not only to Chinese students but to all concerned.

Chinese students and the UK educational context

In 2002/3, international students from all over the world constituted 17 per cent of all UK students, with Britain being the highest recruiter after the United States. Figures from the Higher Education Statistics Agency suggest that between 1997/8 and 2002/3, the number of Chinese students in UK HE rose from 2883 to 32,000 (provisional figure for 2002/3, Universities UK 2005). The modernising agenda in mainland

China especially since Deng Xiao Ping's economic reforms, the one-child policy instigated in China in 1979, the cachet and employment advantage to be gained from a British education for one's only child, together with the relaxing of visa restrictions for travel have all led to an increase in the numbers of Chinese students.

However, this rising trend showed signs of reverse in 2003/2004 (Universities UK 2005). According to the information released by UCAS, the UK universities admission system, overseas students from non-EU backgrounds have shown a sharp decline in number. Initial reasons given for the decrease suggest the kinds of difficulties that are most easily quantifiable: the disproportionate costs for non-EU students, problems in obtaining visas to do part-time jobs or work placements and so on. Since Chinese students often stay on to pursue postgraduate study, a decline in the figures represents, in purely statistical terms, a significant loss to the UK economy as far as HE funding and associated consumer spending are concerned. Far more importantly, in terms of the increased cross-cultural experience, for students and also for all those who have regular contact with them – British teachers, native students and host families, for example – the decline in numbers represents an even greater loss in the potential for heightened cultural awareness.

That the Chinese presence in the United Kingdom and links with China are increasingly valuable is not in dispute. The state visit by the Chinese President Hu Jintao in November 2005 signals Britain's desire to acknowledge and be part of China's increasingly important world role. At the same time, Jacques (2003) sounds a note of warning: 'given the extraordinary provincialism of our culture, we remain blissfully ignorant of the speed with which the world's most populous county … is being transformed. … The world's centre of gravity has already shifted to the Pacific, and east Asia has already displaced Europe as the second most powerful economic region' (http://www.dawn.com/2003/12/05/int1.htm).

His argument is reinforced when he states that Asian studies is 'an impoverished, marginal discipline in British universities' and that it is 'virtually impossible to learn Chinese' in British secondary public or private schools. This is echoed by Sakuragi (2006), who reports a similar situation for the United States. Global economic opportunities are quickly grasped by those with the resources to do so, but unless attempts are made to improve how we communicate with each other through language, behaviour and intercultural understanding, then the charge of ethnocentric opportunism, cultural and linguistic imperialism,

Westernisation will always be levelled. Without harnessing the potential in these fields, national and international agendas across all fields are not optimally compatible and advances will be made in spite of themselves, rather than efficiently.

Little qualitative research has been done with Chinese students to suggest the extent to which more 'invisible' factors such as differences in educational expectations and delivery, transferability of knowledge and skills from the United Kingdom to the home employment market, the cross-cultural experience itself and the level of host country service, support and hospitality might also play a part. Such research, if conducted, would almost certainly implicate cultural difference over more obvious differences such as language.

Language education per se is often perceived as the curricular interface to mutual understanding and educational success. Its wider role in the dialogic process of meaning negotiation and the developing of intercultural relationships is often lost, not least because the use of English as a *lingua franca* can render culturally blind those who speak it as a native language themselves. Gudykunst (1991: 2) states, 'if we understand each other's languages, but not their cultures, we can make fluent fools of ourselves'. Few language professionals are trained to teach language with the specific purpose of addressing culture and intercultural communication. A higher profile inclusion of intercultural learning on the curriculum, together with more equal and inclusive participation amongst staff and students could contribute to redressing this imbalance.

Today, the enormous role played by language and culture in the acquisition of new knowledge and the ongoing negotiation of social identity is well recognised. However, it was not until the late 1950s in the United States that interest in Intercultural Communication (ICC) first came about. Intercultural Communication

> refers to the symbolic process by which people from different cultural backgrounds interact with each other. This process includes language, but also encompasses the background of the participants, stereotypes or prejudices they may hold of the other cultural group, social roles they each hold in their respective cultures and culturally appropriate norms they have each learned for communicating with strangers. (Lucas 2003: 302)

Intercultural communication competence, which involves a number of skills from language competence, adaptation, social decentring, communication effectiveness, social integration and knowledge of the host culture (Redmond 2000), became an area of interest as events such as the Second World War, mass migration, international trade and ease of travel affected intercultural contact on a more global scale. Previous to this, culture and language had seemed to be on more separate trajectories, with anthropologists studying culture and social behaviour through contact with small-scale societies and linguists teaching language primarily through literature for the understanding of civilisation and for grammar translation purposes. From the 1950s onwards, ideas, research and methods in culture and language became more interdisciplinary and, outside academia, pragmatic.

The term 'culture' itself has for decades been a highly contested one, from Kroeber and Kluckhohn's many definitions (1952) to more recent attempts to define cultures as 'dynamic, changing, developing processes' and 'chaotic systems', rather than monolithic 'endstates' (Casrnir 1999). Our cultural identities are complicated by the fact that we, as individuals, come from different social and regional backgrounds, speak different languages and dialects, and inhabit not single but multiple social roles. How we communicate is a part-universal, part-cultural, part-personal reflection of our identities.

Communicating across cultures is complex not only as a result of identity issues, but because of the communication process itself: the multi-layered, explicit and implicit ways in which our messages are transmitted and the inequality in power relationships between those communicating. Success depends on the individual's ability to 'read' the situational context and to feedback appropriately, in cultural, linguistic and paralinguistic terms. For non-native students in UK HE, all of this may be occurring not only in a new territorial setting but also via an area of unfamiliar subject matter. This can be an enormous challenge and one which we as educators would have trouble with ourselves, were we to find ourselves as students in China, for example.

Success in adapting to a new culture is achieved over time through the transitional process of *acculturation*, described by Barnard and Spencer (1996: 594) as 'the process of acquiring culture traits as a result of contact'. This process involves the individual in the often painstaking cognitive, affective and behavioural activities of negotiating, making sense of, and incorporating new patterns of context-based understanding. It takes place where there is the will (opting out and spending time with fellow nationals is another possibility) and where the communication across cultures is ongoing. It is also an intensely personal experience.

Yet until recently ICC and identity issues have not been included as a requisite transferable skill in education. Even in the field of EFL, in which a focus on context, situation and authenticity has long been the 'constitutional' bedrock, culture has tended to be dealt with through micro-topics such as traditions and festivals, cultural 'dos and don'ts', rather than as generic concepts which underpin all cultures albeit in very different ways. Atkinson expressed surprise that there was no mention of the role that culture would play in the future of English Language Teaching, as late as the 1991 volume of the *Teacher of English to Speakers of Other Languages* (TESOL) *quarterly* (1999). However, 'Today, the relationship of language and culture in language study is one of the most hotly debated issues at the present time' (Kramsch 1998: 79). Dealing with cultural issues should not be left to EFL or to the realms of language teaching. It has a wider role to play, not only as subject matter but in the pedagogy and method underpinning the rapidly changing educational context.

The majority of courses undertaken by UK HE students are knowledge and text oriented, and most academic assessment still takes place in traditional, written form. However, what may appear to be the straightforward linguistic and intellectual requirements of the academic environment, quasi-universal the academic world over, can mask varying behavioural responses in the approach to learning and the way in which tasks are carried out. Just as cultures differ, student responses to the university experience will differ, through diverse 'cultures of learning'. These are defined by Jin and Cortazzi (1998: 749) as being 'at the interface between culture, socialization and education. They are influenced by tradition but can change in response to circumstances or other traditions. A Chinese culture of learning might be expected to underlie many of the ideas and practices involved in the dialogue in large classes in China.' Language and intellectual knowledge are tools with which we operate, but the real cultural currency is meaning, which is deeply embedded in social semiotic practice. Fairclough (1995: 6) points out this link when he states that 'cognition and representation of the world and social interaction' all occur simultaneously. For teaching and learning to be optimised, academics universally would have a raised awareness of generic concepts of culture and the effects of more localised pedagogical methods and communicative styles and their influence on student learning.

Different cultures in the classroom

The Western literature on students of Chinese origin, in mainland China, Hong Kong, Taiwan and, to a lesser degree, Singapore (the so-called 'Confucian Heritage Cultures', see Biggs 1996) has tended to lay emphasis on the way in which history and socialisation processes have produced students with behaviours, learning styles and expectations at cultural variance with 'progressive Western-style' education.

Much of the intercultural literature derives from the research done by Hofstede (1980), Bond (1988) and Triandis (1995), using dimensions of cultural variability as a framework for comparing the cultural values underpinning behaviour, though not specifically addressing what occurs in situations where ICC actually takes place. Whilst Hofstede's original study focussed on employee values in the workplace, its findings were so influential that they are widely used as reference points in other fields, the literature of intercultural education being no exception. Bond's research highlighted the 'long-term' orientation of the Chinese people, characterised by a long-term attitude towards overcoming obstacles, perseverance, frugality, respect for social status, virtue and subordin-ation of self to a purpose, amongst other things. Socialisation and enculturation, the inter-generational transmission of behaviours, values and world view begin at home, and the research has tended to show that affluent, technologically advanced societies rate more highly in terms of

> individualism…in which the ties between individuals are loose: everyone is expected to look after himself or herself and his or her immediate family. Collectivism as its opposite pertains to societies in which people from birth onwards are integrated into strong, cohesive in-groups, which throughout people's lifetime continue to protect them in exchange for unquestioning loyalty. (Hofstede 1994: 51)

Western as well as Asian literature has suggested that China has tradi-tionally tended towards a stronger, more collectivist family and work group ethic, based on a Confucian heritage fostering strong respect for certain role relationships within society and strong social groupings such as the commune, collective and work unit under socialism. Respect for relationships, together with other Confucian values such as a strong internal sense of responsibility for outcomes (success and failure occur-ring largely as a result of one's own efforts), hard work, face-saving, careful observation and adaptability in relation to all tasks, tend to be cultivated at home in pre-school years and are then reinforced through state intervention in education by 'equating politics with morality, phrasing them both in the same language, and then...encouraging correct moral and political relations and behaviours through education' (Li et al. 2004: 449).

Achieving standards and obtaining good exam results are crucial (Ran 2001: 311). In China, the originally Marxist policy of *deyu*, or moral education, capitalising on Confucian ideology has adapted and developed with the changing times, 'exhorting China's citizens, from generation to generation, to hold lofty ideals, to behave with moral integrity, to achieve high levels of education, and to exemplify a strong commitment to social order' (Li et al. 2004: 455). Archer and Francis (2005: 167), in gauging teachers' opinions of the children of Chinese immigrants in Britain, note, in an article entitled 'They never go off the rails...', that

> it was...unanimously thought that British Chinese pupils' 'success' was attributable to family and home culture – namely a high valuing of education in 'Chinese culture', high parental expectations and strong 'pushing' or encouragement of their sons and daughters. References were also made to 'stable' and 'supportive' Chinese family structures that promote 'obedience to authority' and/or 'respect' for teachers, parents, combined with a 'natural ethic' to work hard.

The values, attitudes and behaviours which result from the strong didactic force of family, education and state working together extend to the role and perception of the teacher. Jin and Cortazzi (1998) document the conflicting opinions of British and Chinese students on the qualities of a good teacher. For the Chinese, deep knowledge and the human qualities of the teacher as a 'moral example' are important, whilst for the British students organisational skills and the ability to explain clearly rank highly.

However, increasingly, there are those who argue that much of the Western literature serves to essentialise Asian students of all backgrounds, and with economic and social changes in China since the early 1980s, the tendencies that contributed towards a cultural profile might be changing. Indeed, evidence from the arts such as the 'Between Past and Future' photography exhibition (V&A September 2005–January 2006) suggests that today's more technology- and media-savvy, young, urban Chinese may be more creative, independent and daring than their predecessors might have been. Matsumoto (2002) reinforces this in the Japanese context, discussing how inter-generational change due to increased resources and falling birth rates have created a society in which there is an 'individualism–collectivism duality' emerging.

Until the early 1990s, much of the literature on Chinese education describes large class sizes and a teacher-fronted, textbook approach to education in which students are passive, learn by rote and engage in what appear to be 'surface' (Biggs 1993) forms of learning. More recently, however, such views have been challenged (Biggs 1994, Biggs and Watkins 1996, Jin and Cortazzi 1998), and a reappraisal of the ways in which learning actually takes place in the Chinese classroom has occurred. As Biggs (1998: 725) suggests, 'Western observers perceive fierce and overcrowded classrooms, filled with docile rote learners cramming for exams. The evidence is that CHC [Confucian Heritage Culture] students use highly adaptive learning strategies and achieve better than most Western students in high level academic tasks.' For the Asian student, rote learning, it appears, can be both a 'surface' or a 'deep' memorising strategy, depending on the longer-term aim (Biggs 1993, Tang 1996).

Beyond the boundaries of one's native culture, the impetus for change can be strong. On (1996: 32) argues that while individualism is subjugated to collectivism in the Chinese context, as a result of consideration for those in one's familiar circles, this 'culture of restraint' can be liberated when the Chinese leave their relational networks. Volet and Renshaw (1996) too highlight Chinese students' adaptability and achievement orientation, when studying in Australian HE. Evidence shows both strong intrinsic and extrinsic motivations for Chinese students: 'Internally, education is important for personal development, and associated with it is the notion of human perfectibility, which is believed to be achievable by everyone. Externally, education is important for social mobility, and is also believed to be achievable by whosoever aims to do so' (On 1996: 39).

It would appear that many Chinese students are motivated, willing to work hard and to adapt to whichever instrumental methods are likely to bring them success. In subjects less reliant on language ability such as maths and science, they even tend to outperform their Western counterparts at universities in the West (Stevenson and Lee 1996). In the arts, to a greater extent, the evidence points to a match that is more problematic. The classroom, with its superficially familiar resources, desks, chairs, whiteboards, technology, is the crucible for very different teaching and learning expectations, which are rarely fully explored but which can significantly affect outcomes.

Cultural learning is never a one-way process. Teske and Nelson (1974) highlight the dynamic nature of the process and the way that changes that take place can occur in one or both cultural groups, involving possible changes in values. As the numbers of international students increase, so the number of different experiences in the classroom increases too. Educators should be trained to question this intercultural context.

The paucity of provision of both theory and practice in cultural learning contradicts the messages about 'internationalisation' that are widely promoted, and suggest a gap in vocational training, that would be widely suitable not only for non-natives, but for staff and native students too. It will prove ever more necessary to raise our own awareness at the same time as helping students negotiate their own, 'third place' (Kramsch 1993) or 'small culture' (Holliday 1999) as a necessary foundation for academic success and for the confidence and motivation that will come as the new context is mutually habilitated. Casrnir (1999: 94) uses the term 'third culture' to describe 'the construction of a mutually beneficial interactive environment in which individuals from two different cultures can function in a way beneficial to all involved'.

The danger and the difficulty will be to avoid succumbing to the all-too-marketable idea of teaching culture as 'product', so compatible with the university modular system and with students' short-term, quantifiable goals: a degree, a contract, prestige or promotion. It is difficult to disassociate the neatness of an educational package and rigid forms of assessment from the messy lifelong process of negotiating cultural learning. This is a particularly difficult problem when the Chinese place such high value on external measures of success: league tables, exam results, paper qualifications. Academics, too, are pressured, and making messy, long-term, human goals practice-based and academically valid may seem difficult and unappealing.

Although the research is limited, previous studies have shown that intercultural experience leads to increased knowledge of other cultures causing individuals to communicate more effectively across cultures (Martin 1987). Gibson and Zhong (2005) found positive correlations of empathy and experience with successful ICC competence for those having lived in a foreign culture, in a study undertaken between natives and non-natives in the United States health-care environment. On the other hand, their hypothesis that bilingual participants would be more competent intercultural communicators compared to natives was disconfirmed. The results supported earlier work by Bennett (1979) and Gudykunst (1993) that empathetic individuals are also proficient in ICC.

Thus, one might suggest that today's academics would ideally them-selves have experienced cultural learning at first hand. In reality, the comfortable roles of knower, teacher and host may make educators less likely to perceive the necessity for cultural explanation than for the students who are in the process of actually having to deal with change.

Otherness is a dialectical concept. It implicates two parties, both of whom are 'strangers'. Teachers in classrooms, like anthropologists in the field, need to be trained to observe better and to reflect on their own cultural behaviours and teaching methods, which act as pedagogical models in the classroom. Empathy is partly intuitive and partly train-able, but to develop it consciously awareness-raising needs to be done. Everything from the material culture, to social behaviour, organisation and institutions, the language, paralanguage and non-verbal commu-nication needs first to be problematised. Difference cannot be passed over if educators and students are to endeavour to build bridges to communication in unfamiliar contexts.

To this end, transmissionist methods of teaching, the teaching of content over behaviour and an old Anglophone paradigm that requires students to submit unquestioningly to the discourse practices, conven-tions, behaviours and norms of the English-speaking academic environ-ment do not lend themselves to learning that stretches easily beyond the boundaries of the classroom. Nor do they enhance the awareness and sensitivity of teachers.

In reality, it is evident in HE that an increasingly international envir-onment is leading to a 'global university contact zone' (Singh and Doherty 2004: 9) and, further, that students will be likely to take their learning with them to use in parts of the world that are not necessarily English-speaking. An understanding of the concept of culture in general, of 'culture franca', would be useful not only to students or language teachers but to all practitioners in education interested in a world where citizens need to be more tolerant and adaptable.

From both policy and pedagogical perspectives, we are still a long way from the fluid, mutually supportive, problem-seeking/problem-solving learning environment required before all can begin to recognise the taken-for-granted concepts on which cultures are founded, enabling students and educators to gain the confidence and skills to balance the pressures of conforming with the new conventions, with maintaining their own changing identities. There is often an expectation of enough similarity in the nature of the human condition for meaning to be made across cultures. While partially true, of course, this may as a classroom strategy be over-simplistic, if it is considered at all.

Worth and Gross (1974) describe the process by which people learn to make and interpret meaning from signs in their own culture. They propose as cumulative the way in which a child comes to distinguish between a natural event requiring a straightforward response and a much more sophisticated symbolic or communicative event requiring interpretation through a developmental process of increasing interpretive complexity. As the child's understanding increases, so does the ability to make correct inferences based on the relationship between signs and contexts: 'being a member of a culture "tells" one that certain events are communicative. Interpretive problems which arise in clearly marked communication situations will concern the assignment of a specific meaning or meanings to be inferred from some specific event' (Worth and Gross 1974: 28).

This cumulative process of cultural learning explains how correct inferencing can occur more reliably as the context becomes more familiar and suggests that investigating cultural systems will reveal information that might enable students to make more situated cultural assumptions and lead them to more reliable reasoning of their own. It also explains how spontaneous use of 'ethnocentric' cultural criteria from the 'home' culture might result in faulty inferencing when cultural boundaries are crossed. Since the outcomes of reasoning are most often behavioural and communicative, we could look to the anthropologists to find a method to underpin such practical learning.

Revising the methodology – An anthropological perspective

An anthropologist is defined by their training and research methodology, namely ethnography. Ethnography is a methodology based on an understanding of cultural concepts, which engages with culture empirically, through fieldwork, participant observation, and various forms of written and visual documentation. In addressing what Holliday refers to as 'small cultures', it attempts to deal with behaviour as it emerges on the ground, rather than as the 'cohesive process of any social grouping' (1999: 241). It is with the methodology rather than with the content that educators might usefully reorient the work they do and simultaneously provide students and themselves with the opportunity of becoming more comfortable in the cultural context.

Referring to Ballard and Clanchy (1991), Kirby et al. (1996: 142) suggest that 'Asian cultures and educational systems emphasise a view of knowledge as that which should be conserved and reproduced.' This is in contrast with Western systems, which emphasise a more speculative, questioning approach. For some groups of Asian students, 'the individualist emphasis of the Western academic system may require that students develop a whole new "identity" to approach tasks in the expected way.' However, by requiring Chinese students and educators to become actively involved in an approach which analyses cultural concepts and engages in the discovery and documentation of culture in all its forms, participants may be able to

- engage with the new culture both inside and outside the classroom in an active, participative and purposeful way;
- engage with the new culture both intellectually and behaviourally;
- observe and record the material culture, practices, behaviours and discourse within it;
- analyse their findings in a supportive and empathetic classroom environment;
- make connections and account for observations that are relevant to individual experience, as norms and values are revised, and so reflect and locate themselves in the new cultural context; and
- forge connections both interdependently and independently, both interculturally and intraculturally, between the social context and the academic context of learning.

In the marriage of content and method, the aim is to bridge the gap between what is known and what is unknown, through a personal, reflexive exploration rather than at the sole discretion of syllabus or textbook. The means will be through language, communication and content both inside and outside the classroom but the target will be more holistic than the memorisation or internalisation of pure facts.

Xiaoming and Haitao (2000: 104) see China wishing to contribute to the idea of 'internationalisation', but not as a means of 'simple standardisation, even less Western standardisation ... what internationalisation emphasises is not the elimination of cultural differences but international exchange on an equal footing'. This is a potentially more equalising agenda, where educators and students explore the liminal and articulate independent findings, within the collaborative classroom context. As field workers in a variety of cross-cultural situations, everyone is 'non-native' and all can attempt to question and understand each other's worlds and respond in a new way in a new cultural context. By removing the authoritative status of the teacher and the teacher-dictated curriculum, all are encouraged to re-evaluate their roles and the cultural preconceptions they bring to the classroom. The primacy of the written word, much prized in Chinese education, is combined with practice-based research. Project work with a more ethnographic agenda can be incorporated into the field of language or any other subject, since it can focus on any aspect of the native language and target any aspect of life in the local environment.

Fieldwork should be preceded by theory and practical exercises. As preparation for practice, the incorporation of chosen texts from the literature of ICC can provide a framework for discussing culture. Ideas such as kinship, social organisation, ritual, ethnocentrism, verbal and non-verbal communication, time and space, dimensions of cultural variability, values and ethics provide starting points with which non-native students will be able to identify.

Also as useful background, comparative analysis of culture through 'outsider' accounts of students' own cultures can help students to critique the authority of non-native text, by beginning with familiar subject matter. Chinese students diverged greatly in their opinions on chapters from *Encountering the Chinese: A Guide for Americans* (Hu and Grove 1991), finding sections of the work outdated and with variety of opinion occurring significantly between Taiwanese and mainland Chinese students.

The analysis of such texts addresses the advantages and disadvantages of making generalisations about culture, debunking stereotypes by showing up cultural and individual variation within what might seem from the outside to be 'homogenous groups' and showing how economic, social and political factors change aspects of culture even within relatively short spaces of time. Students can gain the vocabulary of their own cultures from the perspective of the outsider and from the insights into how 'the other' sees them and can learn to reflect on, evaluate and criticise the written word. Ethnographic writing from the target culture can also provide a useful reference point in attempting to gauge an insider perspective and in interpreting and analysing student data. Attempts to analyse such accounts involve discussion of the cognitive, affective and linguistic complexity of culture and parallel what occurs as insider/outsider boundaries are crossed and identities renegotiated.

Any attempt at ICC competence, however, implies also incorporating practical exercises, which focus on behaviours, attitudes and beliefs (see EMIL 2006), since knowledge is important to provide a rationale for choice, but behaviour is notoriously hard to change without practice. Both are necessary for empathy to be developed. Some degree of familiarity with ethnographic methods is also a prerequisite.

These days the power of the visual in such projects should not be underestimated. The 'media age' has brought with it an explosion of images and visual technology, and young people today are more visually literate than their predecessors. The realisation that members of different cultures see with different eyes, a concept neatly encapsulated in the visual anthropologists' term 'scopic regimes' (Foster 1988) is well recognised within certain disciplines but seems neglected in the field of pedagogy. Although vision requires no verbal language, our vision nevertheless is controlled by a 'semiotic grammar' linked to the ways we see the world. Different cultures and subcultures have different scopic regimes that can be harnessed through the methodology of visual ethnography as an approach of particular interest in attempting to bridge the gap between what native and non-native cultural participants see.

Visual anthropologists distinguish between 'vision' (what the human eye sees) and 'visuality' (the socially constructed nature of what we see) (Rose 2001) and students of visual anthropology typically employ camera and video as data-gathering tools for empirical documentation of cultural practices and products. A visual approach, to some extent, gets around the difficulty of a shared linguistic code, at least in the data-collection phase and provides a visual record as a 'site of production' (Rose 2001) for further investigation into society, history, geography and behavioural practice. It can therefore serve to equalise power roles in the classroom. Presentation is possible of what might otherwise remain 'verbally unrealised' (Ruby and Chalfen 1974).

Both the methods and the visual materials that result thus become the locus of cultural investigation as forms of representation are analysed and interpreted according to relative semiotic systems. Chinese students respond well to the use of the technologies and can take up the challenge of engaging with the social and physical environment visually. Chinese students are users of a powerfully visual language: Chinese ideographs, or characters, need to be practised and memorised and are therefore learnt through the eyes and disciplined control of the hands and body. Confucian heritage cultures also have an educational tradition that values metonymy particularly in the form of analogy and metaphor, so students are well disposed to observe, document and draw parallels between cultures and societies. Such work enables them to bridge the gap between the classroom and the outside world, encouraging them to be active participants in transformative learning and literally to negotiate the new space around them.

Although researchers in the field of visual anthropology argue about the lack of a clearly defined 'scientific' theory as a base for analysis, the four activities of photographic criticism as listed by Barrett (1990: xi) – 'describing, interpreting, evaluating and theorizing' – allow for a systematic reading of the surface-level content of the photographs. Cross-referencing research findings with other students allow the invisible slowly to become visible. A negotiation and potential accommodation follows the reconstruction of the context and recognition of differing values and attitudes. The influence of globalisation/Westernisation can be acknowledged at a superficial level, and the influences that underlie the local culture gradually surface. Students begin to analyse their own role as viewers/voyeurs/photographers and participants in a second culture, having to account for both the representation and interpretation of their photographic choices and the subsequent evaluations they make about the world around them.

The important point in such projects is that students are actively involved in collecting and recording data individually according to given criteria, and they learn to articulate, evaluate and write about what they see, with the teacher as cultural mediator but not authority. The process is behavioural as well as intellectual and the teacher often has as much to learn as the students. With discussion and research and with time for reflection, views are tested against a range of sometimes conflicting opinions from the 'host culture'. Since all the students are themselves accommodated within the urban landscape under consideration, reflexive insights from findings can help make them feel more integrated, if not always more comfortable. Inferences are given reason or rejected, so that more reliable attributions can be made. Attributions and interpretations come to be made more soundly in the wider context and not just in the limited context of the project undertaken. As with language and cultural concepts, vision can be seen to be in part universal, in part relative.

The value of ethnographic and visual ethnographic investigations is evident, both being situated within the wider social fabric and practices of the local culture, whilst also providing a link to the requirements of the academic culture of learning through the language and method. Findings themselves afford insights into cultural concepts such as space and time, social and institutional organisation, individual practices and behaviours. Students' work reflects not only the task but their own interpretation of it in accordance with their 'visuality' or 'scopic regime', their culturally tinted way of seeing the world. Learner autonomy and active participation are encouraged around a subject that is crucial to individual acculturation. Visual data can be employed in numerous other meaningful ways, for example in the form of personal ethnographic diaries to record the acculturation process and provide a reflexive record of personal stages in the adaptation to the new cultural environment.

Projects such as these do not preclude the need for more traditional forms of study; they only refocus and underpin it by providing an intellectual foundation to the study of culture and a practical project in the wider environment, improving the visual and contextual grammar. With critical observation skills more in line with cultural norms, the environment in its broadest sense can be revised, and the semiotic and semantic transfer of knowledge gradually become more situated. Inferencing skills improve and students can begin to provide social reasoning more appropriate to the new context. Diversity of opinion experienced first hand makes it clearer that human voices and actions create culture rather than humans having cultural practices inflicted on them.

Researchers have questioned the generalisability of findings in large-scale cultural research. Casrnir (1999: 91), for example, questions the relevance in emic studies (such as Bond's) that have been based on etic generalisations (such as Hofstede's), since etic generalisations originate in the specific background of the researcher. The over-simplicity of research based on such binary distinctions as high and low context (Hall 1959) has also come into question. Holliday (1999: 243) argues for a 'small culture', heuristic approach, as an alternative to the 'large culture' which so often 'supports various spheres of political interest'.

This chapter has attempted to provide a rationale for incorporating ICC and ethnographic learning into the curriculum, with particular reference to educators and Chinese students. It has attempted to show that the educational context is changing with the influx of international students and that research on how students learn changes too. Teachers could not possibly hope to know about all the cultures or 'cultures of learning' of their students, and therefore an approach that deals with cultural concepts and then relies on students' own data collection within the culture is likely to prove the most genuinely awareness-raising and efficient. Chinese students have been seen to be hard-working, adaptable and receptive to change. Cheng (2000: 445) argues that the causes of reticence and passivity in Chinese students are often related to 'unsuitable methodologies and lack of required language proficiency'.

If Chinese students are involved in the process of acculturation and interested in the subject of culture itself, it seems likely that the majority will be motivated to work with language and with culture, since it can facilitate both their everyday and academic lives simultaneously. Working in a supportive environment, with an open-minded and empathetic mediator, within a project framework, whether in EFL or other subject disciplines, can give the student an opportunity to develop an individual voice, a degree of autonomy, and the confidence to ask more effective, analytical questions.

Research by Castro et al. (2004) suggests that teachers wish to spend more time teaching culture but are hampered by institutional constraints and the deep-seated belief that language teaching is more important. This seems to be based on the fact that teachers continue to do what they themselves were taught and know how to do best. The question of resources is necessarily a limitation. However, with interest in culture in education proliferating and conferences and journals increasingly addressing ways in which to deal with this in relation to the academic context (Jiang 2001, Guest 2002, Tseng 2002), it must be time to call into question the need for a wider cultural training agenda for educators at every level. As the number of students from ethnic minorities in UK HE increases too, educators need the skills and behaviours to be able to apply knowledge and use methods in appropriate and empathetic ways. Too few currently have relevant acculturation experience or actively use such experience in their classrooms.

In order to deal with this, UK HE needs to recognise that real internationalisation cannot occur without issues of culture being addressed universally with staff and administrators, in the form of intercultural skills training. For many of the newer universities, with a more vocational emphasis, this proposal may not sit too uncomfortably. These are after all 'transferable skills'. The concept of culture need to be more widely incorporated into teacher training programmes and study-abroad or residence-in-ethnic-communities' programmes, ethnographic field projects and even a measure of language learning (particularly of the less familiar languages) should be incorporated in the training of today's teachers of every discipline.

For Chinese students in UK HE in particular, the transition from a culture of learning which may be more teacher-centred can be encouraged, as long as the methods can be seen to be rigorous, generative and engaging in the widest sense. For the Chinese student particularly, for whom the distance between his/her culture and the British one is greater than for his future EU classmates, this process needs to be supported and collaborative, since 'empirical evidence has consistently shown that social support diminishes psychological distress during cross-cultural transition' (Adelman 1988, Fontaine 1986).

A two-way acculturation process will then be seen to operate – a classroom microcosm of what needs to happen on educational, political and global levels if equality of experience is to be accepted. The issue of internationalisation will be addressed at the level of the classroom and students given a forum in which to express their thoughts and concerns. Perhaps the raising of confidence, the increased contact with the community and a more direct engagement with society at large, on a more equal footing, will begin to address some of the 'invisible' reasons why Chinese students to the United Kingdom are declining in number.

As more and more people negotiate new intercultural spaces in both the physical and the metaphorical sense, with the expectation of concrete outcomes that will influence their lives, success can surely no longer be a matter of receiving transmitted knowledge but learning to transform knowledge for one's own ends. Language, power and identity are all implicated. Culture has long been the preserve of the anthropologists and sociologists but in a rapidly changing world, ICC and ethnographic fieldwork, and the real difference their insights and methods can bring, should be a matter for debate and action for all educators and policy makers too.

References

Adelman, M. (1988) 'Cross Cultural Adjustment: A Theoretical Perspective on Social Support', *International Journal of Intercultural Relations*, 12, 183–205.

Archer, L. and Francis, B. (2005) ' "They Never Go off the Rails like Other Ethnic Groups": Teachers' Constructions of British Chinese Pupils' Gender Identities and Approaches to Learning', *British Journal of Sociology of Education*, 26 (2), 165–82.

Atkinson, D. (1999) TESOL and Culture, *TESOL Quarterly*, 33(4), 625–54.

Ballard, B. and Clanchy, J. (1991) *Teaching Students from Overseas: A Brief Guide for Lecturers and Supervisors*. Melbourne: Longman.

Barnard, A. and Spencer, J. eds (1996) *Encyclopaedia of Social and Cultural Anthropology*. Routledge: London.

Barrett, T. (1990) *Criticizing Photographs: An Introduction to Understanding Images*. California: Mayfield.

Bennett, M. J. (1979) 'Overcoming the Golden Rule: Empathy and Sympathy', in D. Nimmo ed., *Communication Yearbook, 3*. New Brunswick, NJ: Transaction Books, pp. 407–22.

Biggs, J. (1993) 'What do Inventories of Student's Learning Processes Really Measure? A Theoretical Review and Clarification', *British Journal of Educational Psychology*, 63, 1–17.

Biggs, J. (1994) 'What are Effective Schools? Lessons from East and West', *The Australian Educational Researcher*, 21, 19–40.

Biggs, J. (1996) 'Western Misperceptions of the Confucian-heritage Learning Culture', in D. Watkins and J. Biggs eds, *The Chinese Learner: Cultural, Psychological and Contextual Influences*. Hong Kong: Centre for Comparative Research in Education; Camberwell, Vic.: Australian Council for Educational Research, pp. 45–68.

Biggs, J. (1998) 'Learning from the Confucian Heritage: So Size Doesn't Matter?', *International Journal of Educational Research*, 29, 723–38.

Biggs, J. and Watkins, D. (1996) 'The Chinese Learner in Retrospect', in D. Watkins and J. Biggs eds, *The Chinese Learner: Cultural, Psychological and Contextual Influences*. Hong Kong: Centre for Comparative Research in Education; Camberwell, Vic.: Australian Council for Educational Research, pp. 269–86.

Bond, M. (1988) 'Finding Universal Dimensions of Individual Variation in Multi-cultural Studies of Values: The Rokeach and Chinese Value Surveys', *Journal of Personality and Social Psychology*, 55(6), 1009–15.

Casrnir, F. (1999) 'Foundations for the Study of Intercultural Communication Based on a Third Culture Building Model', *International Journal of Intercultural Relations*, 23(1), 91–116.

Castro, P., Sercu, L. and Méndez García, M. (2004) 'Integrating Language-and-Culture Teaching: an Investigation of Spanish Teachers' Perceptions of the Objectives of Foreign Language Education', *Intercultural Education*, 15(1), 91–104.

Cheng, X. (2000) 'Asian Students', Reticence Revisited', *System*, 28, 435–46.

EMIL (2006) *European Modular Programme for Intercultural Learning in Teacher Training and Continuing Training*. Munich: Socrates Comenius Project in Intercultural Competence, Ludwig-Maximilian's University.

Fairclough, N. (1995) *Critical Discourse Analysis*. Harlow: Longman.

Fontaine, G. (1986) 'Roles of Social Support in Overseas Relocation: Implications for Intercultural Training', *International Journal of Intercultural Relations*, 10, 361–78.

Foster, H. ed. (1988) *Vision and Visuality*. New York: Dia Art Foundation.

Gibson, D. and Zhong, M. (2005) 'Intercultural Communication Competence in the Healthcare Context', *International Journal of Intercultural Relations*, 29, 621–34.

Gudykunst, W. (1991) *Bridging Differences: Effective Intergroup Communication*. Newbury Park, CA: Sage.

Gudykunst, W. (1993) 'Toward a Theory of Effective Interpersonal and Inter-group Communication: An Anxiety/Uncertainty Management Perspective', in R. Wiseman and J. Koester eds, *Intercultural Communication Competence*. Newbury Park, CA: Sage, pp. 33–71.

Guest, M. (2002) 'A Critical "Checkbook" for Culture Teaching and Learning', *ELT Journal*, 56(2), 154–61.

Hall, E. (1959) *The Silent Language*. New York: Doubleday.

Hofstede, G. (1980) *Culture's Consequences: International Differences in Work-related Values*. Newbury Park, CA: Sage.

Hofstede, G. (1994) *Cultures and Organizations, Software of the Mind*. New York: McGraw Hill.

Holliday, A. (1999) 'Small Cultures', *Applied Linguistics*, 20(2), 237–64.

Hu, W. and Grove, C. (1991) *Encountering the Chinese: A Guide for Americans*. Yarmouth, ME: Intercultural.

Jiang, W. (2001) 'Handling "Culture Bumps" ', *ELT Journal*, 55(4), 382–90.

Jin, L. and Cortazzi, M. (1998) 'Dimensions of Dialogue: Large Classes in China', *International Journal of Educational Research*, 29, 739–61.

Kirby, J., Woodhouse, R. and Ma, Y. (1996) 'Studying in a Second Language: The Example of Chinese Students in Canada', in D. Watkins and J. Biggs eds, *The*

Chinese Learner: Cultural, Psychological and Contextual Influences. Hong Kong: Centre for Comparative Research in Education; Camberwell, Vic.: Australian Council for Educational Research, pp. 141–58.

Kroeber, A. and Kluckhohn, C. (1952) 'Culture: A Critical Review of Concepts and Definitions', *Papers of the Peabody Museum of Harvard Archaeology and Ethnology*, 42(1), Cambridge, Mass: Museum Press.

Kramsch, C. (1993) *Context and Culture in Language Teaching*. Oxford: Oxford University Press.

Kramsch, C. (1998) *Language and Culture*. Oxford: Oxford University Press.

Li. P., Zhong, M., Bin, L. and Zhang, H. (2004) 'Deyu as Moral Education in Modern China: Ideological Functions and Transformations', *Journal of Moral Education*, 33(4), 449–64.

Lucas, J. (2003) 'Intercultural Communication for International Programs', *Journal of Research in International Education*, 2(3), 301–14.

Martin, J. (1987) 'The Relationship between Student Sojourner Perceptions of Intercultural Competencies and Previous Sojourner Experience', *International Journal of Intercultural Relations*, 11, 337–55.

Matsumoto, D. (2002) *The New Japan: Debunking Seven Cultural Stereotypes*. Yarmouth, Maine: Intercultural Press.

On, L. (1996) 'The Cultural Context for Chinese Learners: Conceptions of Learning in the Confucian Tradition', in D. Watkins and J. Biggs eds, *The Chinese Learner: Cultural, Psychological and Contextual Influences*. Hong Kong: Centre for Comparative Research in Education; Camberwell, Vic.: Australian Council for Educational Research, pp. 25–43.

Ran, A. (2001) 'Travelling on Parallel Tracks: Chinese Parents and English Teachers', *Educational Research*, 43(3), 311–28.

Redmond, M. (2000) 'Cultural Distance as a Mediating Factor between Stress and Intercultural Communication Competence', *International Journal of Intercultural Relations*, 24, 151–9.

Rose, G. (2001) *Visual Methodologies*. London: Sage.

Ruby, J. and Chalfen, R. (1974) 'The Teaching of Visual Anthropology at Temple', *SAVICOM Newsletter*, 5(3), 5–7.

Sakuragi, T. (2006) 'The Relationship between Attitudes towards Language Study and Cross-cultural Attitudes', *International Journal of Intercultural Relations*, 30, 19–31.

Singh, P. and Doherty, C. (2004) 'Global Cultural Flows and Pedagogic Dilemmas: Teaching in the Global University "Contact Zone' ", *TESOL Quarterly*, 38(1), 9–42.

Stevenson, H. and Lee, S. (1996) 'The Academic Achievement of Chinese Students', in M. Bond ed., *The Handbook of Chinese Psychology*. Hong Kong: Oxford University Press, pp. 124–42.

Tang, K. (1996) 'Collaborative Learning: the Latent Dimension in Chinese Students' Learning', in D. Watkins and J. Biggs eds, *The Chinese Learner: Cultural, Psychological and Contextual Influences*. Hong Kong: Centre for Comparative Research in Education; Camberwell, Vic.: Australian Council for Educational Research, pp. 183–204.

Teske, R. and Nelson, B. (1974) 'Acculturation and Assimilation: A Clarification', *American Anthropologist*, 1, 351–67.

Triandis, H. (1995) *Individualism and Collectivism*. Boulder, Colorado: Westview Press.

Tseng, Y. -H. (2002) 'A Lesson in Culture', *ELT Journal*, 56(1), 11–21.
Volet, S. and Renshaw, P. (1996) 'Chinese Students at an Australian University: Continuity and Adaptability', in D. Watkins and J. Biggs eds, *The Chinese Learner: Cultural, Psychological and Contextual Influences*. Hong Kong: Centre for Comparative Research in Education; Camberwell; Vic.: Australian Council for Educational Research, pp. 205–20.
Worth, S. and Gross, L. (1974) 'Symbolic Strategies', *Journal of Communication* (Autumn), 27–39.
Xiaoming, Z. and Haitao, X. (2000) 'Internationalisation: A Challenge for China's Higher Education', *Current Issues in Chinese Higher Education*, OECD, pp. 101–10.

Websites

Curtis, P. (2005) 'Universities Warn UK Could Lose Students to US', *The Guardian*, http://education.guardian.co.uk/students/overseasstudents/story/0,12743,1415060,00.html.
Jacques, M. (2003) 'The End of the West', *The Guardian Online*, http://www.guardian.co.uk/comment/story/0,3604,1099256,00.html.
Universities UK, 'Impact of China on the World & UK Economy – Memorandum from Universities', http://www.universitiesuk.ac.uk/parliament/showEvidence.asp?id=26.
Universities UK (2005) 'Universities UK Launches New International Strategy, as Survey Shows "Worrying Downturn" in International Student Numbers', http://www.universitiesuk.ac.uk/mediareleases/show.asp?MR=413.

Exhibition

Between Past and Future – Victoria and Albert Museum, London, 15 September 2005.

9
Faith, Language and Identity: Muslim Migrants in Scotland and Northern Ireland

Gabriele Marranci

There are about 32 million Muslims living in Europe and forming about 40 per cent of the labour migration (Brown 2000). They come from different Islamic countries; they have different ethnic origins and traditions; they are affiliated to different Islamic sects; they are not only individually different from each other but are also individually different in their personal understanding of Islam. Furthermore, Muslims live in European countries that have developed diverse national histories, albeit entangled ones. European countries have possibly less in common than is claimed by politicians. Each European country has its own impact on migrants' lives. To speak of Muslims in the West is over-simplistic (Haddad 2002). Let us wonder to which degree Muslims could act, think and believe in similar fashions. Let me be clear, 'the Muslim', as an archetype, exists only in our need for generalisations.

In this chapter, I shall discuss the relationship that my Muslim respondents, in Northern Ireland and Scotland have with language and worship. Indeed language is one of the most complex and fascinating human skills, from physical, cognitive, and social-cultural viewpoints (Taylor 1991). Language is more than a medium of communication. It often becomes a symbol of membership in and belonging to a group or (as in the case of Arabic) to a religion (Giles and Saint-Jacques 1979). However, as Dorais (1988) emphasises, languages are not abstract objects but are linked to the environment in which people live and its cultural, social, and political realities. As we shall see in this chapter, environment plays a fundamental role in the decision on which language to select in relation to faith.

Kay Milton (2005: 31) has argued that 'emotions are ecological rather than social phenomena'. She defines 'ecological' as 'mechanisms through which an individual human being is connected to and learns from their environment'. Of course Milton does not deny the social aspects of the emotions involved, but reminds us that such social elements are 'only one part of the story'. I agree with Milton's interpretation of human emotions (Marranci 2006) and concur with the view that they are universal in their ecological mechanisms. Now we can understand why emotions are so important in studying attitudes towards language and faith. Muslims charge Arabic with particular emotional meanings, since it is the language in which Allah has revealed the Qur'an. The words of the Qur'an form a Holy sound which Muslims see as part of their devotion. For this reason Muslims claim that the Qur'an could only be 'interpreted' but not literally translated. The divine sound is lost in the process of translation. Arabic is central to the concept of *ummah*, which has been often translated as the community of believers (Al-Ahsan 1992), although I would prefer (following Maffesoli's idea of community 1996) the notion of 'community of emotions'.

After briefly summarising the two Muslim communities in which I have conducted my research, I shall discuss the official role of Arabic within the *ummah*. Then, I shall discuss the manner in which Muslims in Northern Ireland and Scotland tend to differ in their use of language during *khutbas* (Friday sermons). This would help us to understand the indirect influence that host societies have in such decisions. In particular in the case of Northern Ireland, we shall observe how political sectarianism and what I call 'symbolphagy' have induced the Muslim community to adopt English as the main language for their *khutbas*.

Muslims in Northern Ireland and Scotland

The presence of Muslims in Northern Ireland is not a recent phenomenon. The first Muslim, a South Asian member of the East India Company, had reached Ireland around 1780 settling in Cork. Ulster saw its first Muslim, an Indian, in the 1920s (see also Donnan 1993, Donnan and O'Brien 1998, Corrigan 2001). According to the 2001 census, 1993 Muslims live in the region. Yet my research suggests that the number is possibly 2500 while the President of the Belfast Islamic Centre (BIC) is convinced that the overall Muslim population in Northern Ireland is some 4000 members (Marranci 2003).

These first Muslim immigrants were self-employed in the rag trade and sold their products door to door. Their degree of success was so high that it allowed them to invite other members of their family to join these entrepreneurs. Before the end of the 1930s, several South Asian families lived in what, after 1921, had become Northern Ireland, a controversial region of the United Kingdom. From the 1940s to the 1950s, the majority of Muslims arrived from west Punjab, Mirpuris, Azad, Kashmir, and other frontier provinces. Then, an increasing number arrived in Northern Ireland from England, in particular from Birmingham, Manchester, Yorkshire, Cardiff, and Glasgow through family networks.

The Arab Muslims reached Northern Ireland mainly as doctoral and post-doctoral students. Most of the South Asians settled in the city of Craigavon (about 50 kilometres from Belfast), and the Pakistani businessmen in Craigavon bought a semi-detached house, located in Legahory, a Protestant neighbourhood, transforming the premises into a mosque. Even though religious affiliations and sectarian divisions mark Northern Ireland, the decision to build the mosque in a Protestant-British estate did not express a political act, but, since many Pakistanis living in Craigavon came originally form British cities, they were expected to know British Protestants better than Irish Catholics. The Craigavon mosque provided them with the Islamic facilities they needed.

Although Pakistanis in Craigavon had established a mosque, the Muslims in Belfast lacked one. In 1972, with the support of the Pakistani businessmen, the Muslims in Belfast started the 'Islamic Society of Northern Ireland' (ISNI), which, among other activities, had to collect the funds to build the first 'real' Northern Irish mosque in the capital. Despite dreaming of a mosque comprehensive of minaret, the degeneration of the Northern Irish political scene as well as a lack of funding forced the Muslims in Belfast to follow the path of those in Craigavon: to buy a small property and to transform it into a 'mosque'. When the terrorist activities increased in the 1970s, Shi'a Muslims, coming from Lebanon, Iran, Iraq, some parts of Yemen, as well as Pakistan, Bangladesh, and India joined the Sunnis in Belfast. This increased the differences among the members of the community and facilitated rivalry. In 1985, the Muslims in Belfast bought a new semi-detached house in order to accommodate the community. It became the BIC, and since then influential Pakistani businessmen have controlled its committee, though an Arab has often been the President.

In 1998, the Good Friday Agreement established the Northern Irish peace process. Many in Northern Ireland hoped that inter-religious relations would improve. The BIC's committee were also hopeful of a new era. The Pakistanis were enjoying the new peaceful atmosphere when the atrocity of 11 September 2001 shocked Muslims and changed their lives. I have discussed elsewhere (Marranci 2003, 2004) how Northern Irish society has a peculiar capacity for changing the meaning of symbols and setting them in the context of the Northern Irish conflict. 'Symbolphagy' is the term I have given to this process. After the atrocity of 11 September 2001, Islam has become part of the dynamics of symbolphagy, transforming Muslims there into potential victims of sectarianism, rather than Islamophobia. As we shall see, this had an effect on the manner in which my respondents understood the use of Arabic.

There are 42,600 Muslims living in Scotland. Although they constitute less than 1 per cent of the overall Scottish population, they are 45 per cent of the non-Christians. The history of the Scottish Muslim community is not very different from that of the Northern Irish. Sixty-seven per cent of these early south Asians were Pakistani migrants who reached Scotland during the 1960s. As in the case of Northern Ireland, Middle East migrants arrived in Scotland at a later date and mainly as students or as part of an internal migration from the United Kingdom. The Muslim community in Scotland has the youngest age profile. According to the Census of 2001, 31 per cent of those who responded were under 16 years of age. The Muslim families in Scotland tend to have more than one child and maintain extended networks with their relatives both in the United Kingdom and in the Islamic countries. While some migrants may have some issues in speaking English, their children struggle with the languages of their family of origin, such as Arabic, Urdu, and Farsi.

We have seen that in Northern Ireland the majority of Muslims live in the capital, Belfast. Yet this is not the case in Scotland, where Edinburgh has only 16 per cent of the overall Muslim population. Indeed, Muslims are primarily concentrated in Glasgow (42 per cent). Two other cities have relevance in this study, although they have a lower proportion of Muslims: 7 per cent of Muslims live in Dundee, and 4 per cent in Aberdeen. Although Glasgow has the largest South Asian community, Edinburgh, Dundee, and Aberdeen host the highest number of Arab families as well as students. Of these Aberdeen is the only city to have only one official mosque, while Edinburgh, Glasgow, and Dundee have developed more than one alongside the sectarian divisions among the Muslim community.

Muslims in Scotland (in particular the Pakistani) have high rates of unemployment. Unfortunately, Muslims continue to represent the highest proportion of people with no qualifications in the region, facilitating, in this way, the issue of unemployment and underpayment. A high proportion of employed Muslims in Northern Ireland and Scotland tend to be self-employed. This means that many Muslims (in particular,

South Asians) depend on their family networks and tend to live with their families. Although Catholic discrimination exists in Scotland, it is not as evident as in Northern Ireland. Many Muslim respondents had no idea that such tensions within and between the Christian communities existed in Scotland. Yet, while Muslims in Northern Ireland played down the idea that Islamophobia may exist in everyday life, Muslims in Scotland are highly convinced that racism and Islamophobia have an impact on their everyday lives.

Although in Northern Ireland, Muslims have organised some religious education for their children, this was more informal than official. Indeed, many Muslim parents in Northern Ireland rejected the idea of a Muslim school, since they were very critical of the faith-based system of education in Northern Ireland. By contrast, in Scotland there is a wide support for the idea of an Islamic School, as demonstrated by the case of St Albert's Primary school in Pollokshields, Glasgow. This was a Catholic school but now 90 per cent of its pupils are Muslims. Both the Muslim parents and the local Roman Catholic Church would agree to a transformation to Islam. At this stage the debate has opened in the Scottish parliament. As we shall see, the difference in opinion between the Scottish and Northern Irish Muslim parents on this matter has relevance in our understanding of the relationship between language and faith.

Arabic, the language of the *Ummah*

Since my first approach as a young anthropologist to Islam, I became immediately aware of the relevance that Arabic has for Muslims, despite their ethnic, national, and Islamic affiliations (Marranci 2003). This idea was reinforced in France when I observed that some very religious parents allowed their sons (but not their daughters) to listen to the so-called 'raï music' (Marranci 2000, 2001, 2002, 2003, 2005). This repertoire is often considered too mundane and sensual to be acceptable from an Islamic viewpoint. Yet the decision of these parents has nothing to do with the music itself; they just hoped that their sons would develop an empathy with Arabic through the songs which they could not understand. Of course, the Arabic of the singers was an Algerian dialect. Yet it was enough to reinforce the hopes of these parents that their children could in future approach the Arabic of the Qur'an. Sometimes, I have to admit, the system worked; some children from the raï-consuming group began to attend the mosque and started to chant the Qur'an. As Abdullah, one of the imams I met in north Paris, used to say, 'we do not know what Allah may use to bring people to the Qur'an and its perfect language'.

Muslims consider Qur'anic (or classical) Arabic a superior language, and a considerable distinction is made between it and Arabic dialects (Strijp 1998). In the case of mosques with a majority of members coming from non-Arabic-speaking countries, Arabic classes are organised with many Muslims willing to learn the language of the Qur'an. There is a 'collective awareness' among the European Muslims about the centrality of Arabic as a medium of resistance against the pressure to assimilate into the host societies, and it is a way to maintain a sense of unity and identity (Khellil 1991). The use of Arabic as the (theoretically) only acceptable language within the Muslim communities allows an emphasis on the participation of the individual Muslim within the Islamic *ummah* (Muslim community of believers). Indeed, as Anderson (1991) has observed, language is a powerful tool in the formation of 'imagined communities'. Yet I have argued in my book *Jihad Beyond Islam* (Marranci 2006) that young Muslims particularly tend to reject cultural aspects of Islam for the sake of a mythical 'pure Islam'.

Therefore, the *ummah* seems to acquire a different meaning from the 'community of believers' as it tends to be known. Muslims, migrants, and their children increasingly look for Islamic knowledge from Islamic websites (Brückner 2001 and Bunt 2003) rather than from imams and Islamic scholars. Furthermore, Muslim migrants' ideas of local and global are increasingly becoming similar to their non-Muslim peers. Hetherington (1998) has suggested that communities form so that people could share emotions and empathetic identifications. These communities 'of emotions', Hetherington has observed, 'are achieved as intentional "communities", that can be seen as either moral communities or emotional communities' (1998: 50). Although this process implies forms of identification, Maffesoli has argued that personal identities find their expression through the community in a mutual transformation (1996: 98, emphasis in the original): 'this bond is without the rigidity of the forms of organisation with which we are familiar; it refers more to a certain ambience, a state of mind...It is a case of a kind of collective unconscious (non-conscious) which acts as a matrix for varied group experience, situations, actions or wanderings.' Maffesoli has described communities as places in which interactions generate 'general emotions'. My respondents have experienced the meta-space of the *ummah* in a similar fashion.

During my research, I became aware that Arabic has a vital role in the 'moral' or 'emotional community' that Muslims call *ummah*. Though the majority of Muslims in the world do not speak Arabic, they show great respect not only for the language but also for those who can properly read and understand it. The language has symbolic status and my recent research on Muslim inmates in UK prisons has confirmed such a process. South Asians are in the majority in the UK Muslim community and they are also the main ethnic group among Muslim detainees. Yet in many UK prisons it is not difficult to find at least one person able to read and speak Arabic. In a short time, this inmate becomes the leader of the Muslim prison community, the 'official' imam, and the person leading the prayer and presenting the *khutba*. Actually, as I observed in Bralinnie (the prison in Glasgow), the most important thing is not the ethnic origin of the Arabic-speaking person, but the fact that he could claim that he speaks and understands Arabic. In this prison an Ethiopian became the internal imam of that Muslim prisoners' community. Arabic has the spiritual power to captivate individuals.

Other scholars, in different contexts, have also observed such a process. For instance, Ismail (2000) and Kepel (1997) have observed that the process of mastering Arabic could become a matter of personal honour. Yet it is not only important to speak Arabic, but also to listen to it, as Iqbal, a 32-year-old Muslim of Pakistani origin, told me after the Bangladeshi imam had finished his *khutba* in Arabic at the Edinburgh mosque:

> I have not understood one word of the khutba, I speak a bit of Urdu, but English is my language since I am born and bred Scottish. So you may wonder why to pay attention to it [the khutba] because Arabic is the language of the Qur'an and God. It is important to show respect to it. I want to learn Arabic, but working all day it is very difficult. I know only how to recite my prayers but I cannot read the Qur'an in Arabic, I know some of it by heart. So you see, all Muslims have to pay respect to this language because is the language that God has selected to give us His message.

Others in the mosque agreed that Arabic is fundamental to the *ummah*, since it is the only recognised language. Yet some Moroccans of Berber origin spoke against the Arabisation project that is being implemented by the Moroccan government. Nonetheless, this group of Berbers explained that rejecting the political aspects of the Arabisation process did not mean the rejection of Arabic as God's langue. They emphasised that Arabs should allow other ethnic minorities to keep their identities and leave the Arabic to the spiritual dimension of all Muslims; in other words, Arabic for the *ummah*, local languages for everyday lives.

Differences in the use of language during *Khutbas*

In this section, I shall compare two different attitudes towards language within the Northern Irish and Scottish communities. The comparison would be based on the observations I have conducted during the Friday sermons. First of all, let me explain the structure of Friday prayer, since some of my readers might never have attended one. Muslims try to pray five times per day. Although they could pray everywhere, the mosques organise congregations when *salat* (prayer) should be performed. The five times when Muslims performed such prayers are at dawn, after midday, at mid-afternoon, at sunset and about an hour and a half after that. All of them are performed without any sermon and tend to be very short. The attendance may vary considerably from prayer to prayer, since it is not compulsory to attend them in a mosque.

Friday is the most important day in the Islamic week; although the five daily prayers are also performed, a special congregational prayer (*yawm al-jum'a*) is organised around midday and the imam who leads the prayer also has to deliver a sermon. Most of the Muslims (even those avoiding the prayers during the other days) try to attend the *yawm al-jum'a*, since it is an important part of the *sunna* (tradition of the Prophet). The standard *khutba* is divided into four parts: first, the imam (or the person in charge of the prayer) introduces the sermon by praising Allah and reciting a prayer celebrating the Prophet; then, standing up, he delivers the first section of the *khutba* in which he discusses a specific Islamic topic or a current event affecting the community or the Islamic world. At the end of the first sermon, the imam sits down and, together with the congregation, concentrates on a silent *du'a* (supplication to Allah). Then, after standing up again, he presents the second part of the *khutba*: a shorter sermon summarising the first speech, or the translation of the *khutba* in the local idiom, or other general comments on the selected topic. Finally, the imam recites two supplications, one standardised (a prayer asking Allah for forgiveness for all believers) and a second one of his choice. Islamic scholars tend to state that the Friday *khutba* must be conducted in Arabic (De Ruiter 1998: 28), yet, as we shall see in the case of Belfast, there are some exceptions among the Muslim communities in the United Kingdom, although the Qur'an and the two *khutba*'s supplications are always recited in Arabic.

In Scotland, I have observed that the majority of the mosques adopt the use of Arabic as the preferred language for the *khutba*. Some mosques, such as Aberdeen, adopt a bilingual approach and give summaries of the *khutba* in English. Very few Muslims complain that they could not understand the sermon; instead the majority blames itself for not understanding Arabic. In Dundee, the three mosques (Jamia Masjid, also known as Dundee Islamic Society; Jamia Masjid Tajdar-E-Madina, also known as Tayside Islamic and Cultural Education Centre; and Jama Masjid Bilal, also known as Scottish Islamic and Cultural Centre) have two different approaches to the *khutba*. While in the main mosque (Jamia Masjid – Dundee Islamic Society) the imam conducts the *khutba* only in Arabic, the other two opt for Urdu. The recitation of the Qur'an in Arabic is in this case followed by an Urdu translation or, better, as my respondents emphasised by an Urdu interpretation. Indeed, both the Jamia Masjid Tajdar-E-Madina and Jama Masjid Bilal mosques are linked to the Barelwi School and are attended by Pakistani migrants and their children. The Barelwi was funded by Ahmad Riza Khan, who lived in the city of Barelwi. The movement is strongly influenced by Sufism and contrasts sharply with Deobandi interpretations of Islam. In these two mosques, Urdu is purposely used in the hope that the new generations will maintain it as their language. This has less to do with nationalistic or ethnic ideologies than with religious necessities: all the Barelwi's primary scholarly books are in Urdu and the traditional teaching in the Pakistani Barelwi madrasat is conducted in this language (Rahman 1998).

In Northern Ireland, by contrast, English seems to be the only acceptable language within the central mosque. Although hardly less multicultural and multiethnic than the Scottish Central mosque, the BIC has decided to use English during the *khutbas* and for all its communication. Even the quotations from the Qur'an are then translated for the congregation. Clearly, the Muslim community in Northern Ireland seems to be very aware of potential problems for Arabic within the context of Northern Irish society. Indeed, in Northern Ireland, Irish and other local accents are used as symbolic political systems. The following anecdote may demonstrate the pressure to maintain English as the *khutba* language within the Northern Irish Muslim community.

An Islamic scholar from England was invited to deliver one of the Friday sermons. He adopted the same system that I have seen in Aberdeen. He presented the first three *khutbas* in Arabic, providing a short summary in English at the end of his sermon. Nevertheless, some Muslims, both Arabs and South Asians, complained about the scholar's decision to use Arabic in the longest part of the *khutba*. Yet this scholar rebuked the Muslim community reminding them that their complaints were unacceptable according to the tradition of the Prophet, who, of course, delivered his *khutba* in Arabic. The second Friday the invited scholar still delivered the *khutba* in Arabic. Concerns started to develop within the Muslim community. Finally, under pressure from the community, the scholar was gently, but firmly, asked to preach in a more neutral-safe English. Indeed, in the context of Northern Ireland, Muslims have fully adopted English in their *khutbas* to symbolise their 'peaceful', 'non-sectarian', and 'open' contribution to their host society.

We have seen different patterns of language use during worship among Muslims in Scotland and Northern Ireland. Other scholars have discussed this relationship between worship and language among Muslims (De Ruiter 1998, De Ruiter and Obdeijn 1998, Ngom 2003, Rahman 1998, Rampton 1995, Seymour-Jorn 2004, Strijp 1998), yet these studies have overlooked two important factors: environment and emotions. We have observed that in Northern Ireland Muslims have adopted English as the main religious language (of course, the Qur'an is recited in Arabic), while in Scotland we have found a similar pattern to other European locations (see for instance Alsayyad and Castells 2001, Haddad 2002, Kepel 1997, Lewis and Schnapper 1994, Nielsen 1988, Werbner 2002), with Arabic being used in the central mosque as well as local languages, in this case Urdu, among mystical groups. If we analyse the elements involved, we may observe that social and political local realities have an impact on the use of language among Muslim migrants' decision on which language to use during worship.

In Scotland, sectarian divisions among communities still exist but are less strong and Muslims have developed different attitudes towards the language of worship. Indeed, in Dundee this has meant the formation of three different mosques, which tend to criticise each other exactly on the language selected to deliver the *khutba*. Yet emotional elements also play a role in these decisions. In the Central mosque, Muslims strongly agreed that Arabic should be at the centre of Islam and *ummah*: 'one language, one people'. The sound of Arabic is itself part of the worship and formation of the 'emotional community'. Yet in the case of the two Barelwi mosques, Urdu, rather than Arabic, has a central role in maintaining a spiritual, often linked to an ethnic, identity. Arabic is the language of Allah, Urdu becomes the language of the believer's soul.

If the Muslim community of Northern Ireland were not affected by the symbolphagy attitude of the Northern Irish society, it is likely that the language dynamics would be the same as those in Scotland. Indeed, now that the peace process is taking place and the Irish Republican Army has issued a statement (29/07/2005) ending its long campaign, the issue of language and its emotional values have started dividing the Muslim community. By contrast, the 7/7 terrorist attacks in London are producing the opposite effect in Scotland. The environment in which Muslims in Scotland now live is much tenser than before, and the perspective on language use is changing. While previously language was regarded as a marker of identity, it is now seen as a potential cause of conflict.

References

Al-Ahsan, A. (1992) *Ummah or Nation: Identity Crisis In Contemporary Muslim Society*. Leicester: Islamic Foundation.

Alsayyad, N. and Castells, M. eds (2001) *Muslim Europe or Euro-Islam: Politics, Culture, and Citizenship in the Age of Globalisation*. Oxford: Lexington Books.

Anderson, B. (1991) *Imagined Communities: Reflections on the Origin and Spread of Nationalism*. London and New York: Verso.

Brown, M. (2000) 'Quantifying the Muslim Population in Europe: Conceptual and Data Issues', *International Journal of Social Research Methodology*, 3(2), 87–101.

Brückner, M. (2001) 'IslamCity, Creating an Islamic Cybercity', *ISIM Newsletter*, 8, 12.

Bunt, G. R. (2003) *Islam in the Digital Age*. London: Sterling and Virginia: Pluto Press.

Corrigan, M. (2001) *A Sociological Study of Pakistani Muslims in Northern Ireland*. Belfast: Queens University, PhD Thesis.

De Ruiter, J. (1998) 'Language and Religion. Moroccan and Turkish Communities in Europe', *ISIM Newsletter*, 1, 28.

De Ruiter, J. and Obdeijn, H. (1998) *Le Maroc au coeur de l'Europe: l'enseignement de la langue et culture d'origine (ELCO) aux élèves marocains dans cinq pays européens*. Tilburg: Syntax Datura.

Donnan, H. (1993) 'New Minorities, South Asian in the North', in T. Eriksen ed., *Ethnicity and Nationalism: Anthropological Perspectives*. London: Pluto Press.

Donnan, H. and O'Brien, M. (1998) ' "Because you stick out, you stand out": Perception of Prejudice among Northern Ireland's Pakistanis', in P. Hainsworth ed., *Divided Society, Ethnic Minorities and Racism in Northern Ireland*. London: Pluto Press, pp. 197–221.

Dorais, Louis-Jacques (1988) '*Sois belle et tais-toi*: The Language of the Inuit in Today's Canada', *Études Inuit Studies*, 12, 235–43.

Giles, H. and Saint-Jacques, B. (1979) *Language and Ethnic Relations*. Oxford: Pergamon.

Haddad, Y. ed. (2002) *Muslims in the West: from Sojourners to Citizens*. Oxford, NY: Oxford University Press.

Hetherington, K. (1998) *Expression of Identity: Space, Performance, Politics*. London: New York, Sage.

Ismail, E. (2000) *The Dar al-Islam and the Dar al-Harb: A Discourse on the Crafting of a Muslim State*. Austin: University of Texas, MA Thesis.

Kepel, G. (1997) *Allah in the West: Islamic Movements in America and Europe*. Cambridge: Polity Press.

Khellil, M. (1991) *L'Intégration des maghrébins en France*. Paris: Presses Universitaires De France.

Lewis, B. and Schnapper, D. eds (1994) *Muslims in Europe*. London and New York: Pinter.

Maffesoli, M. (1996) *The Time of the Tribes*. London: Sage.

Marranci, G. (2000) 'La Musique Raï: Entre Métissage et World Music Moderne', *Cahiers de musiques traditionnelles*, 13, 137–50.

Marranci, G. (2001) 'A Complex Identity and its Musical Representation; Beurs and Raï Music in Paris', *Music & Anthropology*, 5 (http://www.muspe.unibo. it/period/ma).

Marranci, G. (2002) 'First and Second Generation Muslim Immigrant Women in Europe: Transnational Identity vs. Cross-cultural Identity?', Florence: Paper presented at the Third Mediterranean Social and Political Research Meeting, Mediterranean Programme, Robert Shuman Centre for Advanced Studies, European University Institute, March 20–24.

Marranci, G. (2003) ' "We Speak English." Language and Identity Processes in Northern Ireland's Muslim Community', *Ethnologist*, 25(2), 59–77.

Marranci, G. (2004) 'Constructing an Islamic Environment in Northern Ireland', *Built Environment*, 30(1), 5–17.

Marranci, G. (2005) 'From Orano to Paris: Identity, Raï Music and Algerian Immigrants', in D. Cooper and K. Dawe eds, *The Mediterranean in Music*. Lanham, MD: Scarecrow Press.

Marranci, G. (2006) *Jihad Beyond Islam*. London and New York: Berg.

Milton, K. (2005) 'Meanings, Feelings, and Human Ecology', in K. Milton and M. Svasek eds, *Mixed Emotions: Anthropological Studies of Feelings*. New York and London: Berg, pp. 26–42.

Ngom, F. (2003) 'The Social Status of Arabic, French, and English in the Senegalese Speech Community', *Language, Variation and Change*, 15, 351–68.

Nielsen, J. (1988) 'Muslim in Britain and Local Authorities Responses', in T. Gerholam and G. Lithman eds, *The New Islamic Presence in Western Europe*. London and New York: Mansell, pp. 53–77.

Rahman, T. (1998) 'Language, Religion and Identity in Pakistan: Language-Teaching in Pakistan', *Madrassas' Ethnic Studies Report*, 16(2), 197–214.

Rampton, B. (1995) *Crossing: Language and Ethnicity among Adolescents*. London: Longman.

Seymour-Jorn, C. (2004) 'Arabic Language Learning among Arab Immigrants in Milwaukee, Wisconsin: A Study of Attitudes and Motivations', *Journal of Muslim Minority Affairs*, 24(1), 110–22.

Strijp, R. (1998) *Om de moskee: Het religieuze leven van Marokkaanse migranten in een Nederlandse provinciestad*. Nijmegen: Proefschrift Katholieke Universiteit, PhD Thesis.

Taylor, D. (1991) 'The Social Psychology of Racial and Cultural Diversity: Issues of Assimilation and Multiculturalism', in A. Reynolds ed., *Bilingualism, Multiculturalism and Second-Language Learning*. Hillsdale, NJ: Lawrence Earlbaum, pp. 1–19.

Werbner, P. (2002) *Imagined Diasporas among Manchester Muslims*. Santa Fe, NM: School of American Research Press.

10
Language, Faith and Communication

John Dunlop

> My companion laid hands on a friend and violated a covenant with me with speech smoother than butter, but with a heart set on war; with words that were softer than oil, but, in fact, were drawn swords. (Psalm 55: 20–21)

What have been called the Peace Process and, before that, the scandalous murderous terrorist activity of paramilitary groups have made their tortuous way through myriads of press conferences, speeches, sermons, statements from governments and political parties, newspaper articles, countless books as well as comments from public bodies. The whole long journey has been mapped by words, many of them carefully chosen to serve the purposes of the speakers and writers, some of them rooted in a search for truth, others in the service of propaganda, many of them duplicitous.

The two parts of the community which make up the population of Northern Ireland have found themselves on the narrow ground of contested space, each with umbilical cords connected either to Britain or to the Republic of Ireland, reaching out beyond them to a world some parts of which were sympathetic, some antagonistic, many confused, most bored. The participants in the long conflict used words as weapons, to explain, to excuse or to inflame. While many who lived outside the contested space listened with incomprehension, those within the conflict had finely tuned receptors and had learned how to listen in order to have their convictions and prejudices reinforced like walls around citadels of settled contentious conviction.

The print and electronic media have meticulously reported what has been said and what has been done but have often failed in a higher obligation to facilitate sympathetic understanding across the divides.

The media has often been the arena for verbal contests. The two sides in the conflict have lived beside each other for a long time. At one level we understand one another very well but at another level there has been the absence of sympathetic understanding of the other and commitment to one another's well-being.

Words as symbols

The Irish School of Ecumenics carried forward an important *Discussion Document on Sectarianism* (The Irish Inter-Church Meeting 1993) into the *Beyond Sectarianism Project* (Liechty and Clegg 2001). This is a programme which correctly analyses legitimate identity issues which have become diseased into sectarianism through centuries of division. The project invites people from different churches and communities to be involved in a process of interaction which may move them from resignation through toleration towards empathy with others. Such empathy does not imply complete identification with the other community. Instead the original identity is maintained, but one has arrived at a form of understanding and toleration of others.

Not too many people have made that journey and even those who have got there have not always been able to hold the position gained as some new atrocity or seeming duplicitous statements have caused them to abandon the new ground and retreat to more familiar territory. At the time of writing many would reckon that we are living in a community the two parts of which continue to segregate into comfort zones of homogeneous familiarity.

Peter Shirlow and others have researched this in North Belfast (2001). They describe how people avoid communities within which they fear they will experience the chill factor of verbal abuse or violence. The political process has delivered a welcome and hard-won political accommodation in the complex Belfast or Good Friday Agreement, which has achieved much but has fallen far short of reconciliation, all of which would indicate that the subject of 'Language, Communication and Reconciliation' still needs to be on the agenda.

Words are very powerful symbols. They can humiliate, deceive and destroy or, on the other hand, they can confirm, clarify and mobilise. In the Epistle of James we read the following:

> How great a forest is set ablaze by a small fire! And the tongue is a
> fire. The tongue is placed among our members as a world of iniquity;

it stains the whole body, sets on fire the cycle of nature, and is itself
set on fire by hell. For every species of beast and bird, of reptile and
sea creature, can be tamed and has been tamed by the human species,
but no one can tame the tongue – a restless evil, full of deadly poison.
With it we bless the Lord and Father, and with it we curse those who
are made in the likeness of God. From the same mouth come blessing
and cursing. My brothers and sisters, this ought not to be so. (James
3:5–10)

Words can be informative, such as 'a concert is taking place in the Magee
Campus of the University of Ulster'. It is a safe way of saying where a
concert is taking place. I could go on to say that 'the concert is tonight
in Derry or is it Londonderry?' Whichever word is used for the name of
this city will be noted by those who listen and may well please some and
irritate others. Words can be informative and simultaneously divisive.

There are words which may also be intentionally performative; they
do more than inform, in the uttering of them something is done. In
a marriage ceremony in a church when two people exchange vows,
the reciprocal words used lead on to a subsequent declaration that the
singleness of the two people has been transformed into a marriage.
The performative effect of words may be constructive as in a marriage
ceremony or destructive as in a quarrel.

Like somebody who takes a passing dog by the ears is one who
meddles in the quarrel of another. Like a maniac who shoots deadly
firebrands and arrows, so is one who deceives a neighbor and says, 'I
am only joking.' For lack of wood the fire goes out, and where there
is no whisperer, quarreling ceases. As charcoal is to hot embers and
wood to fire, so is a quarrelsome person for kindling strife'. (Proverbs
26:17–21)

Carefully chosen words, delivered in a specific context can be expressive
of what people feel. Following the bombing of the London Underground
on 7 July 2005, Ben Macintyre, writing in *The Times* on the following
day, observed about Tony Blair's use of language: 'Blair is a master of
rhetoric: he can deploy words to dissemble and demean, but he can also
use them to articulate the feelings, fears and hopes of his listeners. He
did this over the death of Diana, Princess of Wales, and he did it even
more dramatically on Thursday, offering a resonate response to terrorism
even before the scale of the devastation was known' (MacIntyre 2005).

MacIntyre then quoted William Hazlitt's definition of the purpose of oratory: 'Not to inform but to arouse the mind'.

John F. Kennedy once observed that Winston Churchill 'mobilized the English language and sent it into battle' (Kennedy 1961). Not many people could better Martin Luther King's capacity to deploy language to inspire and motivate. But his capacity to do that depended on his words being heard by a community of people gathered together, so that interaction took place between King and the audience. It is said that Martin Luther King's famous Washington speech 'I have a dream', delivered at the Lincoln Memorial on 28 August 1963, did not include the best-known section in the previously circulated text. It was only as he sensed the mood of the crowd that he then drew on previously used material to deliver one of the greatest speeches of all time. It is necessary to hear the words to appreciate their impact. How impoverished we would be if we only had the words to read and had never heard the voice with its measured cadences of protest and hope?

Many children have been turned against Shakespeare because they have never got beyond the words on a page. It is one thing to read a Shakespearean play but it is an experience of a different order to watch the play on television or to enjoy it in the company of others in a theatre, although the words used in all three experiences are the same. Shakespeare intended the words to get off the page and onto the stage of spoken speech and shared experience.

The ancient text in the Gospel according to John declared that 'In the beginning was the Word, and the Word was with God, and the Word was God' (John 1:16). The Word became flesh and witness is borne to that event in the words of scripture. The Word became flesh but did not become a book and however useful the book may be it is no substitute for the Word becoming flesh.

Who knows what words might do or where they might end up? Paul Muldoon's translation of an Irish poem refers to something placed in the little boat of the language of poetry, which is set at the water's edge

> only to have it borne hither and thither,
> not knowing where it might end up;
> in the lap, perhaps,
> of some Pharaoh's daughter.

> (Nuala Ni Dhomhnaill 1990: 155)

Rachel Campbell-Johnston in a review of 'Gilgamesh' translated by Stephen Mitchell, wrote, 'Gilgamesh is the oldest recorded story in the world… they are stories that explore timeless human themes. They are stories of lust and love, of passion and arrogance, of retribution and remorse. And at root lies the most fundamental of all human fears: the fear of death' (Campbell-Johnston 2004: 15).

It is inconceivable that those who wrote the ancient piece of text could have imagined it being translated thousands of years later into a then unknown tongue and reproduced on a word processor. Who knows where the words may end up? Who can quantify what they may do for good or ill? I have written about the subject of words and language in *A Precarious Belonging – Presbyterian and the Conflict in Ireland* (Dunlop 1995), a book published by the Blackstaff Press in 1995. Those of you familiar with the book will be familiar with some of what follows.

That book was written from the perspective of someone who is a minister of the Presbyterian Church in Ireland, which is the largest Protestant denomination in Northern Ireland and second in size to the Church of Ireland in the whole of Ireland; both of course smaller than the membership of the (Roman) Catholic Church in both political jurisdictions. For those of you who are unfamiliar with the history of churches in Ireland, let me explain, briefly, that the Presbyterians trace their history back to Scotland and through the Scottish Reformation to Geneva and John Calvin and the Reformation in Europe, through the pre-Reformation Western Church, through the great schism of 1054, and then to the apostles and to Christ. The first presbytery was organised in Ireland in 1642.

In the book, I have explored the use of language within the Presbyterian tradition and suggested ways in which it affects the ethos of the church and, through it, the wider community. I have suggested ways in which it may differ from other religious traditions. The Word of God, contained in the scriptures of the Old and New Testaments, is central in Presbyterian thinking. In most Presbyterian churches the pulpit is in a central and dominating place. The reading and preaching of the Word probably occupy between one-third and one-half of the service. Should a worshipper be blind, very little would be missed in a Presbyterian worship service, for there is little to see, but much to hear. The service is dominated by words. It is easy to broadcast such a service on the radio; it does not work well on television.

Preaching is based upon the scriptures, and theology and preaching are tested against the Word of God. Congregations will not necessarily believe a preacher as what is heard will be tested against what the hearer understands to be the truth. Truth is an elusive concept and the scriptures of the Old and New Testaments are complex documents, rich and varied in theology, prophetic utterances, historical reflections, poetry, worship songs, apocalyptic complexity, gospel witness as well as letters to churches and to some individuals. The issue of Biblical authority and the terms used to give expression to it have been the cause of deep controversy within Protestant theology.

The basic code of the Presbyterian Church in Ireland (1980) states that 'The Word of God as set forth in the Scriptures of the Old and New Testament is the only infallible rule of faith and practice and the supreme standard of the Church.' There being controversy about what the Word of God teaches on certain important points of doctrine and worship, the Presbyterian Church in Ireland has adopted subordinate standards set down in the Westminster Confession of Faith and in the Larger and Shorter catechisms.

It is written that 'All scripture is inspired by God and is useful for teaching, for reproof, for correction and for training in righteousness, so that everyone who belongs to God may be proficient, equipped for every good work' (2 Timothy 3:16). Whether inspiration is to be confused with infallibility is a matter of importance. They are, to my mind, two different concepts. To say that the love poetry of the Song of Solomon is infallible is to attribute to it an inappropriate descriptive category.

A story is told about how Francis Hutcheson, who later became Professor of Moral Philosophy at the University of Glasgow, was sent as a young preacher by his father, who was afflicted with rheumatism, as a substitute to conduct the service:

> The weather clearing meanwhile, the father, out of paternal curiosity, proceeded towards the church, two miles distant, that he might collect the opinions of his hearers as to the pulpit powers of his son. Mr Hutcheson was surprised to meet the people returning home long before the usual hour for dismissal. He interviewed an elder, a Scotsman, concerning this remarkable occurrence, and received as reply, *Your silly son, Frank, has fashed a' the congregation with his idle cackle; for he has been babblin' this oor aboot a good and benevolent God and that the sauls o' the heathen themselves will gang tae heaven if they follow the licht o' their ain consciences. Not a word does the daft boy ken, speer, nor say about the gude auld comfortable doctrines of election, reprobation, original sin, and faith'.* (Stewart 1950: 39)

Presbyterian churches usually have little artistic adornment. I told a Catholic friend once that I liked well-lit churches and didn't like Catholic shadows and candles and narrow windows; to which he said, 'You Presbyterians think you understand everything. I like shadows and the contemplation of mystery – there are some things we do not understand.'

W. Rogers (1993: 147), writing about speech patterns, expressed the abrupt nature of Protestant people:

> Who like the spiky consonants in speech
> And think the soft ones sissy ...

He continues by describing the Protestant people as an 'angular people'

> For whom the word is still a fighting word,
> Who bristle into reticence at the sound
> Of the round gift of the gab in Southern mouths.

Presbyterians are suspicious of those who come bearing a wealth of vocabulary, wondering what might be hidden in the multiplicity of words. If it can't be said simply, perhaps there is something to hide. Being careful with words, they follow the preacher's injunction in Ecclesiastes, 'Let your words be few; think before you speak ... and don't say any more than you have to' (Ecclesiastes 5:2), and the words of Jesus, 'let your "yea be yea and your nay be nay"; whatsoever is more than these cometh of evil' (Matthew 5:37).

Words, relationships, power

On Good Friday, 5 April 1985, Oliver Messiaen was interviewed on the *South Bank Show* in a programme entitled 'Music of Faith'. He spoke of the radiance of Christ at the Transfiguration and the Resurrection being like the radiance of snow in bright sunlight, which is nothing compared with the radiance of the sun itself. He described a glorified body as one with 'agility'. In the prison camp where Messiaen was interned during the Second World War he composed a '*Quartet for the End of Time*'. They would not have had adequate instruments in the prison to perform the work – indeed he might have been killed before it could be performed, but he said, 'even if I died, I knew there would be paradise; it is certain, joy exists beyond sorrow, beauty beyond horror' (Messiaen 1985).

That is an eloquent testimony of Christian hope. All preaching and Christian worship; all celebration of the sacraments should be marked with the agility of the transfiguration and resurrection, and should be filled with Christian hope. 'But', said Messiaen, 'strict beat belongs to the military march which is unreal.' He said that his music belongs to birdsong which he likens to 'the branches of a tree or the waves on the sea, all of which are uneven'.

Irish Presbyterians are more influenced by the strict beat of scholastic thoroughness than by the agility born of grace. If preaching is preoccupied with orthodoxy and is formed 'in conformity to the [orthodox theological] standards rather than as the truth most surely to be believed' (Burleigh 1960: 307), that is to theological formulations rather than an exploration of the complex text of the scriptures and the implications of the grace of God made manifest in Jesus Christ, then it may produce congregations which are submissive to orthodox conformity rather than people excited by the living truth 'most surely to be believed'. The former may produce a culture of rigid inflexibility rather than a community of faith ready for journeys, especially when people are further influenced by the interpretive icons of their own situation in the words and images of siege and survival associated with Derry, which resonates with the history of their precarious existence as an Irish minority.

This is not unrelated to our understanding of God. If we think primarily in terms of sovereignty, power and authority and overlook relational concepts which lie at the heart of the Trinity (Moltmann 1981: 198, 202, 216), we are not likely to produce congregations and communities which major on the importance of relationships. The nature of the relationships between a child and a parent ought not to be primarily those of authority and submissiveness. Children ought to obey their parents, and parents ought to provide a secure environment which will include boundaries, but the relationship ought to be marked by warmth and love, which encourage obedience, love, trust, freedom and creativity.

God has given us the capacity to imagine as well as to think logically. The left and right hemispheres of the brain work in two different ways. In most people the left hemisphere functions logically and analytically and looks for literal meanings. The right hemisphere processes information holistically. Many scientific breakthroughs come from intuitive artistic imagination located in the right hemisphere and not from logical deduction. Theology which is dominated by the left hemisphere will be logical and rigid and its associated preaching will be analytical. Right-brain theology will be imaginative and creative. There are dangers if the two are disconnected. While the first kind will be extraordinarily dull, there is no way the second can be checked against anything. What is needed is a dynamic relationship between both. Presbyterianism is marked by too much left-brain strict beat. We could do with more of our life marked by agility; more affirmation of joy beyond sorrow; more celebration of apocalyptic extravagance using the doxologies sung by choirs composed of millions from all over the earth (Revelation 5:11–13). More of that might provide us with a mind set which could celebrate diversity and make space for legitimate difference.

Presbyterian language does not have too many layers to it; it does not possess too much flexibility. Presbyterians are probably not very good negotiators. The opening political statements of political negotiators influenced by Presbyterianism tend to contain an analysis of the situation along with their bottom line. There is no movement either contemplated or even possible unless you can convince them that the analysis is wrong. If you can't convince them of that, the bottom line will not move, on principle. Maurice Hayes (1995: 219) observed this characteristic in his position as a senior civil servant:

> There is…an inevitable and real problem in any negotiations in Northern Ireland arising both from the evangelical Protestant tradition of commitment to the Word, to revealed truth, and from the Presbyterian suspicion of rulers and hierarchies. That, and a more relaxed attitude among Catholics to broad moral principles, made any meeting of minds highly unlikely, and made negotiations in any real sense almost impossible.

Presbyterians like the words to be precise. Generally, they try to get the language right first and then build the relationships. If they can't agree on the words, then the relationships suffer; even disintegrate. The fractured nature of Reformed Churches is evidence that perceived truth, verbally expressed, takes precedence over sustaining communities. This is not an exclusively Northern Ireland phenomena, it is reproduced worldwide in the experience of reformed churches. The fractured characteristics of Protestant ecclesiology is reproduced in the fractured characteristics of unionist and loyalist politics. While the nationalist/republican section of our community is represented by one church and two political parties, the unionist/loyalist section of our community is riven by division and rivalry in church and politics.

Clearly there is some strength in proceeding with precision. People know where everyone stands. There are areas of life which need absolute clarity and the elimination of ambiguity. If there is to be a merger between two insurance companies, the lawyers would rightly crawl all over the documents for ambiguities and inconsistencies. Among other things the life savings of customers may be at stake so it is important that everything is accurate. There are great strengths in clarity of discourse, where what is being said can be believed.

There are times when one needs to be precise and accurate, but the demand for too much precision at all times, at every stage of the negotiation, may result in deadlock. Compromise becomes impossible. It may not facilitate the creation or preservation of good human relationships. There are times when intransigence is a sign of weakness and not of strength. There are times when a refusal to try to settle a dispute with an opponent is not in the interest of either party.

There is a difference of emphasis when we compare the Presbyterian and Catholic communities on the issue of the priority given to Church allegiance as against theological statements. Many Catholics find it possible to stay within the Catholic Church while disagreeing with some of its teachings and some of the statements in papal encyclicals. Many Protestants would be much more likely to leave a denomination or a congregation if they disagreed with official statements made or policies being pursued.

Compared with the Protestant part of the community, the Catholic part of it exhibits a greater cohesiveness and a willingness to stay together. Looking at it from the outside, relationships and cohesiveness have a high priority, and words are found which meet the perceived needs of the hour to keep the relationships intact. I suspect that the Catholic culture of cohesive internal hospitality is gentler and more accommodating with sinners. Within that culture of hospitality, everyone seems to belong; no one is finally put outside. The prodigal son never ceases to be a son, even if he is in the far country. Even Irish Republican Army (IRA) gunmen were still part of the family at the end of the day. If they were killed, the Church did not condone what they had done but neither did it disown them; it compassionately prayed for them and buried them.

Presbyterian belonging is much more conditional. In Presbyterian culture there are many outsiders. The Church and the society within which the church lives its life are not one and the same thing. Presbyterians are suspicious of a culture which gives greater priority to maintaining relationships if the price to be paid is diminished honesty. Catholic culture is much more unified and cohesive, more capable of mobilisation, more capable of accommodating diversity and possesses greater community capacity. It has consequently been much easier to organise community development groups in Catholic than in Protestant areas. Protestant culture is deeply individualistic. There are of course exceptions to these caricatures. Presbyterian precision may mask a hidden generosity of spirit. The relaxed surface of Catholic Ireland may hide deeper hidden unexpressed animosity and ancient resentments of disputes between neighbours. The current relationships between the Social Democratic and Labour Party and Sinn Féin are hardly marked by generosity and trust.

Reading 'between the lines': Text and meaning

Following the publication of one of the many position papers which have been produced by the British and Irish Governments over many years of tortuous negotiation, I had a conversation with a senior civil servant who was involved in the discussions, a person who was intelligent, thoughtful and committed to finding a solution to our problems. He urged me 'to read between the lines' of the actual text, to which I replied that 'there was nothing written between the lines'.

I think that conversation illustrated two approaches to text and language: on the one hand, a desire for subtlety and some necessary ambiguity, illustrating a desire to keep people involved in a complex political process, thereby keeping the dialogue alive, preventing people from walking away in what was a preliminary stage of what turned out to be a long process; and on the other hand, a desire to ascertain exactly what the text was saying, it being an important position paper from two governments.

Barry White after an interview with Padraig O'Malley, the influential Irish-American expert on divided societies, reported O'Malley's conviction that 'language is central to the lack of understanding between Roman Catholics and Protestants. Nationalist leaders talk about *frameworks* while Unionists prefer to deal with definite proposals. These two approaches can be traced back to their theological roots before and after the Reformation.' He argues that if the religious element is not addressed, it could seriously handicap the search for a solution. If any progress is to be made in the talks, the two sides would have to understand each other, knowing that they used language in two different ways, coming from different modes of thought. 'Both the Anglo-Irish Agreement and the Downing Street Declaration were written in a language which Protestants could not understand. They were devised to allow for latitude – and that's what Protestants can't deal with' (White cited in Dunlop 1995: 99).

Let me suggest three ways of looking at the use of language in facilitating understanding and honest discourse. Let us assume for a moment that we are looking at three paintings. In the first, the perspective narrows to a point in the distance and the lines converge. In the second, the controlling point of perspective is somewhere behind the artist, and the painting invites one to contemplate wide horizons; it is like looking through a window with the shutters thrown back. In the third, there is no perspective, there are impressions.

For some people, a piece of text is to be dissected for meaning, the meaning being within the text, within ever narrowing horizons. One needs a microscope. It is believed that this will disclose the truth hidden in the text. For others, the text points beyond itself to a reality greater than the text itself. One needs a telescope to discern what lies beyond what is immediate. For others, this may refer to poetry, the meaning is multifaceted and subtle. I think it was Seamus Heaney who, having been asked to explain a poem, said that if he could explain the poem there would have been no need to write it in the first place. One needs neither microscope nor telescope, one needs imagination. In an interview conducted with Seamus Heaney in 2002, the poet wrote that

> [U]tterance is the basis of poetry – poetry is a new way of seeing it, of saying it – as a refreshment of what you know. People can enter the kind of thing that poetry is without any technical knowledge. I think of the old fellow down in Donegal beside the sea. He looked at the waves and said 'It's very shabby out there today'. It's seeing the thing absolutely refreshed – the world seen again. (Johnson 2002: 4–5)

There are many Presbyterians who have difficulty with processes which allow for latitude. They are much less likely to separate form and substance. For them, the meaning of a document is the sum total of the words used. If they want to understand a document they don't look for spaces, they delve into the meaning of the words, and may thereby fail to understand the purpose of the text, or may, perhaps rightly, discover it to be an exercise in deception. Is it the case that the intention behind a document – for example perhaps that of keeping options open, in the case of the conflict in Northern Ireland, keeping disputants at the table – is greater than the meaning of the actual words used? Is it important to look for spaces as well as specific details?

There are times when creative flexibility is needed to give people necessary space; but too much of it may cover duplicity and lead ultimately to the total destruction of trust. The Belfast (or Good Friday) Agreement was the result of long and detailed negotiations (http://cain.ulst.ac.uk/events/peace/docs/agreement.htm). The Agreement involved many drafts of key paragraphs. Two that subsequently caused enormous difficulties had to do with the exclusive use of peaceful means in the pursuit of political objectives and the expectation that the total disarmament of paramilitary organisations and the decommissioning of all paramilitary arms would follow within 2 years.

Two key paragraphs are paragraph four of the Declaration of Support and paragraph three of the section on Decommissioning which read as follows:

> We reaffirm our total and absolute commitment to exclusively democratic and peaceful means of resolving differences on political issues, and our opposition to any use or threat of force by others for any political purpose, whether in regard to this agreement or otherwise.
>
> All participants accordingly reaffirm their commitment to the total disarmament of all paramilitary organisations. They also confirm their intention to work constructively and in good faith with the Independent Commission, and to use any influence they may have, to achieve the decommissioning of all paramilitary arms within two years following endorsement in referendums North and South of the Agreement and in the context of an overall settlement. (http://cain.ulst.ac.uk/events/peace/docs/agreement.htm)

The meaning and implication of these paragraphs proved to be contentious. Did these paragraphs unambiguously commit Sinn Féin and the IRA to decommissioning within two years? They might be deemed to be ambiguous if it was believed that Sinn Féin and the IRA were two separate organisations and not two parts of the same organisation.

Prior to the parties signifying their acceptance of the Agreement on 10 April 1998, the British Prime Minister Mr Tony Blair MP reassured David Trimble MP, the Leader of the Ulster Unionist Party, that if the provisions in the Agreement proved to be ineffective in excluding people from office who did not meet their responsibilities set out in the Pledge of Office, he would support changes to be made to make them properly effective and that he further believed that the process of decommissioning should begin straight away. The Pledge commits holders of Ministerial Office 'to pledge commitment to non-violent and exclusively peaceful and democratic means;' (Annex A (b), http://cain.ulst.ac.uk/events/peace/docs/agreement.htm). This reassurance was given by the British Prime Minister in a letter delivered to David Trimble in the latter stages of the negotiations. What was the status of this letter? Was it a last-minute attempt to cover David Trimble's embarrassment and therefore of no significance as it was not included in the text of the Agreement or was it, as David Trimble maintains, 'an authoritative interpretation of the Agreement'? Dr Mo Mowlam, the then Secretary of State for Northern Ireland said subsequently that while IRA decommissioning was not a precondition for Sinn Féin entering the devolved government, decommissioning was 'an obligation' under the Agreement (in Millar 2004: 70–73).

There then followed statements by the Prime Minister regarding his understanding of the Agreement and his commitment to its implementation. On Wednesday 20 May, 2 days prior to the referendum, the Prime Minister made the following pledge in a speech at the University of Ulster in Coleraine:

I pledge to the people of Northern Ireland:

- no change in the status of Northern Ireland without the express consent of the people of Northern Ireland;
- power to take decisions returned to a Northern Ireland Assembly, with accountable North/South co-operation;
- fairness and equality guaranteed for all;
- those who use or threaten violence will be excluded from the Government of Northern Ireland;
- prisoners kept in unless violence is given up for good.

Whatever the Referendum result, as Prime Minister of the United Kingdom I will continue to work for stability and prosperity for all the people of Northern Ireland (http://cain.ulst.ac.uk/events/peace/docs/tb20598.htm).

On 22 May 1998, on the morning of the referendum Blair wrote in the two Belfast-based morning newspapers that

representatives of parties intimately linked to paramilitary groups can only be in a future Northern Ireland government if it is clear that there will be no more violence and the threat of violence has gone. That doesn't just mean decommissioning but all bombings, killings, beatings and an end to targeting, recruiting and all the structures of terrorism. (Blair 1998a and b).

This was even more explicit than the pledges given in Coleraine.

These promises were designed to encourage the suspicious voters in the Unionist part of the community to vote 'Yes' in the referendum. Their concerns lay primarily in the areas of the continued existence of the armed Provisional IRA and the release of prisoners, with no guarantee that prisoner releases would be accompanied by the decommissioning of weapons. The problem was that these pledges were never rigorously honoured, which gives rise to a consideration of the seriousness of the language being used.

All paramilitary prisoners were released without violence being given up for good. Beatings, targeting, recruiting, and training continued. The later Reports of the Independent Monitoring Commission in 2004 and 2005 on the activity of paramilitary groups, including the Provisional IRA which is closely connected with Sinn Féin, gave details of the kinds of illegal activities which were still continuing even then. The International Decommissioning Commission was not able to report the completion of decommissioning of the arms of the Provisional IRA until 2005, that is 7 years after the promises were made and 5 years after the deadline in the Agreement.

The language used in the text of the Agreement took account of the complexity of the situation being addressed. Sinn Féin promised to 'use any influence they may have' to achieve the decommissioning of weapons within 2 years after the endorsement of the Agreement in concurrent referenda in both political jurisdictions, North and South. Given the overlap between Sinn Féin and the IRA it was reasonable to assume that such an undertaking would deliver the intended result. It is widely felt that the commitment 'to use any influence they may have' to achieve the desired result was never properly exercised and the result was not delivered until it suited them, 7 long years later. Republicans would maintain that it could not have been delivered earlier.

The republican movement engaged in a long-drawn-out strategic retreat from the unwinnable goal of achieving a United Ireland through what they called 'armed struggle'. Their original strategy was predicated on a profoundly flawed analysis of the challenge which they faced, which had to do with resistance to their goal lying with their Unionist neighbours rather than, as they said, with the government in London. As they retreated, they kept their own movement intact, increased their electoral support at the disadvantage of their closest nationalist colleagues in the Social Democratic and Labour Party, caused confusion among their political adversaries and Assembly colleagues in the Executive, and saw the political defeat of their principle co-negotiator

David Trimble, the leader of the Ulster Unionist Party, and the rise to unionist supremacy of their principle opponent Dr Ian Paisley and the Democratic Unionist Party.

Decommissioning and the declaration that 'the war was over' were delayed until further concessions were wrung from the British Government in 2005 on the issue of the return to Northern Ireland of 'On the Runs', that is those who had fled the country to avoid arrest. Fergus Finlay, an early participant in the process as an adviser to Dick Spring, one-time Minister of Foreign Affairs in the Irish Government, accused Gerry Adams of Sinn Féin of misusing the Peace Process as a Power Process. He wrote, 'Gerry, for you it's just a power process – not a peace process' (Finlay 2005).

In order to achieve an accommodation it is reasonable that leaders cannot be pushed beyond their capacity to deliver their people. However, that concession cannot be made to weigh more heavily on one side than the other, especially if the latter is afforded special consideration due to their association with an armed illegal organisation. If a Peace Process is used to destroy political adversaries, it will never engender reconciliation, it will deepen mistrust. If the building of confidence is a necessary precondition for political accommodation, the consolidation of trust is a necessary part of that process. This is not easily achieved, as witnessed by the multitudes of drafts of documents preceding agreements. There are people who will scour the text to make sure there are spaces within it, while others will scour the same text to eliminate any ambiguity.

David Trimble said that '…the Agreement isn't a legal document, again that's another mistake a lot of people make. They assume that this is a big legal document and they're looking for the certainty that a conveyancing lawyer would have about anything…And how many treaties are precise, without their opacities and all the rest of it' (in Millar 2004: 77). Some matters in the Agreement are implicit, for example the connection between decommissioning and the release of prisoners within a 2-year time frame. Ed Moloney, who wrote *A Secret History of the IRA* (2002), maintains that to have made the connection explicit would have pitched the whole process into a real and possibly fatal crisis, and key British officials believed this to be the case. If the text is too ambiguous, people may be unwilling to have confidence in what is being said. Or, if people are persuaded that imprecise language is being exploited by an opponent to achieve sectional advantage or to maintain organisational coherence at the expense of a partner in the process, then the apparent exploitation of ambiguity will erode trust and will destroy the political accommodation.

Multinational and multiparty agreements are only arrived at after long and tedious negotiations, as evidenced by talks about European budgets, global warming and world trade agreements. When it comes to the very final stage, negotiators have to weigh narrow self-interest against wider community concerns. Self-interest may dictate getting less than is hoped for. To collapse an agreement at the very last minute may not ultimately be in the interest of the nation or the party so doing. On the other hand, to threaten to do so is part of the negotiating process and a threat is empty if the possibility is not there.

Following political discussions in Downing Street, after the 2004 General Election, which saw David Trimble losing his Westminster parliamentary seat, the respected columnist David McKittrick wrote concerning Dr Paisley:

> He and his party have learned much from David Trimble's experience in negotiating with republicans. They have learned that every last detail of any accord has to be nailed down, with no room for ambiguity... They have also learned from republicans, for like them the DUP is on a journey from the politics of automatic opposition to a new phase of negotiation. Republicans showed that caution and time may be needed to bring the more militant grass roots along on the odyssey. The DUP may well conclude that a year as the top dogs in Unionism has not been long enough to accustom its own militants to the realities of the peace process. (Mc Kittrick 2004)

Stephen Dempster echoed this assessment the next day. 'Party leader Ian Paisley offered the first official response to the package on the table indicating the DUP could work with the government's package but still required a few 'i's dotted and 't's crossed.' Dempster then proceeded to quote Dr Paisley:

> Initial scrutiny shows that there are some areas of confusing ambiguity and even apparent inconsistency. We will want to have clarification on a number of matters where there is a lack of detail or the use of imprecise text. While on one construction it is possible, if our outstanding concerns were removed, to see a basis for agreement, other interpretations of some sections would require a less favourable judgement. We must not allow a lack of clarity to lead to misunderstanding and dispute at a later stage. (Dempster 2004)

At the time of writing, it remained to be seen whether it will be possible for Sinn Féin and the Democratic Unionist Party to reach some kind of workable accommodation.

The resistance to terrorism, the patience and generosity of many victims of violence, the long negotiations, with the deployment of position papers and statements produced by highly intelligent people, the taking of risks and a colossal commitment of time and energy have delivered a political accommodation which has been accompanied by ceasefires and a significantly less violent but still polarised society, still marked by mistrust. Levels of unemployment have been substantially reduced and the quality of life and freedom greatly enhanced. There remains some way to go before this could be described as reconciliation, should that ever be reached. Communication between people who mistrust one another will be needed. It will be necessary for people to continue to engage with one another and to build trust, which will be consolidated if truthful discourse is used, but will be destroyed if duplicity is deployed in pursuit of power. 'Language, communication and reconciliation' still need to be on the agenda.

Acknowledgement

Parts of this chapter draw on the author's material in *A Precarious Belonging – Presbyterians and the Conflict in Ireland* (Belfast: Blackstaff Press, 1995). The material has been used with the permission of the publisher.

Note from editor

Since this chapter was written, the Northern Irish Assembly has reconvened. The DUP leader Dr Ian Paisley is now Northern Ireland's First Minister. The Deputy First Minister is Martin McGuinness of Sinn Féin.

References

Blair, T. (1998a) 'Press Release', *The Irish News*, 22 May.
Blair, T. (1998b) 'Press Release', *The Newsletter*, 22 May.
Burleigh, J. (1960) *A Church History of Scotland*. Oxford: Oxford University Press.
Campbell-Johnston, R. (2004) 'Back to Babylon', *The Times*, 20 November, p. 15.
Dempster, S. (2004) 'Makings of a Deal', *The Newsletter*, 19 November.
Dunlop, J. (1995) *Precarious Belonging – Presbyterians and the Conflict in Ireland*. Belfast: Blackstaff Press.
Finlay, F. (2005)'An Open Letter to Sinn Féin Leader Gerry Adams', *Irish Examiner*, 1 February.

Government of the United Kingdom of Great Britain and Northern Ireland and Government of Ireland (1998), *Agreement Reached in the Multi-Party Negotiations*, Belfast (http://cain.ulst.ac.uk/events/peace/docs/agreement.htm).

Hayes, M. (1995) *Minority Verdict: Experiences of a Catholic Public Servant*. Belfast, Blackstaff Press.

Johnson, S. (2002) 'Interview With Seamus Heaney', *The Independent*, 31 October, pp. 4–5.

Kennedy, J. (1961) *On the Occasion of Declaration of Honorary American Citizenship to Winston Churchill*, 9 April (http://www.winstonchurchill.org).

Liechty, J. and Clegg, C. (2001) *Moving Beyond Sectarianism: Religion, Conflict and Reconciliation in Northern Ireland*. Dublin: Columba Press.

MacIntyre, B. (2005) 'Two Moments in a Week that will Define Blair's Place in History', *The Times*, 9 July, p. 16.

McKittrick, D. (2004) 'Here's One Peace Process that Wont Be Unravelling', *The Newsletter*, 19 November, p. 37.

Messiaen, O. (1985) *The South Bank Show*, ITV 5 April.

Millar, F. (2004) *David Trimble, The Price of Peace*. Dublin: Liffey Press.

Moloney, E. (2002) *A Secret History of the IRA*. New York: W.W. Norton & Company.

Moloney, E. (2005) 'Was There a Stormontgate', *The Belfast Telegraph*, 18 November.

Moltmann, J. (1981) *The Trinity and the Kingdom of God: The Doctrine of God*, translated by Margaret Kohl. Norwich: SCM-Canterbury Press Ltd.

Ni Dhomhnaill, N. (1990) 'The Language Issue', poem from *Pharaoh's Daughter*, translated from the Irish original by P. Muldoon. Co. Meath: The Gallery Press, p. 155.

Oetting, D. (1999) 'Distribution Statement: Accepted as Part of the Douglas Archives of American', *Public Address*, 26 May (http://www.douglas.speech.nwu.edu).

Presbyterian Church in Ireland (1980) *The Code: The Book of the Constitution and Government of the Presbyterian Church in Ireland*. Belfast: Presbyterian Church in Ireland.

Rogers W. R. (1993) 'Epilogue to the Character of Ireland' from W. R. Rogers *Collected Poems*, Oxford: Oxford University Press, p. 147.

Shirlow, P., Murtagh, B., Mesev, V. and McMullan, A. (2001) *Spaces of Fear: Modelling and Measuring Chill Factors in Belfast*. Belfast: University of Ulster.

Stewart David (1950) *The Seceders in Ireland, with Annals of their Congregations*. Belfast: Presbyterian Historical Society.

The Irish Inter Church Meeting (1993) *Discussion Document on Sectarianism*. Belfast: The Inter Church Centre.

11

9/11 and the War on Terrorism: The Clash of 'Words', 'Cultures' and 'Civilisations': Myth or Reality

Javaid Rehman

Words represent striking modes of expression and communication. In this capacity they have always had a sensitive role to play in the debate of cultures, traditions and civilisations. A reckless and uncaring usage of words could jeopardise relations between various communities and societies, and can easily provoke anger and resentment. In the existing multi-cultural, multi-religious global society, the significance of values as understood and expressed through words cannot therefore be under-estimated. A general obligation to act responsibly with phonetics lies upon all individuals, although words, expressions and terminologies adopted by political figures and statesmen are open to a particularly close scrutiny. Words and expressions have also had a significant contri-bution in the long-standing debate of differing ideologies and values of the world of Islam and the 'West'.[1]

This debate has been reinvigorated by the unfortunate events of 11 September 2001: Islam and the Islamic civilisation have been castigated as inferior, advocating recourse to violence, terrorism and destruction. 'Many horrific acts have been, and continue to be carried out in the name of Islam, just as they have in the name of Christianity. But unlike Islam, Christianity does not justify the use of all forms of violence. Islam does' (Sookhdeo 2001: 22).

This chapter aims to address two fundamental questions. First, it considers the extent to which the application (or misapplication) in the usage of words has a role in exacerbating divisions between contem-porary Muslim societies and the Western world. Secondly, there is an assessment of the usage of words and values and a consideration of the problems that have arisen as a consequence of their application since 11 September 2001. In order to examine and assess the two afore-mentioned questions, the chapter will rely on certain key words and expressions. For many of those engaged in this debate – and in particular for many Westerners, words such as 'terrorism', 'civilisation' and 'democracy' characterise major point of difference between the West and Islam. In formulating explanations, the chapter examines the impact and influence of the usage of the aforementioned words.

Words and the clash of 'Civilisations'

> We must be aware of the superiority of our civilisation, a system that has guaranteed well-being, respect for human rights – and in contrast with Islamic countries. (Berlusconi 2001)

This message of superiority of the Western civilisation has been a consistent theme emanating not only from statesmen and politicians, but also from scholars and political scientists. *The Clash of Civilizations and the Remaking of World Order*, the infamous work by Samuel Huntington, is the ultimate expression of superiority of the West and damnation of Islam as a peaceful religion. In engineering the 'clash of civilisations', Huntington views Islam as 'a religion of the sword … glorify[ing] military virtues' (1996: 263). In his perceptions, '[t]he Koran and other statements of Muslim beliefs contain few prohibitions on violence, and a concept of non-violence is absent from Muslim doctrine and practice' (ibid.). Similar sentiments are expressed by Payne, who contrasts what he perceives as the 'Western view of what religion is and ought to be, namely, a voluntary sphere where coercion has no place' with that of Islam. In this comparison the 'emphasis on non-violence is not the pattern in the Muslim culture. To the contrary, violence has been a central, accepted element, both in Muslim teaching and in the historical conduct of the religion. For over a thousand years, the religious bias in the Middle Eastern Culture has not been to discourage the use of force, but to encourage it' (Payne 1989: 122).

Words and terms employed by some other Western writers are profoundly insensitive and offensive. In assessing the Islam and Arab relationship with the West, Cruise-O'Brien makes the observation that 'Muslim society looks profoundly repulsive … It looks repulsive because it *is* repulsive. … A Westerner who claims to admire Muslim society, while still adhering to Western values, is either a hypocrite or an ignoramus, or a bit of both … Arab and Muslim society is sick, and has been sick for a long time' (italics original in 1989: 11).

It would perhaps be less worrying if these words and views were the sole domain of isolated individuals, and did not bear any relevance to the real politic. The superiority of the West and the neglect of the Islamic world is unfortunately omnipresent in the entirety of the prevailing legal and political order. The edifice of modern international law is built upon exclusion of Islamic communities and the domination of the West – according to the modern phase of international law, the 'West' epitomises 'civilisation'. The position is established by the Statute of the International Court of Justice of the existence of 'civilised nations'. In its search for sources of international law, Article 38(1) of the Statute undertakes to apply 'the general principles of law recognized by civilized nations' (See Brierley 1963: 56).

The Statute, which has its origins in the Statute of the Permanent Court of International Justice established in 1920, clearly viewed only a few states (principally victorious states of the West) as civilised; the majority of the world – including the whole of the Islamic world was at that time under colonial occupation and perceived to be 'uncivilised'. The reference to Article 38(1)(c) of the Statute of the World Court also confirms the relativity and the difficulty in establishing the meaning of words such as 'civilised' or the 'superiority of a civilisation'. During its developmental stages, modern international law sanctified all acts of mass terrorism so long as these were conducted by 'civilised nations' over colonised indigenous people.

The contemporary post-colonial world that emerged in the aftermath of the Second World War has been fashioned in the vision of the imperialist political elite. New states were carved out in a design hitherto established by the European powers, containing a recipe for future ethnic and political conflicts. A cursory examination of existing borders of modern African states establishes the reality of European hegemony as well as the artificiality of international boundaries. More problematic have been the schemes and designs for preserving the global political and legal order since 1945. The tool of Western imposition has been formed through the powers and composition of the Security Council (See Bailey 1992: 304–36, Higgins 1970: 1, Sands and Klein 2001: 39–55). This continues to be a body designed to maintain and to enforce international peace and security. A designation of permanent membership and veto power was introduced to ensure that law or politics could not adopt a course detrimental to specific interests. It is a legal order in denial of justice, equity or fairness for all of the peoples of the world.

The Islamic world has suffered at the hands of this unfairness of international law. The Security Council has proved to be least supportive in matters which mean the most to the Muslim people – the role of individual members of the Council, particularly the United States, in support of Israel has been disappointing and provoked resentment. The clash, if there is one – between the Islamic states and the West – is not so much about values, but is more a manifestation of control, domination and exploitation. The West, led by the United States, is controlling legal avenues for challenging this domination and exploitation. As the bombings of Afghanistan and the more recent invasion of Iraq establish, Muslim communities are left without a voice in the Security Council and the United Nations more generally.

9/11 and the 'war on terrorism'

The post-9/11 world is increasingly becoming familiar with the so-called 'war on terrorism'. Within international law, the usage of the word 'war' has carried a specific meaning, and its current expansion into hitherto unchartered territories is problematic. The United Nations Charter avoids the terminology of 'war' but places reliance on a prohibition on the use of force. Article 2(4) of the United Nations Charter provides, 'All Members shall refrain in their international relations from the threat or use of force against the territorial integrity or political independence of any state, or in any other manner inconsistent with the Purposes of the United Nations' (The Charter of the United Nations 1945: http://www.un.org/aboutun/charter/chapter1.htm). If the word 'war' has been given an exceptionally broad meaning, the concept of 'terrorism' has from time immemorial been a problematic one. There is significant truth in the sentiments of Professor Baxter, who in his moment of frustration noted that '[w]e have cause to regret that a legal concept of "terrorism" was ever inflicted upon us. The term is imprecise; it is ambiguous; and above all, it serves no operative legal purpose' (Baxter 1974: 380).

Explanations for the difficulty in defining the word 'terrorism' includes varied perceptions over the characterisation of the terrorist acts, purpose and motivation behind such acts and the variable identity of the perpetrator. Indeed the issue has been so controversial that divisions have emerged not only in the proposed definitions but also more fundamentally as to whether it is worthwhile attempting to define such an elusive concept. Bassiouni makes the point that

> there is . . . no internationally agreed upon methodology for the iden-
> tification and appraisal of what is commonly referred to as 'terrorism';
> including: causes, strategies, goals and outcomes of the conduct in
> question and those who perpetuate it. There is also no interna-
> tional consensus as to the appropriate reactive strategies of states
> and the international community, their values, goals and outcomes.
> All of this makes it difficult to identify what is sought to be
> prevented and controlled, why and how. As a result, the pervasive
> and indiscriminate use of the often politically convenient label of
> 'terrorism' continues to mislead this field of inquiry. (Bassiouni
> 1988: xvi)

Efforts to reach an agreement on issues of definition is confronted with complications (Higgins 1997: 14).

One immediate question relates to the identification of the 'terrorists'. In any ideological and political conflict, is it possible to objectively distinguish between a terrorist from a freedom fighter? In contemporary politics, our perceptions of acts of violence conducted by such groups as the Palestinians, the Kashmiris, the Tamil Tigers and Northern Irish Republicans is variable (McCoubrey 1997: 258). There is a great measure of truth in the well-known cliché that 'One man's terrorist is another man's freedom fighter' (Bassiouni 2000: i, Rosand 2003: 33). It is also the case that views and values of whether a particular individual or entity is pursuing terrorists acts is subject to political persuasion and change. Saddam Hussein, Osama Bin Laden, the Taliban have all been at one stage hailed as friends: they were then regarded as freedom fighters and those fighting a just war by the United States and its allies (Thomas 2002: 366).

Furthermore, there is also the complexity of finding agreement in relation to the entities, which could conceivably perpetrate terrorism. In this context there has remained a major ideological conflict between the developing states, many of whom represent the Islamic block on the one hand and the developed world on the other. While the developing and Islamic states have emphasised state-terrorism largely in the context of racial oppression and colonial regimes, the developed world has concerned itself with individual acts of terrorism. Levitt correctly points out that

> governments that have a strong political stake in the promotion of
> 'national liberation movements' are loath to subscribe to a defin-
> ition of terrorism that would criminalise broad areas of conduct

habitually resorted to by such groups; and on the other end of the spectrum, governments against which these groups' violent activities are directed are obviously reluctant to subscribe to a definition that would criminalise their own use of force in response to such activities or otherwise. (Levitt 1986: 109)

In the post-colonial, post-cold-war era, a number of Islamic states such as Libya, Iran, the Sudan and Iraq have protested against what they believe as American-sponsored 'state-terrorism'. An example could be found in the position adopted by Iraq. In its letter dated 26 December 2001, the *Charge d'Affaires* of the Permanent Mission of Iraq to the United Nations addressed the Chairman of the Security Council Committee established pursuant to Resolution 1373 (2001) concerning Counter-terrorism. The letter noted that

> Iraq is the foremost victim of terrorism, including state terrorism. Its leaders, officials and citizens have been exposed to many terrorist kidnapping attempts and its cities and villages have been the target of terrorist acts committed by terrorists who slip across borders – terrorists that receive patronage, training, finance and armament within a framework of state terrorism i.e. terrorism carried out by states themselves. One such state is the United States of America which openly spends tens of millions of dollars on troops of mercenaries to carry out terrorist operations against Iraq pursuant to what is referred to as the 'Iraq Libera-tion Act'. (http://ods-dds-ny.un.org/doc/UNDOC/GEN/N01/723/00/ PDF/N0172300.pdf?OpenElement)

According to conventional wisdom, the motive, characteristics and underlying causes of any terrorist action must not provide a justification. On the other hand, depending on one's moral and political views many of these actions have been justified or condoned. Analysing statistic-ally, the Islamic world has a forceful argument to make. State-sponsored terrorism is far more devastating in its impact than individual acts of terrorism. This is particularly the case, where state-terrorism is generated by militarily powerful states. According to one estimate the twentieth century has witnessed 70 million casualties of state-sponsored terrorism as opposed to 100,000 deaths which were caused by individual non-governmental acts of terrorism (Bassiouni 2001: 46).

Substantively, the confrontations between the world of Islam and the West over accusations of terrorism and identification of terrorists have been deep-rooted and significant. For decades, indeed for centuries, the two camps have held antithetical visions of what constitutes violence and terrorism. During the colonial era, it was perfectly acceptable to use violence and aggression to invade and occupy foreign land, and kill and terrorise the indigenous population. European colonialism legitimised racial superiority, slavery, ethnic cleansing and genocide (Strawson 2002: xix–xx). In its historic developments, international law sanctified all acts of mass terrorism so long as these were conducted by 'civilised nations' over colonised indigenous people. The contemporary postcolonial world that emerged in the aftermath of the Second World War has been fashioned in the vision of the imperialist political elite. New states were carved out in a design hitherto established by the European powers, containing a recipe for future ethnic and political conflicts.

The great colonial empires were built not on the concerns and welfare for indigenous peoples but upon their abuse and exploitation. Once the United Nations became operational, the meaning of aggression and terrorism retained its controversial character, although the protagonists were more or less the same. The Islamic world, in association with other colonial entities of the developing world, wanted action taken against what was considered state-terrorism – in other words those who were alien occupiers of foreign lands. For much of the history of the United Nations, the word 'terrorism' has been the battleground of these two opposing parties.

In the aftermath of the Second World War, state-sponsored terrorism was deployed to resist granting the right of self-determination to many of the oppressed nations and peoples (Elagab 1995: IV). Colonisation provided a *de facto* lawful mechanism to violate human dignity, to terrorise the indigenous peoples into submission and humiliation. The terrorism of colonialism produced a backlash. Terrorism was often met with counter-terrorism; the colonisers using terror as an instrument to maintain their hold over their overseas territories, whereas the indigenous peoples and their national liberation movements resorting to terrorism and political violence as a means to gain emancipation and independence (cf. Minority Rights Group 1997). In their effort to rid themselves of what they perceived as alien, foreign and unlawful domination, resistance movements were formed. Many of the so-called 'national liberation movements' such as the African National Congress (South Africa) (Beinart and Dubow 1995, Dubow 2000), Algerian Liberation Movement (FLN), (Kuper 1977), Irish Republican Army (Ireland) (Patterson 1997, Smith 1995), Indian National Congress and Muslim

League (British India) combined nationalist sentiments with political violence (Hardy 1972, Jalal 1985, Tomlinson 1976).

The subject of terrorism became a matter of serious contention between states with overseas colonies on the one hand and the newly independent and communist states on the other. Even at the end of the decolonisation period, the legacy of colonial times render the subject often an unpalatable one. There is a substantial relationship with the right to self-determination for such groups or peoples as the Palestinian, which is complicated by the definition of 'peoples' and 'indigenous peoples' (Rehman 1998: 165). In this context it needs to be noted that Osama Bin Laden has repeatedly emphasised the rights of self-determination for the Palestinian peoples as a prerequisite to world peace and security (Bell 2000, Guyatt 1998, Takkenberg 1998). Another particularly controversial area is the right of the Kashmiri Muslims to self-determination; the conflict between India and Pakistan on the territory of Kashmir already having produced three wars (Rehman 2000: 454).

For the societies in the Islamic world, the crashing of planes into buildings on 11 September 2001 was an act of unforgivable cowardice, an unacceptable and a terrorist act. However, these societies also demand retribution and punishment of all those states – including militarily powerful states such as Israel and the United States – which have for so long violated the rights of Muslim peoples in the world. Since the commencement of the 'war on terror' Muslims have demanded accountability for allied actions in the Middle East, Afghanistan and Iraq. It is also hugely unfortunate that the events of 9/11 and the commencement of the 'war on terror' have not brought about any changes in the psychological approaches of the West. Revisiting the episode of the US invasion of Iraq and subsequently witnessing each of the arguments presented in justification of such an invasion fall to pieces, brings out the *déjà vu* of age-old economic and political expansionism. The divisions over the meaning of terrorists persist, with the West continuing with its agenda of duplicity and double standards. The clash of perceptions over the meaning of terrorism and its causes often becomes apparent in the choice of words – for example, in many of countries of the Islamic world, the acts of defiance in Iraq and Afghanistan have been varyingly described as resistance movement, national liberation movement and Jihad (Ali and Rehman 2005, Zawati 2001). The United States and its allies on the other hand exclusively perceive such resistance as either militancy or terrorism.

Whilst, as argued above, the psychological approaches of the West have not altered despite the events of 9/11, there certainly has been a much greater stigmatisation of the Islamic world. In so far as the United States is concerned, the enemy is no longer the stubborn though visible regimes of the former Soviet Empire. Instead the enemy in this war on terror, we are told, comes from the ranks of the Muslim communities. These are the Islamic extremists – members of the Al-Qaeda, its associates and other Jihadis. It has been argued that the world is no longer a safe place. We need strong, fearless leaders who are capable of taking pre-emptive action; security of nations is more important than that of the respect for civil liberties or human rights.

This undue deference to national security has resulted in undermining minority rights, with a growth in Islamophobia, that is fear or hatred of Muslims. The consequences for Muslim minorities in the United States, the United Kingdom and many parts of Western world have been particularly deplorable. The United States and the Western Europe witnessed a serious public and political reaction to the attacks on 11 September. In many quarters, Muslim minorities were immediately castigated. Their physical presence was questioned and their loyalties were doubted. There were attacks on Muslim communities leading to loss of life.

There was a dramatic rise in hate crimes against Muslims in the United States, with the Federal Bureau of Investigation reporting a dramatic escalation of 1600 per cent in incidents largely consisting of assaults and intimidation (Thomas 2002: 366). An unfortunate example of hate-crimes was the murder of at least eight persons belonging to ethnic minority communities in the aftermath of 11 September 2001. One tragic case was that of a turbaned Sikh, Balbir Singh Sodhi, who was shot five times on 15 September 2001 by a gunman in Phoenix, United States – Mr Sodhi died instantly (http://www. east-valleytribune.com/index.php?sty=48149). He was targeted because of his turban and beard that bore a resemblance to orthodox Muslim believers. Within the United States, hundreds of young Muslim men were detained, interned, incarcerated or deported by security and immigration services. Vulnerable members of the Muslim communities such as elderly women were forced to replace their traditional dress, the *Shalwar-Qamiz*, with the American-style clothing. Tens of thousands of terrified young Muslim men were coerced into an enforced scheme of compulsory registration and finger printing. Minority communities were reluctant to express their fear (even in private) lest they might be arrested, deported or even stripped of their nationalities. Words such as *Hijab* (Islamic headscarves), *Madrisas*

(Islamic Schools) and the *Hawala* (Islamic Finance) system became too sensitive to articulate.

Having itself not been the subject of an attack, a more sober response from the United Kingdom was anticipated (Thomas 2002). However, there was an unprecedented surge in violence against Muslims in the aftermath of 11 September 2001 within the United Kingdom. According to the Islamic Human Rights Commission, during September 2001, a total of 206 incidents of assault, violence, verbal and physical abuse and other forms of malicious acts were recorded in Britain. Expanding on some of these incidents, a recent report notes that in the aftermath of 11 September 2001

> Muslim adults and children were attacked, physically and verbally. They were punched, spat at, hit with umbrellas at bus stops, publicly doused with alcohol and pelted with fruits and vegetables. Dog excrement and fireworks were pushed through their letterboxes and bricks were thrown through their windows. They were called murderers and excluded from social gatherings. One woman in Swindon was hospitalised after being beaten with a metal baseball bat; two Cambridge University students had their headscarves ripped off, in broad daylight outside a police station; Saba Zaman, who, in July 2001, had her scarf pulled off and two of her ribs broken in Tooting, London was stopped and searched by the police three times in two weeks following the terrorist attacks in the United States of America (USA). In west London, an Afghani taxi driver Hamidullah Gharwal, was attacked shortly after 11 September, and left paralysed from the neck down ... Vandals attacked mosques and Asian-run businesses around the country. Nine pigs' heads were dumped outside a mosque in Exeter. Many [Muslims] were said not to have reported attacks because of fear of reprisals. (Ansari 2002: 4)

The UK government also adopted a series of draconian legislative and administrative measures which included *inter alia* indefinite detention (for foreign terror suspects) and the acceptance of evidence which may have been obtained through torture in a foreign jurisdiction. There are currently legislative proposals to criminalise 'glorification' of terrorism and stripping off dual British nationality for those whose conduct is 'not deemed for public good' (Immigration, Asylum and National Bill C1.56). The government has also introduced proposals for screening clerics and closing down mosques. There now remains the concern that the new Identity Cards scheme would turn into a witch-hunt for targeting and harassing Muslim men (http://www.publications.parliament.uk/pa/ld200506/ldbills/071/2006071.htm).

'Democracy', 'human rights' and 'regime change': The tools of Western imposition

> Every impulse to protect the weak and help the infirm is noble. The impulse to use the means at our disposal to liberate a people from a government that poses no imminent or prospective threat to us, but is so despotic, violent, and vicious that those suffering under it cannot shake it off, is also noble. The action that gives effect to that impulse may sometimes be internationally lawful. It may sometimes be feasible. It is often – but not always – misconceived. (Reisman 2004: 516)

In the modern international human rights discourse there is no one solid definition of what constitutes a 'democracy'. A generally useful starting point and the basis of all human rights could be taken from the Universal Declaration of Human Rights adopted on 10 December 1948 (http://www.un.org/Overview/rights.html). The Universal Declaration although adopted as a General Assembly Resolution and not binding *per se* has attained universal respect and approbation. There is a strong contention that most provision if not the entire document now binds states of the world in general international law. Although the Declaration does not use the term 'democracy', Article 21 provides as follows:

(1) Everyone has the right to take part in the government of his country, directly through freely chosen representatives.
(2) Everyone has the right of equal access to public service in his country.
(3) The will of the people shall be the basis of the authority of government; this shall be expressed in periodic and genuine elections, which shall be by universal and equal suffrage and shall be held by secret vote or by equivalent free voting procedures.

Other components of the so-called 'bill of rights' also elaborate these notions. Article 25 of the 1996 International Covenant on Civil and Political Rights (http://www.unhchr.ch/html/menu3/b/a_ccpr.htm) for example provides that

Every citizen shall have the right and opportunity, without any of the distinctions mentioned in article 2 [i.e. distinctions such as race, colour, sex, language, religion, political or other opinions, national or social origin, property, birth or other status] and without unreasonable restrictions:

(a) take part in the conduct of public affairs, directly or through freely chosen representative;
(b) to vote and to be elected at genuine periodic elections which shall be by universal and equal suffrage and shall be held by secret ballot, guaranteeing the free expression of the will of the electors;
(c) to have access, on general terms of equality, to public service in his country.

These ideals are also reflected in a number of regional instruments, for example Article 3 of Protocol 1 of the European Convention on Human Rights (http://conventions.coe.int/Treaty/EN/Treaties/Html/009.htm), which states that 'the High contracting parties undertake to hold free elections at reasonable intervals by secret ballot, under conditions which will ensure the free expression of the opinion of the people in the choice of the legislature'.

Article 23 of American Convention on Human Rights (1969) (http://www.oas.org/juridico/english/Treaties/b-32.htm) provides that 'every citizen shall enjoy the following rights and opportunities':

(a) to take part in the conduct of public affairs, directly or through freely chosen representatives;
(b) to vote and to be elected in genuine periodic election, which shall be universal and equal suffrage and by secret ballot that guarantees the free expression of the will of the voters; and
(c) to have access, under general conditions of equality, to the public service of his country.

Moreover, 'the law may regulate the exercise of the rights and opportunities referred to in the preceding paragraph only on the basis of age, nationality, residence, language, education, civil and mental capacity, or sentencing by a competent court in criminal proceedings'.

From the aforementioned descriptions it is clear that democracy is a noble ideal. Having said that, the practical application of the concept remains difficult for there is considerable ambiguity as to their precise contents. In historical as well as contemporary terms, explanation of democracy has provoked considerable discussion. There are also cultural and sociological variations as what meaning should be imparted to the conception of democracy or with whom should popular sovereignty be ultimately placed. In Islam, for example, sovereignty lies with Allah alone, who is almighty, and His will is to be implemented through his chosen representatives.

In the modern era, a right to democratic governance is being increasingly asserted; there nevertheless remains substantial misgivings when militarily powerful states invade another state ostensibly for the projection of human rights and democracy. A useful though unfortunate example was the invasion and occupation of Iraq in March 2003. The build-up to the invasion saw *inter alia* 'democracy' and 'human rights' arguments advanced by the United States and the United Kingdom. President Saddam Hussein's dictatorial regime and Iraq's repression of its ethnic and religious communities were put forward as grounds for justifying invasion and removal of the regime. The induction of 'democracy' and 'human rights' were ostensibly the highest priorities of the US administration for Iraq and for the states of the Middle East. The arguments advanced by the United States were nevertheless fallacious in that substantial violations of human rights and democratic governance within the region have been conducted at the behest, knowledge or support of the United States. Furthermore, the promotion and projection of democracy has only been a factor, when it suits the political ambitions of the United States and other powerful states; the worst violators of democratic principles and rule of law in the Middle East and the Islamic world continue to be the closest allies and friends of the United States.[2]

Indeed this so-called 'war on terrorism' has presented an excuse to dictatorial and autocratic regimes across the globe to repress, torture and violate fundamental human rights – the world is silent and even appreciative of such actions so long as these regimes continue to purport allegiance to the ambitions of the US foreign policy.[3] A recent Amnesty International Report reinforces this point when it notes:

> the impact of the so called 'war on terror' (henceforth 'war on terror') on human rights in the Gulf and the Arabian Peninsula has been profound and far reaching. Governments in the region and the US government have treated nationals and residents of the area with a disturbing disregard for the rule of law and fundamental human rights standards. The results have been mass arrests, prolonged detention without charge or trial, incommunicado detention, torture and

ill treatment, strict secrecy surrounding the fate and whereabouts of some detainees, and apparent extra-judicial killings. These human rights violations have had profound effects not only on individual victims but also on their relatives and the general human rights situation in the region. (Amnesty International 2004)

Such duplicity, double standards and selectivity have not only troubled the Muslim communities but also others who retain an objective vision of law and politics. According to a leading international lawyer, Professor Brownlie:

The issue of selectivity can lead to claims of human rights violations being used as a powerful political weapon. Probably the most egregious example of this is provided by the case of Iraq. The Iraq–Iran War raged for eight years (1980–88). Iran was not the aggressor. During the conflict leading Western powers gave assistance to the Iraqi Government in the form of matrices for chemical weapons (which were used against Iran) and satellite intelligence. The Security Council took no action under Chapter VII of the Charter. In contrast, in the period from 1991 up to the United States attack on Iraq in March 2003, the same state took a strong line on the bad rights record of the Iraqi regime and the attack was justified in public statements in part by reference to human rights factor. Here is revealed a purely cyclical version of human rights, contingent upon collateral political considerations. (Brownlie 2003: 557)

The attacks on the World Trade Centre have left a tragic imprint on subsequent global developments. 11 September 2001 sharpened the debate on a probable 'clash of civilisations' between the West and Islam. It weighed in heavily in support of those, such as Samuel Huntington, who forecast the existence of a clash of cultures and civilisations. It provided vital ammunition to critics who had hitherto been restrained though deeply suspicious of Islam and Muslim believers. 'Islamabophia' found a firm place in societal discourses and was also evident in the practices of many states.

A further negative effect of 9/11 and the consequent war on terrorism has been to strengthen the very individuals and organisations that were intended to be censured – it is an unfortunate reality that in the post-9/11 Islamic world there is far greater radicalism and hatred for the West. The indiscriminate killings in Afghanistan, the deceitful and illegal invasion of Iraq and the abuses in the US naval base at Guantánamo

Bay and Abu Gharib detention centres in Iraq have provided a fertile breeding ground of further recruitment for extremist organisations such as Al-Qaeda. For liberals campaigning for moderation and reconciliation between the West and Islam, these are times of great disappointment.

This chapter has argued that it is the economic and political exploitation by the West which has aggrieved and antagonised the Muslim world. Although it would as yet be premature to locate a clash of civilisations between the West and contemporary Islam, in a delicate phase of this the 'new world order' there is a need for great caution and circumspection. In the aftermath of 9/11, words, concepts and old stereotypes were reinvigorated to humiliate Muslim communities in many parts of the world. Muslim minorities in Europe and North America are consistently referred to as followers of a religion that encourages terrorism – a recent tragic reminder in Europe was the publication of cartoons of Prophet Mohammed. One of the cartoons depicted the Prophet as having a bomb over his head. A reckless usage of belligerent words and expressions has accompanied combative and aggressive foreign policies adopted by the United States and its allies. The belligerence and lack of sensitivity on the part of the United States and the West unfortunately presents a prognosis of the self-fulfilling prophecy of a destructive 'clash of civilisations' between the Islamic world and the West (An-Na'im 2002: 164).

Endnotes

1. It is acknowledged that the terms 'world of Islam' and 'West' cannot be defined precisely – certainly it would be impossible to draw any geographical boundaries. Islamic rule stretched as far as Spain in the medieval period, and the Ottoman Turks who captured Constantinople in 1453 ruled over much of Eastern and Central Europe for a number of centuries. There are currently millions of Muslims living in Europe and North America. Islam also influenced the development of culture and values in many parts of the world including Europe (see Rehman (2005). For the purposes of the present analysis, Islamic States are defined as those States which are members of the Organisation of Islamic Conference (OIC), whereas the 'West' connotes a family of those European and Non-European States where Christian Europeans or their descendants are in charge of the legal, political and economic structures. This definition of the 'West' would include most States of Europe, Americas, Australia and New Zealand.
2. Note the criticisms of violations of human rights conducted in the US Middle Eastern allies such as Saudi Arabia and Kuwait. See the Amnesty International's Reports for 2004 on Saudi Arabia (http://web.amnesty.org/report2004/sau-summary-eng) (23 September 2004); and Amnesty International's Report for

2004 on Kuwait (http://web.amnesty.org/report2004/kwt-summary-eng) (23 September 2004).
3. Amnesty International The Gulf and the Arabian Peninsula: Human rights fall victim to the 'War on Terror' (22 June 2004) AI Index: MDE 04/002/ 2004 (http://web.amnesty.org/library/Index/ENGMDE040022004?open&of= ENG-USA).

References

Ali, S. and Rehman, J. (2005) 'The Concept of Jihad in Islamic International Law', *Journal of Conflict and Security Law*, 10(4), 1–23.

An-Na'im, A. (2002) 'Upholding International Legality Against Islamic and American Jihad', in K. Booth and T. Dunne eds, *Worlds in Collision: Terror and the Future of Global Order*. London: Palgrave, 162–72.

Ansari, H. (2002) *Muslims in Britain*. London: Minority Rights Group.

Bailey, S. (1992) 'The Security Council', in P. Alston ed., *The United Nations and Human Rights: A Critical Appraisal*. Oxford: Clarendon Press, pp. 304–36.

Bassiouni, M. (1988) 'A Policy-oriented Inquiry into the Different Forms and Manifestations of 'International Terrorism', in M. Bassiouni ed., *Legal Responses to Terrorism: US Procedural Aspects*. Dordrecht: Martinus Nijhoff Publishers.

Bassiouni, M. (2000) 'Foreword: Assessing "Terrorism" into the New Millennium', *De Paul Business Law Journal*, 12, 1–20.

Bassiouni, M. (2001) *International Terrorism: Multilateral Conventions (1937–2001)*. Ardsley, NY: Transnational Publishers.

Baxter, R. (1974) 'A Sceptical Look at the Concept of Terrorism', *Akorn Law Review*, 7, 380–88.

Beinart, W. and Dubow, S. eds (1995) *Segregation And Apartheid in Twentieth-Century South Africa*. London: Routledge.

Bell, C. (2000) *Peace Agreements and Human Rights*. Oxford: Oxford University Press.

Berlusconi (2001) cited in 'EU Deplores "Dangerous" Islam Jibe', (http://news. bbc.co.uk/1/hi/world/europe/1565664.stm).

Brierley, J. (1963) *The Law of Nations: An Introduction to the International Law of Peace*, 6th edition, ed. H. Waldock. New York: Oxford University Press, 1963, 1968.

Brownlie, I. (2003) *Principles of Public International Law*. Oxford: Oxford University Press.

Dubow, S. (2000) *The African National Congress*. Sutton: Stroud.

Elagab, O. (1995) *International Law Documents Relating to Terrorism*. London: Cavendish.

Guyatt, N. (1998) *The Absence of Peace: Understanding the Israeli-Palestinian Conflict*. London: Zed Books.

Hardy, P. (1972) *The Muslims of British India*. London: Cambridge University Press.

Higgins, R. (1970) 'The Place of International Law in the Settlement of Disputes by the Security Council', *American Journal of International Law*, 64, 1–18.

Huntington, S. (1996) *The Clash of Civilizations and the Remaking of World Order*. London: Simon and Schuster.

Islamic Human Rights Commission (2001) *UK Today: The Anti-Muslim Backlash in the Wake of 11th September 2001*. London: Islamic Human Rights Commission.

Jalal, A. (1985) *The Sole Spokesman: Jinnah, the Muslim League, and the Demand for Pakistan*. Cambridge: Cambridge University Press.

Kuper, L. (1977) *The Pity of it All: Polarisation of Racial and Ethnic Relations*. Minneapolis: University of Minnesota Press.

Levitt, G. (1986) 'Is "Terrorism" Worth Defining?', *Ohio Northern University Law Review*, 13(1), 97–115.

McCoubrey, H. (1997) *International Humanitarian Law*. Aldershot: Ashgate.

Minority Rights Group ed. (1997) *World Directory of Minorities*. London: Minority Rights Group.

O'Brien, C. (1989) 'Sick Man of the World', *The Times*, 11 May.

Patterson, H. (1997) *The Politics of Illusion: A Political History of the IRA*. London: Serif.

Payne, J. (1989) *Why Nations Arm*. Oxford: Basil Blackwell.

Rehman, J. (1998) 'Minority Rights in International Law: Raising the Conceptual Issues', *Australian Law Journal*, 72, 615–34.

Rehman, J. (2000) 'Reviewing the Right of Self-Determination: Lessons from the Experience of the Indian Sub-Continent', *Anglo American Law Review*, 29(4), 454–75.

Rehman, J. (2005) *Islamic State Practices, International Law and the Threat from Terrorism: A Critique of the 'Clash of Civilizations' in the New World Order*. Oxford: Hart.

Reisman, W. M. (2004) 'Why Regime Change Is (Almost Always) a Bad Idea?', *American Journal of International Law*, 98(3), 516–25.

Rosand, E. (2003) 'Security Council Resolution 1373, the Counter-Terrorism Committee, and the Fight Against Terrorism', *American Journal of International Law*, 97(2), 333–41.

Sands, P. and Klein, P. (2001) *Bowett's Law of International Institutions*, 5th edition. London: Sweet and Maxwell, pp. 39–55.

Smith, M. (1995) *Fighting for Ireland?: The Military Strategy of the Irish Republican Movement*. London: Routledge.

Sookhdeo, P. (2001) 'A Religion that Sanctions Violence', *Daily Telegraph*, 17 September, 22.

Strawson, J. (2002) 'Introduction: In the Name of Law', in J. Strawson ed., *Law After Ground Zero*. London: Glasshouse Press, xi–xxi.

Takkenberg, L. (1998) *The Status of Palestinian Refugees in International Law*. Oxford: Clarendon Press.

Thomas, P. A. (2002) 'September 11th and Good Governance', *Northern Ireland Legal Quarterly*, 53(4), 366–90.

Tomlinson, B. R. (1976) *The Indian National Congress and the Raj, 1929–1942: The Penultimate Phase*. London: Macmillan.

Zawati, H. M. (2001) *Is Jihâd a Just War? War, Peace, and Human Rights Under Islamic and Public International Law*. Lewiston, NY: Edwin Mellen Press.

Websites

Amnesty International The Gulf and the Arabian Peninsula: Human rights fall victim to the 'War on Terror' (2004) – http://web.amnesty.org/library/Index/ENGMDE040022004?open&of=ENG-USA

Amnesty International's Reports for 2004 on Saudi Arabia (2004) – http://web.amnesty.org/report2004/sau-summary-eng)

Amnesty International's Report for 2004 on Kuwait (2004) – http://web.amnesty.org/report2004/kwt-summary-eng

American Convention on Human Rights (1969) – http://www.oas.org/juridico/english/Treaties/b-32.htm

European Convention on Human Rights – http://conventions.coe.int/Treaty/EN/Treaties/Html/009.htm

Identity Cards Bill (2006) (amended) – http://www.publications.parliament.uk/pa/ld200506/ldbills/071/2006071.htm

Immigration, Asylum and National Bill Cl. 56 – http://www.publications.parliament.uk/pa/ld200506/ldbills/074/2006074.htm

Letter dated 26 December 2001, the *Charges d'Affaires* of the permanent mission of Iraq to the United Nations addressed the Chairman of the Security Council Committee established pursuant to resolution 1373 (2001) concerning counter-terrorism, para 1 – http://ods-dds-ny.un.org/doc/UNDOC/GEN/N01/723/00/PDF/N0172300.pdf?OpenElement

Office of the High Commissioner for Human Rights (1966) *International Covenant on Civil and Political Rights* – http://www.unhchr.ch/html/menu3/b/a_ccpr.htm

'Sikhs still living in Shadow of Sept 11' 16 September 2005 – http://www.eastvalleytribune.com/index.php?sty=48149

United Nations (1948) *Universal Declaration of Human Rights* – http://www.un.org/Overview/rights.html

Index